Praise for *Tick Bite Fever* also by David Bennun

'Hilarious.'   BBC Radio 4, *Midweek*

'Matchlessly witty . . . one of the country's funniest writers.'
Steven Poole, *The Guardian*

'A hilarious memoir . . . Enchanting and amazing.'
The Daily Mail

'Simply hilarious. Laugh-out-loud is an understate-
ment . . . A wonderful insight into life in Africa from a
two-foot high point of view, *Tick Bite Fever* is a witty,
touching and above all affectionate look at his unique
upbringing.'
The Press Association

'Exotic hats off to David Bennun, who has written a book
full of warmth and self-deprecating humour . . . The
author's childhood is painted in a wonderfully blurry
way . . . The book continues to amaze with its advice on
how to run from various animals, or its account of the
attempted coup of 1982.'
Word magazine

'A relentlessly bubbling stream of self-deprecating yarns
and misadventures . . . *Tick Bite Fever* itches with mordant wit – there's at least one turn of phrase per para-
graph that gets among your ribs like a feather duster. An
excellent memoir.'
Uncut magazine

'*Tick Bite Fever* is a contemporary version, set in Africa, of
Gerald Durrell's *My Family and Other Animals* . . .
Bennun's writing is often so funny you will find it hard
not to laugh out loud.'
TLS

BRITISH AS A SECOND LANGUAGE

DAVID BENNUN

EBURY
PRESS

First published in Great Britain in 2005

10 9 8 7 6 5 4 3 2 1

First published by
Ebury Press
Random House, 20 Vauxhall Bridge Road, London, SW1V 2SA

Random House Australia (Pty) Limited
20 Alfred Street, Milsons Point, Sydney,
New South Wales 2061, Australia

Random House New Zealand Limited
18 Poland Road, Glenfield, Auckland 10, New Zealand

Random House South Africa (Pty) Limited
Endulini, 5A Jubilee Road, Parktown 2193, South Africa

The Random House Group Limited Reg. No. 954009

www.randomhouse.co.uk

A CIP catalogue record for this book is available from the
British Library.

Cover Design by Two Associates

'First We Take Manhattan' Words and Music by Leonard Cohen,
Stranger Music Inc. Sony/ATV Music Publishing Limited

'Bengali in Platforms' Words and Music by Stephen Street and
Steven Morrissey © 1988, Reproduced by permission of
EMI Virgin Music Ltd, London WC2H 0QY

'Evidently Chicken Town' Words by John Cooper Clarke and Music
by Martin Hannett and Stephen Hopkins © 1980, Reproduced by
permission of EMI Songs Ltd/Dinsong Ltd, London WC2H 0QY

Text design and typesetting by textype

ISBN 0091900344

Papers used by Ebury Press are natural, recyclable products
made from wood grown in sustainable forests.

Printed and bound in Great Britain by Mackays of Chatham PLC

CONTENTS

ACKNOWLEDGEMENTS

MORE PEOPLE DESERVE THANKS from me than space will allow or this book can justify. I trust that they know who they are, and how much I appreciate their help and support. It would be remiss not to single out Jon Wilde, Ben Marshall and Andrew Mueller, mainly for their encouragement, but also to deflect blame from myself. I'm particularly grateful to Karina Mantavia; the chapter on food could not have been written without our many conversations on the subject.

I should point out that with the exception of public figures (politicians, celebrities and the like) and my own family, all names in *British as a Second Language* have been changed. Folk who see their names appear can rest assured that the characters described aren't them. I must also admit to having fused a few characters into composites, although all events are drawn from life.

Finally, let me offer thanks in advance to anyone British who reads this book and doesn't subsequently march up my front path at the head of a lynch mob. Say what you like about Britain – I certainly have – but there aren't many countries where you could get away with this sort of thing. Furthermore, thanks in advance to anyone, British or otherwise, who reads this book, full stop. After all, nobody was ever forced to buy a book at gunpoint. Despite my efforts to persuade my publisher that the idea has its merits.

PROLOGUE

AT THE CONCLUSION OF the Second World War, the British Empire covered nearly a quarter of the globe. Within four decades it had shrivelled like a salted slug. By the mid-1980s it comprised the mainland, an adjacent and disproportionately pugnacious (even for Ireland) corner of Ireland, and a cluster of oceanic fly-specks, which served either as staging posts for narcotics traffickers or trysting grounds for several of the world's hardier seabird species.

I choose this timescale because four decades – forty-one years and the odd month, if you wish to quibble – elapsed between the two events in British history that hold the greatest personal significance for me. The first, the end of the war, is fairly well known; the second, my taking up residency in the country, inexplicably less so. This book may in some small way alter that imbalance. But I don't see how. Unless, by chance, a copy should fall into the hands of a decrepit Japanese jungle warrior in a Guam cave, and alert him to Hirohito's surrender.

In October 1986 I left my home in Nairobi, Kenya – where I had lived for thirteen years, following a two-year stay in Zambia – and flew to Heathrow, college-bound. I was eighteen years old. I had, as the saying goes, a suitcase and a dream. A day later, I was in Brighton and down to just the dream. Lufthansa Airlines, with ruthless German inefficiency, had elected to leave the suitcase in Nairobi. A dream is a fine thing to have, but there are times when you would settle for a change of underwear.

The passport I showed at the Heathrow immigration desk confirmed that I was British, and made a much better job of it than I ever have. I've spent a further eighteen years doing my damnedest to pass for British and only now, when I have all but given up trying, do I seem to be making the slightest headway. It says something about Britain that an Anglophone individual raised in former British colonies and educated in a British curriculum by schools organised on the British model should be wholly baffled by this island. Either that, or it says something even more worrying about the aforementioned individual.

I don't think it's all down to me. I have been to countries where the language sounds like castanets, while the dress calls to mind costumes in an avant-garde puppet play, and not found them one fraction so complicated or strange.

There may – *author clears throat, taps out pipe bowl against leather patches on elbows of tweed jacket, peers over top of half-moon spectacles* – be records of those eighteen years more thorough than this one, more authoritative and of greater value to social historians. To be honest – *author retrieves backrest of disintegrating swivel chair, in the process knocking pile of compact discs and dish of empty pistachio shells over his tattered trainers* – there's no 'may' about it, and to dignify what follows as a 'record' of anything is going it a bit. I've sketched it from memory; or rather, I've assembled a collage/relief portrait of Britain from the marks, knocks and bruises it's given me as I repeatedly bumped into it, tripped over it and cut myself on it.

I now know, to give just a trifling example, that you shouldn't get your dialling codes mixed up, and subsequently – during a telephone call to a business contact in Liverpool – ask how things are in Manchester. But I didn't then. I now know that the word 'knickers' applies only to women's underwear, and that announcing you've run out of clean items of same is liable to bring down ridicule upon a head already reeling with Scouse vituperation. But I didn't then. I now know that it's imprudent to enter into a ding-dong with a tramp who heckles you over your choice of suit. (That one should have been obvious at the time.)

The point is, I've been following a long learning curve where the incline, paradoxically, never eases to a gentler gradient. Britain's like that. If you weren't raised here, it will always be a land of shifting goal-posts. Not to mention abused metaphors. Often, I've felt like a wartime spy, forever mugging up on local customs, quirks and idioms, always in danger of being exposed during interrogation by my ignorance of bus routes and FA Cup finals.

Those who read my African memoir, *Tick Bite Fever* (thank you for your kind words, by the way, and good luck with the upcoming attempt to fit all of you inside a phone box), might expect this book to be a sequel of some kind. I wouldn't make that claim for it myself. If my biography since leaving Africa is of interest, it's not because of what it might tell you about some scribbler you've never heard of, but because of what it might tell you about Britain.

I've tried to recount the story of how I learned simultaneously to be British, and something resembling a grown-up (both projects still require a lot of work). I've documented the people who helped and hindered me along the way, and who introduced me to aspects of British life, sometimes with the best of intentions, sometimes with the most malicious. The friends who schooled me in UK culture. The colleagues who served as role models in inappropriate and self-destructive behaviour. The academics who blitzed my malleable mind with preposterous doctrines imported from the Continent. The market-stall traders, shop-keepers and publicans who seemed convinced that I was engaged in a perpetual wind-up. The patrician acquaintances who treated me with the amused condescension one might show to a monkey in a tuxedo. The scallies who filched my preposterous hat.

I've now resided as long in Britain as outside it. Inevitably, hindsight tints my outlook on this period, at times with rose, at others with jaundice. In writing this book, I saw no sense in trying to avoid such a perspective. Britain then is illuminated by the reflection of Britain now, and vice versa. Frankly, they both remain a bit weird in my incommutably alien eyes.

That Britain made me the man I am today, I would not dare to deny. If I were less civic-minded, though, I might sue for compensation.

CHAPTER ONE

STRANGER THAN KNOWN

A FEW YEARS AGO, a quirky little film by the title of *Galaxy Quest* came scampering off the Hollywood production line, paused briefly to thumb its nose at a nearby clump of lumbering blockbusters, then capered away to seek its fortune. *Galaxy Quest* was an endearing parody of the *Star Trek* series, based on the premise that aliens, exposed to transmissions of a cheap and hammy science fiction show, had concluded that it accurately depicted human life, and taken it as a model for their own society.

Following the normal course of things, you'd assume, the film made a modest worldwide profit of a few million dollars, went out to pasture on satellite TV and was eventually melted down for glue. You'd guess, too, that most of the people who watched it followed its storyline from the viewpoint of its human characters. And they probably did. But not me. I identified squarely with the aliens, because the same thing had happened to me.

I should qualify that: not exactly the same thing. But near as dammit. At eighteen, I came to live in Britain, imbued with an idea of Britishness formed at a great distance. The four thousand miles between Nairobi and East Sussex may not sound much, measured against even the shorter hops across the heavens, but in every way that mattered – bar the spaceship and the tentacles – I too was a creature from a faraway planet. I could not have been less well prepared had I spent my life up to that moment listening to thirty-year-old broadcasts of *The Light Programme*.

My understanding of Britain was based on brief holiday visits, yellowing copies of *Punch* and the opinions of my paternal grandmother, Miriam – a resident of north London whose views, I would discover, were as eccentric on this subject as on so many others. It therefore came as a shock to me that: Britain was not exclusively populated by a mixture of Trotskyite trade unionists, oil sheiks, busty young women and other such staples of the 1970s *Punch* cartoon; there were parts of it which did not resemble Golders Green; and not everybody in the country was after my grandmother's handbag. I was ready to learn, but first I would be required to unlearn everything I thought I knew.

It was probably for the best, then, that I came to Britain intending to further my education. Not for me the University of Life; the entrance qualifications would have been beyond me. I had settled upon the University of

Sussex. I made this decision the way I have always made decisions: by leaving it until the last possible moment, then hastily pulling a number out of the tombola that spins slowly and continually on an imaginary axis between my ears.

My luck held. I arrived in Brighton on a warm autumn day. I have loved the town ever since, although I saw nothing of it that morning save the inside of the train station, a handsome piece of Victorian industrial engineering which had fallen upon hard times. I would soon find out that this held true for the rest of my new hometown. There was something of the ruined duchess about Brighton in the mid-1980s.

I caught a connecting train to Falmer, and sat surrounded by hundreds of other teenagers, all of whom appeared to know each other. I spoke to no one. No one spoke to me. I spent the short journey staring out of the window, as the terraces gave way to hillsides, the hillsides to sullen estates, the estates to college campuses. On one side, Sussex University; on the other, Brighton Polytechnic. The division in status could not have been made clearer; it was signposted. There was a right side and a wrong side of the tracks. Your presumed future was determined by which way you turned as you stepped down from the carriage: left for the footbridge to prestige and excellence; right for the pathway to That'll Have To Do.

The distinction between polytechnics and universities would be eliminated within a few years, to loud disparagement – much of it, I'd guess, from folk who had attended one of Britain's less venerable universities and were eager to cling onto the rank they felt it conferred upon them ('I may not have been to Oxbridge, but at least I didn't slum it at a poly'.)

Sussex University is redbrick made manifest – a collection of rufous rectangular blocks sturdily embellished with uncompromising slabs of concrete, and marshalled with modernist resolve across a dip in the South Downs. It is one of those establishments built in the 1960s with right-angled pride in its purposeful contrast to ancient institutions. No spires and turrets, nor ornaments and filigree. It shrugged the burden of history from its square shoulders.

My elder brother Leon had gone to Cambridge on a scholarship, and it had been mooted I should follow him to the same college there. Two factors mitigated against this. One: where he was both diligent and dauntingly brainy, I was slapdash and half-bright at best. Two: my school in Nairobi, Knollpeak, failed to enter me for the correct papers in the entrance examination. I wound up improvising answers in subjects I hadn't studied for years, and then only to a rudimentary level. When, in the same year that I started at Sussex, I went with my family to Cambridge to mark Leon's graduation, I was surprised my photograph had not been posted at the college gates, along with orders to prevent me sneaking in.

Cambridge did not seem to have changed much since the era of *Chariots of Fire*, a film that, thanks to my father Max's erratic video rental technique, I had seen seventeen times. Here was a Britain I recognised: flagstones; bicycles; the suggested drone of a bearded Greek's synthesiser. While I merely occupied a room at Sussex, my brother dwelt in something called 'digs'. These proved to be an expansive suite directly above the archway into the college quad (they had quads here, too). He commanded this privilege as president of the Students Union – unwillingly carried shoulder-high into the post by cheering comrades, or so I gathered. It was one of the cheering comrades who tipped me off to this, and not my brother. If Leon ever wins a Nobel prize (a possibility I find more than plausible), our family will have to learn of it via the newspapers.

Leon was graduating with a double first in sciences. His friend Alistair had done very well at law. We met up with Alistair's parents in Leon's digs, where my father jovially offered Alistair senior a celebratory malt whisky. This was the cue for my grandmother to launch, bristling, into a fulmination against the evils of drink that would have wowed the severest cadres of the Temperance League a century earlier, but cast something of a pall over the day's jollity.

'You can laugh, but I think it's disgusting,' seethed my grandmother from the sagging depths of Leon's best chair, which by the look of it had last been sprung and upholstered shortly before the influx of the Black Death. An embarrassed silence blanketed the room.

'Thanks, Ma,' my father sighed, with despairing sarcasm. As my grandmother, never reticent in the first place, grew ever more cantankerous with age, he had found himself repeating this at the end of every other conversation.

Among my grandmother's many odd beliefs, none was firmer than the one that held my father to be the Mephistopheles of dipsomania. She had convinced herself not only that he was an irredeemable debauchee in his own right, but also that he had dedicated his life to luring his own children – Leon, my sister Lesley and me – into shameless dissipation. Beer or wine with a meal made her shudder. A liqueur afterwards was incontestable proof of our impending ruin. On those rare occasions when she elected to say nothing, she sat and radiated seismic waves of disapproval. Miriam was not a puritan, by ordinary standards. Drink was her particular bugbear. She also nursed an abhorrence of gambling, but for all her suspicions, was unable to turn up any evidence that my father had warped her grandchildren into the playthings of bookmakers.

My grandmother had lived in Britain since the early 1960s, when she and my grandfather, Toli, disgusted by the white supremacist regime in South Africa and weary of opposing it, left their home in Port Elizabeth and came to London. My parents had followed not long after, returning in 1971 to Africa, where I was raised, first in Zambia, then Kenya. When Toli died in 1973, Miriam remained in their north London flat, which, come 1986, she shared with Lesley. This, it would emerge, was as smart a move as housing a pair of Siamese fighting fish in the same small aquarium.

At the graduation ceremony itself, my grandmother resumed her best behaviour, barring an excited stage whisper that sibilated across the hall when Leon mounted the podium: 'Look! There's our one!'

As we took our leave in the car my father had hired, she remembered that she was meant to be angry. We drove down to Brighton, the plan being to have an early dinner, after which I would return to my residence and they would head back to London. Then we drove around Brighton for two-and-a-half hours, trying to find a restaurant my grandmother would agree to eat in.

'That one, Ma?'

'You know I can't touch Chinese food.'

'How about here, Gran?'

'It looks dirty.'

'This place looks nice, Miriam.'

'Ugh. Fish. Euch.'

We wound up as the only diners in a sepulchral steak-house, by now one of the few eateries left open, gamely hacking at sirloins cut from cattle that had undergone a special toughening regime under the direction of the military, perhaps involving assault courses and parachute jumps into freezing moorland. Even so, the meat had nothing on the vegetables, over which hovered the hard-bitten aura of grizzled mercenaries. To find the worst food in a British town is, as any visitor can tell you, a challenge, but we had met and mastered it.

That Cambridge visit was still some months off when I first came to Falmer. Setting out for Sussex from Kenya, I had travelled light. My worldly goods totalled a brown Samsonite suitcase bearing my brother's initials, two items of kitchenware (a milk pan and a saucepan) and the distinctly unfashionable apparel I stood up in. The suit-case was a solid piece of luggage, but not quite solid enough: it evaporated somewhere between Nairobi and Heathrow, and would re-materialise more than a week

later, begrudgingly lugged upstairs at my hall of residence, Brassic House, by a university staffer (not our regular porter, but an employee from another part of the
campus) who I'll re-name Ray.

'Thanks, Ray,' I said.

'Hnrrr,' muttered Ray, bitterly.

Ray, a compact, lecherous troglodyte who might have
passed for a satyr had he not comprehensively lacked any
kind of charm, let alone the cloven-hoofed variety,
already resented me. It was nothing personal. Ray resented everybody who wasn't either a curvaceous female
undergraduate or Ray. To him, time not spent leering at
the distaff portion of the tenantry was time wasted. Ray
was not, in my view, a nice man, and the day he surfaced
with my luggage is the only time I can recall being
pleased to see him.

In any other environment, wearing the same clothes for
a week might have dented my chances of making a good
first impression. But at the University of Sussex in the
mid-1980s, this was almost de rigueur among the more
seasoned (and I use the word in its aromatic sense) students. On odour alone, I could have obtained unchal-
lenged admission to almost any of the radically minded
clubs, societies and groups which glutted the campus.

That welcome would have lasted only as long as it took
the membership to clap eyes on my increasingly rancid
T-shirt: a black, sleeveless item emblazoned in yellow
with the words 'US Marine Corps – American Embassy –
Nairobi – 1982'. (A few years later, a local hepcat in a
Devon nightclub would ask me to name my price for that
garment. I declined, principally because I didn't fancy

walking topless through the streets of Exeter at two in the morning.)

My Yankee imperialist regalia I tucked into a pair of ill-fitting, lumpy jeans, purchased in a Kenyan backstreet four years of teenage growth previously. I needed only a semi-visible moustache and a cheeseburger clenched in my mitt; then I might plausibly have been teleported in from a convenience store car park in one of the less salubrious districts of New Jersey.

Once my suitcase arrived, I had a chance to make a second impression. This I duly did by donning, for indoor use, a *kikoi* – a brightly coloured and patterned item similar to a sarong – and flipflops, the attire I would have worn around my own home in Nairobi. It was possible that my fellow residents had until then suspected me to be some specimen of nutjob. Now it was certain.

I gave up on this outfit soon afterwards, when I knocked on a neighbour's door in the small hours to remonstrate about the noise – he was playing an electric guitar, very loudly and badly – and he responded with an Indian war whoop, then towed me full-tilt to the far end of the building by the hem of my *kikoi*, my flipflops sliding frictionlessly along the linoleum, and my arms waving in desperate circles as I struggled to keep my balance.

'I'm not going to take that from a guy wearing a skirt,' he sneered.

'It's a *kikoi*,' I protested.

'I don't care who designed it, it's still a fucking skirt.'
It was lucky for me that the new intake of students contained so many poseurs, square pegs and self-styled mavericks that my own idiosyncrasies, rather than singling

me out, acted as a form of camouflage. There were boys in foulards and ruffled shirts who thought they were Lord Byron; girls who came to classes in tutus; female skinheads (a year before Sinead O'Connor made this fashionable, it was seen as outright freakish); a fellow with a spider's-web tattoo across his face (it was unclear whether he was enrolled at the university or loitering around it for less savoury reasons); numerous individuals of indeterminate sex; and a few of indeterminate species. Amid the wider student body, a boy with a militaristic T-shirt and a large, brass, screw-locking bull-ring clamped around his wrist (the previous bearer, who wore it in his nose, had been eaten by my family) didn't draw a second glance.

Until, that is, I opened my mouth. Most listeners took me to be a white South African. This was tantamount to my parading in jackboots across the steps of the Students Union headquarters, Mandela House, with a swastika pennant in one hand and a golliwog dangling from a noose in the other. Explaining that (a) not all white South Africans automatically supported the Apartheid regime, and (b) I was from Kenya anyway, didn't do much good, as I seldom managed to get the first few words out.

My first act of assimilation, accomplished within weeks, was to assume a less infelicitous accent. Many years before, at a colonial-style prep school in Nairobi, I had spoken in Received Pronunciation. I now revived this, and was thereafter routinely disparaged as a bourgeois tool by people from Finchley with newly acquired glottal stops. That was still an improvement, and I was in no position to point the finger at them for changing the way they talked.

In the first week of the university year, Mandela House hosted the Freshers Fair. I went along with the boy from the room next to mine. Rob was as English as it's possible to appear without the aid of a bowler hat and furled umbrella. He had been despatched to Sussex with the advice of his Great-aunt Millicent (until then a type of relative I was convinced existed only in minor pre-war comic novels) echoing in his ears: 'Go to college,' counselled Great-aunt Millicent, 'and meet some well-behaved men.'

When the light struck Rob at a certain angle, he bore a strong resemblance to a young (and, as in the film *Pale Rider*, supernaturally ashen) Clint Eastwood; despite this, he had adopted, in a remarkable facsimile, the mannerisms of a middle-aged John Cleese. Rob was to become, and remain, a very good friend to me. He still looks as if he's stepped out of *Play Misty For Me*, but sounds much less like Basil Fawlty than he used to.

We wandered around the Freshers Fair, a souk for those with hobbies or hobby horses, where eager stallholders chivvied us to throw in our lot with mountaineers, hunt saboteurs, philosophers, motorcyclists, gays and lesbians, winter sports enthusiasts, oenophiles, botanists, pagans, stamp collectors, sci-fi fans, rugby players, cartoonists and – this looked interesting – the Sound Society.

At least, it looked interesting to us. The second-year student manning the table could barely summon enough interest to inspect his fingernails from behind his lank, overgrown fringe. His body language suggested that he had been shackled to his chair with a leg-iron. Rob and I stood over his table, inspecting the gadgets laid out upon it (drum machine, effects boxes, four-track tape recorder) for a minute or two before he noticed our presence. His demeanour changed instantly to that of a castaway catching sight, on the cusp of the horizon, of something which might or might not reveal itself to be the upper edge of a sail.

'HiI'mPete, 'he said. 'Areyouinterestedinjoining theSoundSociety? TheSoundSocietyoffersfreeusetoallits membersofawideselectionofequipment' – here Pete gestured at the goodies before us, still unable to trust his good fortune in inducing this pair of coneys take the bait – 'alongwithanannualbudgetforthepurchaseoffurtheritems.'

'Um, why not?' I said.

'Justsignandprintyournameshere,' said Pete, offering us a clipboard. 'Asnewmembersyouareeligibletostandfor theSoundSocietycommittee. Therearecurrentlyvacancies forchairmanandtreasurer. Youcouldbechairman,' he added, looking at me.

'Um,' I said.

'Greatandyou,' looking at Rob, 'couldbetreasurer.'

'Ah. . .?' said Rob.

'Brilliant! Herearethekeystothesocietyroomrightbehind me. Alltheeequipmentiskeptinthere. Ihavetogonowbutyou cantakeoverthedeskfortherestoftheafternoon. Goodluck andifyouhaveanyquestionsjustasktheoutgoingchairman.'

'Who's that,' I said.

'Me,' said Pete, and – like a genie granting a third wish – vanished into the empyrean and liberty. I never saw him again, which, over a period of three years, on a campus hosting only a few thousand people, cannot have been a coincidence. I suppose he always saw me first.

It didn't take long to work out why Pete had been so keen to rid himself of the Sound Society. It didn't actually do anything. As chairman, your duties consisted only of logging the equipment in and out; you were, effectively, an unpaid rental clerk.

I refused to be downcast about this. Obviously, what the Sound Society needed was a new broom. I discovered the literal truth of this when I opened up the office for the first time and a pall of dust out of the sunken tomb of Cheops settled upon me. The resulting zombie-like effect, combined with a choking fit, scuppered any chances I might have had with our sole female member, a pretty dyed-redhead called Jill, whom I was at that moment halfway to impressing with talk of how very much in charge I was.

I, or so I decided, would be a reforming chairman, revitalising the society, restoring it to its rightful vigour. To foster society spirit and, more pertinently, delude myself as to there being a reason for the society's existence, I organised jam sessions for the membership. Inevitably, this led to seventeen guitarists playing twelve-bar blues for an hour while Rob plunked inaudibly at his electric keyboard. The result was a vile, soul-crushing cacophony; to bring it to an end, I would willingly have bartered my soul to Beelzebub at a crossroads.

Rob, as treasurer, was responsible for the only fun part of the whole farrago: spending the budget. SoundSoc, as we now referred to it, controlled a few hundred pounds furnished by the Students Union, which had been throwing good money after bad for too long to stop now. We elected to buy a drum kit. Maybe if we bought drums, somebody would learn to play them. Not only would that mean SoundSoc boasted a drummer, it might also result in one less guitarist. A small step, but in the right direction.

We fetched up at an instrument shop in Brighton, where an affable garden gnome in a leather jacket – weather-beaten, perhaps, during his years spent holding a fishing rod over a pond – showed us around his selection of drum kit (this was a really tiny shop). The shells were stained a vivid scarlet, inlaid with glitter. It was hideous but cheap.

'Yours for five hundred pounds,' said the gnome.

'We could go as far as four hundred,' said Rob. 'We've got a budget.'

'It used to belong to Showaddywaddy, y'know,' the gnome protested.

'Three-fifty,' said Rob, not missing a beat.

I was impressed by Rob's willingness to haggle. Haggling was something I had grown up with in African markets, where the stated cost of anything was just a starting point, and vendors regarded you with delighted or sometimes affronted incredulity if you attempted to pay it. Arguing the toss over price was not a habit that went down well in Britain. After giving it a go with a fishmonger (who cheerfully refused to bargain), a taxi driver (who acquainted me with some useful Anglo-Saxon phrases) and a girl in a shoe shop (who met my offer with the same vacuous incomprehension she had applied to everything else I said), I got the message. And yet Rob got fifty pounds off the drum kit, which left me more confused than usual.

We packed the kit into the back of Rob's asthmatic Audi, a car that warranted the slogan *Stillstand Durch Technik* ('Going Nowhere Through Technology'). Every journey in that vehicle felt like its last, if not yours, too. I had learned to drive in Nairobi – and if you can survive that, you can survive anything – but all the same I refused to get behind the wheel of this moribund rattletrap. I feared it might give out beneath me halfway up a traffic-snarled 30-degree incline in a hailstorm with visibility at zero and enraged fellow motorists blaring their horns at me from all directions. Which is precisely what happened, about a year later – around the same time I finally found out who the hell Showaddywaddy were, as it happens. Taking the drum kit back to campus, I was so distracted by the rasping and grinding of the gearbox that I had forgotten to ask.

Any youngster moving away from home for the first time is bound to feel disoriented. The additional estrangement of being alone in an unfamiliar country, semi-detached from an unknown continent, had me even further rattled. I had been schooled in institutions over which the musty hangover of British colonialism still lingered. Now I had been dropped into a very different Britain, a country in an unsettled state, undergoing an eerie pause, as the excitements and convulsions of recent years quelled themselves, leaving only the occasional aftershock or shudder.

The drawback with immersing yourself in a country via college is that the college acts as a kind of diving bell. You are inside the country, but still separate from it.

Everything you encounter is filtered through a small, distorting window. As you shed the prejudices and misapprehensions that you brought with you, so you accumulate an entirely new set of prejudices and misapprehensions specific to your place of study.

Sussex may not have been an ivory tower, but in terms of keeping reality at bay, it was certainly a redbrick castle. Like any university – and more so, I suspect, than most – it was crowded with competing ideologies and disparate worldviews, none of which, it slowly became evident, bore a great deal of relevance to anything that went on outside its concrete gateposts. It may have been wonderful for British kids to come browsing at what was, in 1986, not so much a marketplace of ideas as a mini-mall of manifestos. They were well enough supplied with the local cultural currency to shop around: 'How much,' you could imagine them enquiring, 'is that dogma in the window?'

Sussex drew to its lecture halls a large number of youngsters ready for some form of indoctrination. Not that I wish to paint it as a re-education camp in disguise. The doctrines on offer were far too diverse for that. It was undoubtedly the case that the university had a reputation among the kind of teenager who feels impelled to try to change the world – always preferable to the kind of teenager who couldn't care less either way. As for me, I was more intent on trying to change myself. The world, I felt, could struggle on without my intervention for now.

I spent longer than I should have done sitting in my room thinking about all of this. I had been given a room on the north-western corner of the second floor of

Brassic House, a large and featureless cuboid on the edge of the campus. It was around eight feet by nine and contained a narrow bed, a washbasin, a desk and a chair. A single window opened, although not far, onto a steep upward incline, so that the vista consisted of an earth and grass slope a couple of feet away. To see the horizon, you needed to lie supine, parallel to the bed, with the top of your head directly beneath the window and your neck arched back at an unlikely angle. In this position, the horizon would be upside down and, due to the blood pouring into your inverted cranium, bedecked with swirling coloured sparks. But at least it provided proof that you had not, as you often felt, been entombed alive in a coffin the size of a tenement.

Alternatively, you could go and sit in the shared kitchen with the lights off, stare out over the roof of the neighbouring block at the night sky, and scare the Bejesus out of anyone who wandered in to boil the kettle. Evening after evening, I stayed in the soothing gloom until well past midnight, feeling utterly isolated. On one occasion, a girl called Catherine wandered in to make a cup of tea for her boyfriend, Matt.

'Eeek!' said Catherine, as she switched on the light to unveil my motionless frame propped up over the table.

I hadn't met anybody who spontaneously emitted the word 'eeek!' before, but Catherine was small, highly strung and given to vocal self-expression, so it made sense that she would.

'Why do you *do* that?' she said, and put the kettle on.

I wanted to explain that the sky provided the only view around here which bore even the remotest resemblance to where I came from. Instead, I accepted the offer of a cup of tea. Tea in England didn't taste like tea at all. It tasted like the ghost of tea, something brewed from memory rather than leaves. But it was hot and vaguely comforting. That was good enough – vague comfort for the vague malaise of a very vague young man.

CHAPTER TWO

SEXLESS DRUGS AND ROCK 'N' ROLL

SEX. DRUGS. ALCOHOL. Once these qualified as the only ironclad, nickel-plated, copper-bottomed, steel-jacketed and tin-hatted recession-proof industries. To that unholy trinity, we may now add nostalgia.

The boom in cultural necrophilia was still a few years off when I arrived in the UK, and more's the pity. It would have been a godsend to me – a never-ending stream of television programmes and magazine articles evoking a past more fondly recollected than it would appear to deserve. I don't remember going to buy Spangles on my chopper bike with a Rubettes single under my arm, for the pertinent reason that it never happened. But if I watch nostalgic TV programming for long enough, I can start to believe it did.

In 1986, my new-found peers had a vocabulary and a frame of reference I lacked, and felt impelled to attain. They had memories of Morecambe and Wise Christmas shows. They had rocket lollies and Green Cross Codes. They had older siblings who, ten years previously, had brought home punk rock records to antagonise their parents. It hadn't quite worked like that in my household. The only person to bring shocking material into our home was my father, who repeatedly, if inadvertently, rented videos of Hollywood's more risqué 1970s output – films called *Carnal Knowledge* and *Such Good Friends*, which he randomly grabbed off the shelf along with milder titles, and allowed us all to watch anyway, leaving me with the perception that sex was something only divorced New Yorkers did.

My older sister's tastes embraced nothing more esoteric than *The Rocky Horror Picture Show* soundtrack (she had never seen the film, but she knew all the dance steps). If my brother had even heard of punk, he gave no hint of it; he did, however, introduce me to The Beatles, by putting their *Revolver* album on our reel-to-reel tape deck and saying, 'This is pop music. You'll like it.' He was right about that. But it was 1977, the year 'God Save the Queen' unofficially topped the UK charts, and I was listening to John and Paul harmonise their ridicule of Mr Wilson and Mr Heath (who I guessed to be their former schoolteachers).

Eventually playground whispers reached my ears about a pop group called The Sex Pistols, which I thought was the rudest thing I'd ever heard of – and bear in mind, I'd watched some pretty gamey movies. By then, although I didn't know it, The Sex Pistols had already broken up; when you were that far away from the action, information reached you like the light from a dead star – a faint glimmer, opaque and scantly illuminating. One of my schoolfriends did treat a group of us to a couple of verses from 'Friggin' in the Riggin", the ribald traditional shanty recorded by the Pistols near the end of their fleeting career. I forgot all about it until a couple of years after that, when my father absentmindedly struck up a variation on the opening lines during a long car trip – up to Kenya's former Northern Frontier District, I believe – then quickly stopped himself.

> 'Twas on the good ship Venus
> By God you should have seen us
> The figurehead was a whore in bed
> And the mast a giant –

'How do you know that song?' I demanded, appalled.
'How do you know it?' he shot back, even more appalled.

By the time I left Nairobi, I had developed an appetite for British pop culture altogether unsated by my dismal knowledge of it. My experience veered towards the American side of things. American music was aired at school discos and on the national radio. American films and television shows were nightly fixtures on our video recorder. Saturdays were spent at softball games; my father was part of an international side, which, on 4 July, competed against – and to its opponents' chagrin, usually beat – teams from the US Embassy and the US Marine Corps. (That was how I had come by my infra-dig T-shirt.)

In the early eighties, just one shop in Nairobi sold imported records – Assanand's Music Store, on Tom Mboya Street. Where or how they sourced their goods was hard to guess; you might describe their stock as eclectic, but only if the word 'random' had slipped your mind. I would spend hours at a time flipping through their shelves, mulling over such prospects as *The Best of Jimmie Rodgers The Singing Brakeman*, Frank Zappa's *Joe's Garage Acts II & III* (which I bought but wished I hadn't), and *Bunty and Meena Sing Abba's Greatest Hits in Gujarati* (which I didn't buy but now wish I had; only the Cantonese version of Barbra Streisand's 'Woman In Love', overheard in a Chinese restaurant, could come close for entertainment value).

David Bowie had long since gone off the boil, but old albums brought into my school by clued-up chums were borrowed, auditioned and boggled at. The first British music paper I ever saw was a copy of the *New Musical Express*, insouciantly dropped onto the common room ping-pong table by a fellow called Geoff. Geoff spent his summers in England, and plainly rated himself a hipster. Compared to me, of course, he was; but compared to me, so was the slightly backward kid in year two with a picture of Ernie from *Sesame Street* taped to his locker (the picture was inscribed in felt-tip with the legend 'Ernie is my bumchum', so there's a possibility that he hadn't put it there himself).

Geoff was the one-eyed man in this particular kingdom of the blind. To hear him tell it, the UK music industry went on hiatus during Knollpeak term-time, when its teenage prime mover had other commitments near the equator. He spoke in first-name terms of people with whom I wasn't even on second-name terms. Who in holy crackerbarrel were Julian Cope or Pete Wylie? (If you find yourself asking the same question now, fair enough, but at the time, they were quite famous.) What was the function of an Icicle Works? Why should I care that someone called Frankie was en route to Hollywood?

And these were just the subjects of the articles. There was more. A page marked 'Charts' featured a handful of acts that even I had become aware of, but dozens more that were alarmingly obscure. There was something called the 'Indie' chart; as it made no mention of Bunty, Meena or anything else identifiably Indian, I could only assume this to be a reggae rundown from the West Indies. If so, it made no sense for The Smiths to be in there. I recognised The Smiths, although all I knew about them was that they had recorded a song called, 'What Difference Does It Make?', a mournful, self-pitying number with a remarkably lugubrious chorus, which I took to be a deliberate satire on adolescence. It wasn't reggae, but it was hilarious. I would walk around school at break-time with a couple of friends, all of us intoning it in the most funereal moans we could muster.

The Smiths turned up in that year's school general knowledge quiz. 'What name,' read the question, 'does the lead singer of The Smiths go by?' On the basis that the person concerned must have a sense of humour, I took a punt on W.H. Smith.

When I arrived in Britain, The Smiths were at their peak. Even for a straw-chewing colonial hick such as me, it was impossible not to become comprehensively informed of who Morrissey was and what he signified. This did nothing to revise my (still unchanged) opinion that he was a needle-sharp humorist savouring a very long laugh at the expense of his audience, which took him far too seriously.

Smiths fans were easily identifiable, even at college, where 90 per cent of the people you met matched the broad description. You could tell the true devotees from those who happened to wear big, grey overcoats by their demeanour, rather than their dress. They blocked the stairs at parties, or went so far as to lie on the floor – anywhere that they could get in the way and be visibly disconsolate, in the hope that somebody would ask them what was wrong. I'd done the same sort of thing myself, but not since I was thirteen.

Should a compassionate or naive soul (or a soul keen to get past them and reach the toilet) enquire as to their well-being, the Smiths fan would assume an expression of ineffable martyrdom, as of one undergoing an ordeal so far beyond the common lot it defied verbal explication. Then he or she would reply – like a brave little soldier bidding the others to carry on without them – that it didn't matter, there was nothing anyone could do anyway, and they would just have to endure it alone. This begged the question, 'So why did you come to a party?' but to ask it would prolong the conversation, and that was not to be recommended.

Perhaps unwittingly, The Smiths turned passive-aggressive behaviour into one of the definitive pop culture movements of the era. It would take another decade, and the arrival of the Manic Street Preachers, before feeling sorry for yourself would again blossom so spectacularly as a public creed.

It is hard to imagine this mindset coming to the fore anywhere but the UK. In Kenya, a band like The Smiths would have been met with nettled incomprehension. The impoverished majority would have wondered what they had to moan about, and the wealthy minority would have dismissed them as pointlessly dispiriting. Even in those parts of the world where basic survival is not a daily struggle, a band like The Smiths could never have emerged. In America, where – via the sonic equivalent of a tantrum – juvenile angst is generally associated with excruciatingly loud guitars, a homegrown version would have been branded a 'college band' and widely ignored. A French variant might have been admired for its literacy, but derided for its teenage preoccupations. There was something innately British about the mixture of superiority and self-loathing, of arrogance and apology, of precociousness and puerility which characterised followers of The Smiths.

For several of my new acquaintances, Morrissey's lyrics assumed the status of revealed text – from God's mouth to your ears, one might say. I admired The Smiths as artists, but as ever, I was a misfit among the misfits, failing to worship their singer as a prophet of post-adolescent doom. It wasn't until a couple of years later that Morrissey, now a solo performer, came up with something that resonated for me in such a vital way. This was a song called 'Bengali in Platforms', which saw him pilloried in some quarters as, if not a neo-fascist himself, then certainly a comfort to the knuckle-draggers of the National Front and the British National Party.

He only wants to embrace your culture,

sang Morrissey of the titular foreigner,

and to be your friend forever.

Life, Morrissey warned, to the fury of his detractors,

is hard enough when you belong here.

The inference drawn was that the Bengali did not belong here, and should go away. I didn't see it like that. It wasn't the singer who believed the Bengali did not belong; it was the ostracised Bengali who felt it. I knew I had a significant advantage over Morrissey's Bengali, in that my skin didn't mark me out as an immigrant. Otherwise, I felt, rightly or wrongly, a fellowship with the Bengali in platforms. And just as Morrissey forlornly entreated in his song, I didn't blame or hate the messenger for being the one to tell me. But like the Bengali, I was not about to take his advice, and 'shelve my Western plans'. I'd been working on them too long to abandon them now.

The room directly across from mine at the end of the hall corridor housed Sally, the resident adviser on our wing. Sally was also a first-year student, but she had the jump on the rest of us, being an unimaginably advanced twenty-four. She was well equipped for the job of providing help, guidance and sympathy; most of her charges were male, and Sally was a happy, vital odalisque endowed with both a certain maternal quality and a figure by Ingres out of Marvel Comics. She commanded attention, respect and pop-eyed lust in the richly balanced proportions that she herself embodied. When Sally spoke, men listened. Boys, such as myself, stared back at her with puppy-dog devotion.

Sally's room became the wing's salon, an arena for dilettantism and lively conversation. She was the Madame Geoffrin of Brassic House, North-West, Second Floor. In place of Voltaire, Montesquieu and Diderot, she had me, my neighbour Rob and Stephen from seven doors around the corner on the right. It wasn't quite the Enlightenment. Our guiding axiom might be summed up as, 'I disagree with what you say, so shut up and let Sally talk.'

Smoke and music poured out of every door on the corridor: Marlboro Lights (often infused with cheap hashish) and Kate Bush. Everywhere, the sound of Kate Bush, keening and gurgling and making like a tree. Kate Bush had not long before released *Hounds of Love*, as sublime an album as created by anyone in that decade. But that wasn't the record skirling and jarring on everybody's brand-new, poor-quality midi-system. Instead, her hits collection, *The Whole Story* – cluttered with dreadful, affected tripe from her earlier career – seemed to be on a permanent loop. Kate Bush caterwauled as I stumbled groggily to the showers in the morning. She pursued me down the hallway when I hustled tardily to my lectures. When I returned from the Students Union shop in the evening with my sorry haul of tinned ravioli, I would brace myself for her inevitable ululations. Was this what I'd been missing, and so eagerly awaiting?

There was a touch of irony in the fact that whenever Kate took a break, her place would be taken either by the Dire Straits album *Brothers in Arms* – a commercial juggernaut of relentless tedium which had crushed all before it, not excluding Nairobi – or by Paul Simon's *Graceland*. Having got away from Africa, parched for Western sounds, I now found myself pursued to Britain by African music. All things African were very fashionable at Sussex. Except, again, me. I was, reputedly, African, but I wasn't black, which just didn't seem right.

'You should join the Afro Society,' said Rashid, an engineering student, who had done just that. He wasn't African himself – I think this was the first time he'd been south of Hackney – but his father was black, and he qualified on the principle of extraction. Rashid, unusually for a budding engineer, had a keen sense of mischief. After enduring hours of tub-thumping Afrocentrism, he enjoyed the idea of dragging along someone from whom his associates would recoil as they might from a spitting cobra.

'I'm not going to get abused and humiliated just for your amusement,' I told him.

'Pity,' said Rashid.

Every couple of months, a Zimbabwean band called The Bhundu Boys – who must have recognised a sure thing when they saw one – turned up and played at the university. An over-enthusiastic audience in little round hats would crowd into Mandela Hall and pretend to enjoy the show. The sight of several hundred pallid Britons attempting to dance to music for which they felt no affinity, the rhythms of which bewildered them, was something to behold. I would, before long, get used to this scene; I noted that even when the music changed, the dancing remained no less awkward and ungainly. Today, I am just another of those pallid Britons. I can dance as badly as any of them, and worse than most. But I rarely do. Early on my technique was pinpointed as uniquely comical by my college compadres, and dubbed 'the Kenyan Disco Hop, Skip and Jump'. Even when it came to Terpsichorean incompetence, a British hallmark, I was literally out of step. I now dance only when I'm so inebriated that the only alternative is to pass out under a barstool.

Sally had been in her early teens when punk rock plummeted into her consciousness like a meteorite striking the roof of a Wendy house. She spent the next few years hitchhiking from her home in the Midlands to wherever her favourite bands happened to be – at first, other parts of the UK, and later, as far afield as Greece, Hungary and Yugoslavia, where she had met a very likeable chap called Karlo.

Karlo was madly in love with Sally and came to Sussex as often as he could to see her. This wasn't all that often, as he had been conscripted into the army. We sympathised with Karlo; we were all in love with Sally, too, although he was the only one who married her. Sally wanted to get Karlo out of Yugoslavia and into Britain; perhaps she had some notion of the way things were heading in his home country. Karlo wanted to spend the rest of his life with Sally. I wound up standing in as best man in what we all understood to be a marriage of convenience; all, that is, except Karlo. Eventually, he went back to Croatia with his heart broken, just in time for the civil war.

Like me, poor Karlo had no idea what he was getting into by coming to Britain, but was eager to make it work anyway. The consequences of his misunderstandings were immeasurably graver than those which followed mine. I was subject to little worse than embarrassment and the occasional threat of violence. But Karlo was so disenchanted that he was prepared to return to a battlefield rather than exploit the sanctuary Sally had contrived for him. I wanted to become a part of Britain; Karlo wanted no part of Britain, or rather, just one part – the Sally-shaped bit. He was entitled to feel that he had been chewed up and spat out. I was willing to let the country grind me in its molars indefinitely, so long as it eventually deemed me palatable.

You might gather from this episode that Sally was adventurous, impulsive, and at once compassionate and heedless. I certainly did. Her lengthy disappearances from the age of fourteen, living on the road and following bands with names like The Gobbers and Butchered Fraulein, must have had quite an effect on her father, who was by then a widower and her only parent. Visiting Sally at Brassic House, he bore that air of weary resignation common to those whom life has dragged through the rough and can now surprise no longer. When I got tanked up on mudslides (ferocious cocktails that slipped down like milkshake) at the subsidised campus bar in Park

Village and subsequently fell sidelong into Sally's lasagne, he didn't bat an eyelid. It must have been a relief to him, after Sally's years spent fighting off Bulgarian gang-rapists and drooling, soap-averse drummers, to find her in such harmless – not to say hapless – company.

'Where did you say you were from?' he asked me, towards the end of the evening.

'Nrrrrobi,' I replied.

'And you've never been in a rock band?'

'Nrrr.'

'That's good,' he said, looking approvingly at my sprawled, semi-comatose and sauce-spattered form. I think he may have had me down as future son-in-law material.

Via her tiny, tinny, single-speaker cassette deck – known affectionately around the corridor as 'The Abortion' – Sally introduced me to her favourite music. She adored The Stranglers (their tendency towards gruff misogyny, which they brandished as a badge of pride, didn't put her off in the least), The Ruts, and The Anti-Nowhere League, creators of the foul-mouthed anthem to nihilism 'So What'. It would have taken a far better developed eighteen-year-old than I to resist pogoing around her room and bellowing along to its venomous dismissal of a cocky tag-along. And it would have taken a far more self-aware eighteen-year-old than I to twig that I was very likely of a piece with the song's object of derision. Nobody likes a tag-along. But if you don't tag along, you stand no chance of keeping up.

Matt and Catherine, the young couple from Liverpool who had come down to Sussex University together, seemed to find the place as alien as I did, although for very different reasons. To me, it was the country itself that was strange and perplexing; to them, it was the university.

'I never thought I'd be in a place like this,' said Catherine, as a group of us sat at the kitchen table drinking quasi-tea one evening.

'It's not that bad,' I said. 'The people in the next corridor have a much smaller kitchen, and their rubbish bin always smells.'

'I mean at college,' said Catherine, doubtless marvelling at my ability to unfailingly grasp the wrong end of any stick presented to me.

Matt and Catherine did not see themselves as the kind of people who went to university, which is why they were astonished to find themselves there. I was too unworldly to understand how anybody might feel this way. It was completely lost on me that in Britain there might be barriers to overcome – social, financial, educational, psychological. I assumed that everybody took their exams, applied to college and was accepted by somewhere with suitably relaxed entry requirements – end of story.

The university was the only bit of Britain that made sense to me so far. You got up, eventually. You went to lectures, occasionally. You attended tutorials, dozily. You handed in essays, sporadically. It was just like school, only easier. You could more or less keep your own hours. You could eat what you liked (or rather, what you chose, which was not always the same thing). You could call the tutors by their first names; what's more, if you argued with them, they seemed to approve of this, and encouraged you to continue. The preposterous weather, early nightfalls and grumpy populace were mitigated by such prominent advantages.

At first, I pursued my studies energetically. Not because of any virtue on my part, nor because I appreciated my great good fortune in having this opportunity, but because I was too disorganised to buy an alarm clock. Instead I left my radio on overnight, humming with gentle static. When Radio 1 started at 6 a.m., so did I, lurching up in bed at the yammering of Adrian John and the blaring of the station's God-awful playlist. As an unnerving introduction to the day, it was surpassed only by the experience of staying at my grandmother's flat, where she would explode into the room frothing with indignation at the thought of my remaining asleep when she was not; upbraid me at high pitch, volume and pace for daring to be so; fling back the curtains with the brash vehemence of a circus strongman ripping in half a telephone directory; and rattle off a list of tasks she had lined up for me that morning – all inside of nine seconds flat. She prefigured almost exactly the American strategy of 'Shock and Awe' used to such overpowering effect at the start of the second Iraq war. It would take until a little after lunchtime for my pulse to subside to normal.

Duran Duran's 'Notorious' wasn't quite that alarming, but it did the trick, as did The Commodores' 'Goin' to the Bank', which was a brassy, up-tempo gripe at a gold-digging lady friend, and apparently on a permanent loop. That would have been bad enough on its own, but some genius at the record company had elected to dub over a spoken word passage in the middle with a breathless cockney voice, for the benefit of the UK market. Not only did this offer a small but significant indication of Britain's place in the American mind – a distant outpost with locals too insular to accept any accent other than their own on pop songs – it also took a mildly irritating tune and transformed it into one that was intensely aggravating, not to mention blitheringly incongruous. It was as if Max Miller had turned up on *Soul Train* to back Gladys Knight on the spoons.

Still, it got me up, and while I was up, I reasoned, I might as well do some work. That was before dope and Pink Floyd made me their bitch.

I forget how it started, which figures. Anthony may have had something to do with it.

Anthony arrived at Sussex a fully-fledged stoner. I was no stranger to what in Nairobi we had called *bhangi*, but it had always been an occasional and furtive pleasure – the surreptitious teenage equivalent of an after-dinner brandy. Not for Anthony. Here was somebody who, if he ever saw the world through unstoned eyes, might have keeled over in amazement at what it really looked like. His knowledge of life around him was as limited in its own way as mine; the difference was that my limits had been set by circumstance, while his were self-imposed. Where Anthony was oblivious out of choice, or perhaps a malfunction of the psyche, I was oblivious out of sheer witlessness.

The first time I stopped by his room, it was enveloped in a fug worthy of a Yen Shee Doy joint in Qing-dynasty Beijing. Anthony was propped up by one elbow on his bed, the very picture – albeit a blurry one – of an old-fashioned gong-kicker. A version of a familiar tune set to a Lovers Rock beat jinked out of speakers which were, like everything else in the room, hidden.

'That's a Van Morrison song, isn't it?' I asked, pleased with myself for identifying it.

'Who?' said Anthony.

Anthony had the countenance of a cherub – strawberry-blond curls, wide blue eyes, a winsome rosebud smile – an impression reinforced by his appearing to waft around atop a small cloud. But if he was the emissary of any unearthly power, it assuredly wasn't the one on the side of the angels. Dopers have a reputation for being amiably . . . dopey, inevitably. Anthony was neither amiable nor dopey. I came to believe that had he taken the least interest in anything other than reggae and hash, he might have been dangerous. Smothered in that haze was a gleaming edge, a sliver of menace. Fortunately, it was very well smothered. You only saw glimmers of it from time to time. When Sally stopped by the kitchen clad in nothing but a long T-shirt, a lupine flicker darted in his customarily blank pupils.

'Man, what I'd give for a piece of that ass,' he slavered creepily as she left. It wasn't the wish that perturbed me (you would need to have been blind, deaf and dead not to be stirred by the sight of Sally, and even then I wouldn't have bet against it) but the expression of it. We all yearned after Sally, but she was still Sally; anyone who could encompass her solely as 'a piece of ass' was missing something, not just about Sally, but within his own make-up – empathy, a connection to thoughts outside his own.

Whether it was the drugs, or whether a switch in Anthony's brain was already set to 'off', it's impossible to say, but his detachment from both everyday life and common feeling should have served as some kind of warning. It didn't.

Everyone on the corridor smoked dope at least occasionally, except for Rashid, who was an engineer, and like all engineers never did anything untoward; and Chris, who was not only an engineer but the son of a senior policeman. Although rumour had it that Anthony's dad occupied an exalted post in the Church of England – Bishop of Hither and Yon or some such. So paternal membership of the establishment was no marker for filial conduct.

Engineers were much teased by arts students for their unblinking, by-the-book conformity.

> Q: 'How many engineers does it
>   take to change a light bulb?'
> A: 'I don't know, we haven't done it
>   in lectures yet.'

The engineers in turn caricatured the arts students as slack, indolent, soon-to-be-unemployable potheads. They had a point. In my case, they had an irrefutable point.

As any campaigner against the liberalisation of laws governing the use of cannabis can tell you, the problem with this supposedly benign and innocuous drug is that it can act as a gateway to far more toxic and heinous abuses. So it turned out with me. I started innocently enough with Pink Floyd, but wound up listening to Gong.

The hard stuff sneaks up on you. One minute you're appreciating 'Interstellar Overdrive' on your pal Stephen's headphones, because Rob had said, 'You've got to hear this, you won't believe what the stereo does – it really is like a spaceship taking off.' Next thing you know, you're paying rapt attention to songs about Yonis, flying teapots and radio stations run by gnomes.

It's been claimed that Gong's vocalist, one Daevid Allen, persuaded his bandmates that they possessed the ability to walk through walls – and that around this time, photographs of the group tended to disclose a worrying level of bruising around the forehead area. Whether this is true, I wouldn't like to say. But having heard some of their desperately silly and yet desperately solemn recordings, I can certainly vouch for its being plausible.

'I'm living out my clichés,' complained Matt, from behind a spliff the size of his face. 'I'm sitting in a dorm room smoking dope with a bunch of students playing Gong records. What's happened to me?' He took a hefty toke and exhaled glumly, as if the smoke which now covered him might also cloak his shame.

The trouble with never having experienced a British childhood, or a British adolescence, was that I had so much catching up to do. Matt may have been living out his clichés, but it was all new to me. It's to Matt's credit that he was patient about it. I could hardly have blamed him if he had adopted the dismissive attitude of the Lou Reed song, 'Hangin' 'Round', one that he had heard a hundred times but I had only just encountered, crackling with treble via The Abortion.

Matt decided that if I was keen to learn, he ought to

teach me things actually worth knowing. He gave me a crash course in the underside of British pop since the punk era: Magazine; Cabaret Voltaire; New Order; Wire. I was wonder-struck at the realisation that bands like this existed, constructing dark, dense, acrid music seemingly out of right angles.

Matt also instructed me in matters that would have been better left unexplored, such as 'buckets' – a method of inhaling marijuana smoke that involved a bathtub full of cold water and the top half of a large, plastic soft drink bottle.

After trying it, I couldn't move from the bathroom floor. My head felt like a helium balloon tethered to the lead sarcophagus of my body. Abandoned by my fellow psychonauts, I succeeded in switching on the hot tap, and hauled myself into the tub, where I slumped, wobbling in and out of consciousness, until Sally arrived for her morning shower and discovered me stretched out like Marat in fifteen inches of tepid fluid.

'Are you ok?' said Sally.

'Fine,' I said.

She thought about this for a little while, then said, 'You do know that you've still got your clothes on, don't you?'

To deduce that ingesting LSD might not be a bright idea, you had only to look at Charlie and Sam. Not that you would be well advised to look at Charlie or Sam for any length of time, singly or in tandem.

Charlie was the doughy, vacant offspring of a high court judge (there was definitely a pattern emerging here). He always had a mysteriously damp air about him, as if he was drying his clothes by wearing them. Wispily coiffed, he was fond of paisley scarves, louchely unbuttoned shirts and – I could swear to this, but it seems so unlikely that perhaps memory plays me false – the only tie-dyed duffel coat I have ever laid eyes upon.

Sam, a maths student, favoured jeans and leather biker jackets. You wouldn't have noticed much amiss about Sam until the saucer-like eyes beneath the close-trimmed, pudding-bowl haircut lighted upon you. Those eyes were windows into a haunted and broken soul. They had gazed into the abyss, and seen the abyss gaze back into them. They were also eyes in which, owing to their owner's prodigious consumption of psychedelic drugs, the pupils frequently expanded beyond the circumference of the contact lenses resting upon them, inducing even greater hallucinatory panic into the fretful, addled brain behind them than was customary.

Sam and Charlie were textbook acid casualties. If they had ever known when to stop, they had long since blitzed that faculty into mental smithereens. To take as much acid as Sam and Charlie did, you had to have taken as much acid as Sam and Charlie had. To want to take as much acid as Sam and Charlie did, you had to take as much acid as Sam and Charlie habitually would.

Charlie had reacted to this self-inflicted maltreatment by shutting down all but the most essential interactions with the outside world. His movements were those of a man walking along padded streets upon a quilted pavement. He said little, preferring to glassily and non-committally eyeball anything that crossed his vision, his mouth hanging open in perpetual puzzlement. The lights were on, but fitted with a dimmer switch; and as to whether anyone was home, it scarcely seemed worth finding out.

Sam was different. Sam wanted to communicate. He was a good-natured type, and might well have been intelligent – it was impossible to say. Sam talked. A lot. In a unique and agonising way that managed to be both staccato and achingly slow. His voice had diminished to a husky, slurred murmur. He would utter a sluggish phrase, pause for half a minute, then embark on the next one. Had some uncommonly fiendish sadist adopted the use of treacle in the Chinese Water Torture, the torment would have replicated with striking verisimilitude that of Sam's conversation. It wasn't until I saw Keanu Reeves attempt Shakespeare that I beheld anything similar to Sam's delivery, and even then, you'd have to slow Reeves by a factor of ten to approximate the effect.

Worse still, when you hung around long enough to piece together Sam's remarks, you found they made no sense at all. Sam's mind compulsively dismantled everything that was fed into it. If he read a newspaper, he would split up the words and take fright at what he found within. Then he would try to show you what had spooked him.

'It says . . . "skills . . . workshop" but . . . if you . . . cover the . . . "s" . . . with   your . . . hand   it . . . says . . . "kills works". And . . . "hop". I don't . . . know . . . what . . . "hop" means. I mean, I . . . do . . . know what . . . "hop" . . . means but . . . not . . . here.'

Half an hour of this and you were ready to feign death just to make it stop; or failing that, actually drop dead. On more than one occasion when Sam had called round unannounced, I simply fled my room after a while and left him there. I felt bad about this, as he was a well-meaning fellow who had lamentably sabotaged his own ability to associate with others. Invariably, when I went back, Sam would still be there, ready to resume his monologue as if nothing had happened. Perhaps the acid had deprived him of any sense of time, and he was unconscious of the fact I had been absent for hours. Maybe he'd carried on talking regardless – or taken advantage of this helpfully extended lull while he rallied the next two or three words in his head.

'. . . but if you . . . cover . . . up . . . this bit . . . here . . . it says "orks . . . hop" which is . . . spelled . . . different . . . ly . . . but could . . . be . . . some . . . thing out of *The Lord of the* . . .'

He would break off again, sapped by this verbal sprint of seven uninterrupted syllables.

'. . .'

(He nearly had it.)

'. . . *Rings.*'

Still, I was determined to try LSD. Not even Sam and Charlie could put me off. I rationalised my wish with the thought that both of them had bludgeoned their poor brains into submission with ever larger hits every few days. I would be more careful.

Matt procured what he described as 'microdots' – tiny specks of the chemical – which he stored in the freezer. Sally, like a licensed day carer supervising a birthday party for tots, took charge of the proceedings. Rob, Stephen and I each swallowed one dose and sat, waiting, in her room. Nothing happened.

After three-quarters of an hour, I'd had enough. I stood up. 'I don't feel anything,' I announced. 'I'm going to bed.' I fell over, rolled myself up in Sally's tassel-ended rug and bunny-hopped cylindrically to the corner, then refused to budge for the next five hours.

I took acid on two further occasions. Not once did I see God, talking Technicolor salamanders or my feet melting into the carpet (this last hallucination beset Sam all the time, apparently; he would pace the floor so as not to miss out on the sensation, then become so terrified about it that he dared not stop lest he slowly dissolve from the shins upward). I did, however, have a tremendous time. Then I quit while I was ahead.

These stock teenage transgressions meant more to me than a mere experiment in rule-breaking. When I was growing up, The Beatles and the legacy of the 1960s were not woven into life's fabric, as they had been for my contemporaries in the UK. Nor had I been surrounded by adults smugly reiterating, in person and in print, what a marvellous generation theirs had been; how it had meant something, and believed in something; how it had initiated a social revolution and attempted a political one. And maybe it was. Maybe it did. But I swiftly became as weary of hearing it as my British-bred contemporaries must have been. Every so often, from my arrival in the UK onwards, I've watched as politicians in need of an easy target attempt to pin the ills of the moment – crime, illiteracy, poor penmanship – on the 'permissive' attitudes of the 1960s. Each time, I've dismissed this as a cheap diversionary tactic – until the faces of the era duly step forth to protest how wonderful those years really were. At that point, I would gladly blame them for anything.

For most of the adults I knew as a child, the decade had hardly taken place. These folk had been too busy with quotidian chores and demands to attend to anything more radical than a vertical-drum washing machine. They had been as far removed from the hub of revolution by circumstance as I was by time. I came to Britain still accepting the myth of the 1960s as a time of wonder; and I genuinely believed that drug-taking would assist my remedial education – bring me up to speed, so to speak.

In case you're wondering, I didn't move on to speed, even though it might have furthered my understanding of punk rock. If cocaine, in the catchphrase of the day, is God's way of telling you that you have too much money, then speed is His way of telling you that you have too little. Like any student, I had a bank for that.

CHAPTER THREE

LOST IN THE SUPERMARKET

THE BANK I CHOSE was one of two on the Sussex campus. The other one was subject to a boycott from students over its investments in South Africa. Moreover, it was half a mile away, whereas my new British bank stood a twenty-second amble from the door of Brassic House. When the right thing was also the lazy thing, I was happy to stand up and be counted, so long as I could sit down again straight afterwards.

My father had been closely involved with the African National Congress in the 1950s and 1960s. Detestation of the regime in South Africa was taken as read in my family,

as it was in many others. It had not struck me that identifying and condemning something so obviously wrong
could be a cause for self-congratulation. That would be
like patting yourself on the back for recognising that, say,
child molestation or cannibalism was a bad thing. You
simply abhorred it because what else was there to do?

There were those at Sussex who took a different
approach. Apartheid was the great moral luxury of the
era, a monster by which you could define yourself through
your opposition. Which is not to suggest that the British
anti-Apartheid campaign was neither heartfelt nor effective (it was both of those things, and to imply otherwise
would insult many honest and dedicated people); only
that it was also the recipient of a fair amount of lip service, and functioned as a bandwagon for some whose
principal concern was that they be seen to hold the right
opinions.

I could have made life much easier for myself by agree-
ing with those folk at every turn, or at least silently nodding assent until I got my accent straight. Given my bent
for making my life easier in any way possible, I wonder
why I didn't do that. Instead, I primly insisted on contest-
ing the issue.

'Yes, I'm against Apartheid and for the boycott,' I
would find myself saying, over and again, in common
rooms, in cafés or at kitchen tables. It was like a pledge of
allegiance; you couldn't speak out before you offered it.
'I'm also concerned about what a collapse in South
Africa's economy would do to the neighbouring countries,
seeing as it feeds most of them.'

'What are you, some kind of racist Afrikaner boer?'

'"Afrikaner boer" is a tautology.'

'Don't use your racist terminology on me, you racist . . . *racist*.'

There was precious little point, too, in trying to argue that almost all of the major banks had fingers in the Outspan lemon pie cited by a memorable protest song, 'I Support The Boycott', as a symbol of Apartheid-tainted trade. The righteous had picked their target – and their target's competitors, no less complicit, picked up their target's business, mine included.

At the time, a national ad campaign was promoting the new home of my remittance as 'The Listening Bank'. When I walked down to open an account, the first thing I noticed was a giant graffito scrawled on the side of the building: 'If this is the listening bank, then walls have ears.' It didn't fill me with assurance. Passers-by were pointing at the message approvingly, and remarking upon the bank being deaf to grievances about the funding of arms deals. I reckoned that the slogan was not politically motivated, but the work of a disgruntled customer. My own acquaintance with the bank wouldn't do much to alter this interpretation.

Nonetheless, I needed a bank account, and whatever The Listening Bank lacked in sympathy it made up for in proximity. I joined the queue of cheque-carrying applicants, still chuckling at the words on the wall. They had superseded my favourite graffiti, spotted in the narrow, grimy underpass that led from the train station to the university. 'Meat is Murder!' some impassioned vegetarian had scribbled. Another hand had appended: 'It's not as bad as listening to The Smiths.'

Vegetarians were forever invoking the idea of murder, in the hope that it would put the rest of us off our meat. It didn't work. We were already reconciled to the idea that animals had to be killed in order for us to eat them; we weren't under the illusion that they perished of happiness in sunlit fields and willed their bodies to the greater gastronomic good.

'I bet you wouldn't eat it if you had to kill it yourself,' the vegetarians would say.

'I would,' I replied, 'I have, and if needs be I'll do it again.'

The herbivores in Brassic House also started referring to the popular wares of the nearby fast food counter as 'murderburgers'. That didn't work either. The meat-eaters cheerfully adopted the phrase, and used it unselfconsciously.

'I'm off to the murderburger bar. Anybody want anything?'

'Nah, but while you're out I could use a pack of twenty deathsticks.'

Within a few days of opening an account for me, The Listening Bank sent me a cheque book and guarantee card. The card had been issued to somebody named Mr D. Bnnnnvn. 'Come and talk!' ran the bank's advertising jingle. 'Come and talk to The Listening Bank!' So I took the card and went to talk to them.

'And what's wrong with it?' said the teller.

'Look at the name,' I said.

She looked at it. 'Where's the problem?'

'My name's been spelled wrong.'

'Well, you can hardly blame us,' she sniffed. 'With a

name like that, it's easy to get a letter or two out of place.'

'That's assuming you use the right letters in the first place,' I said, allowing myself to be sidetracked. 'Are you telling me that it's beyond this bank's professional ability to copy down an unusual name correctly?'

'If it's *that* unusual, then a mistake is always possible.'

'That,' I said, 'would be no excuse, even if that was my name. But the point is, it's not. It's not anybody's name that I've ever heard of. I know there are lots of foreign students here. I'm one of them. But how many of them come from outside our solar system?'

'There's no need to be sarcastic,' she said.

'Yes, there is. I don't think there's any country in the world where the names don't have at least one vowel in them. Not even Poland.'

'We'll replace the card free of charge,' she said, as if bestowing an extravagant favour upon me.

'I see. So you got my name wrong, but you're not going to make me pay for the privilege. Thank you for that.'

'You're welcome,' she said, investing the phrase with real venom.

In the UK consumers' rights have become a major issue, and expressing your dissatisfaction with substandard merchandise or services is no longer frowned upon. It still gets you nowhere, but it's no longer frowned upon. In the mid-1980s this wasn't so. You took what you were given and offered grovelling thanks to the surly donor in the hope this might cheer them up. I wasn't used to this. I was used to Nairobi. There, while persistent and vigorous complaining might not achieve anything, there remained half a chance that it might; whereas without it, nothing would happen at all.

One of my regular tasks back at home – along with capturing and ejecting poisonous baboon spiders the size and shape of a large, hairy hand, when they crept into the house during the rainy season to escape the wet – was to chase up whichever utility had cut off our supply that week. This might involve driving down to the water company's district office, where a contemptuous young bureaucrat was to be found, feet up on his desk, and toothpick between his lips, idling away the morning with his equally lethargic sidekicks.

'Our water has gone off,' I would say.

'Use what's left in your pipes,' he would dismissively reply, 'and maybe it will be back tomorrow.'

'That's not good enough. We need it today.'

When he realised I wasn't going to go away, he would climb into my car and direct me to whichever local building site, roadworks or irrigation project he guessed had severed the main or hijacked the supply. It generally took a few hours of sleuthing, chauffeuring and remonstrating, but more often than not I would have a result by the end of the day.

Although chronically shy in most situations, I brought with me to Britain this attitude that anyone to whom you paid money should be badgered until they delivered what they owed you. I soon found out I had it the wrong way around. As a rule, unless you were socially assertive, there was no point leaving your room. Nobody would talk to you. But when it came to business transactions, anything other than abject meekness on your part would be met by the employee in question with wounded stupefaction or ill-suppressed pique. That said, approaching them in the first place, no matter how humbly, and obliging them to think about their job, produced the same effect; but having forced this injustice upon them, it was now incumbent upon you to act apologetically from the off.

To ask supermarket staff for assistance was like pleading for a boon from medieval royalty. Your approach had to be sufficiently unctuous to emphasise that you knew your place, and had no business making demands on their time. A sulky girl, propped up against a shelf like a cut-price consignment of shopworn tinned mince, might watch you scrabble through a freezer cabinet for several minutes without betraying the least sign of interest, or even of a heartbeat.

'Excuse me?' you would at last say. 'Excuse me? Excuse me? Yes, hi. Do you have any garden peas?'

'Freezer's over there.'

There were moments, I admit, when I must in turn have tested these people's composure. I still wince when I think of how I approached a scrofulous teenage shelf-stacker in a Gateway supermarket and asked him, in my recently perfected RP, 'Pardon me, do you know where I might find the *sauce tartare*?' Had I been garbed as Mr Peanut, the Planters mascot, complete with top hat, white gloves, spats and a monocle screwed into my right ocular pit, that youth could not have gazed at me with more profound contempt.

After a five-second pause that lasted a week, he said, 'Dja mean tah-tuh sorse?' and gestured towards an adjacent aisle. I went to retrieve a jar. He watched me all the way.

The tartar sauce was indistinguishable from the sandwich spread I sometimes bought, although in the absence of either I could make a meal of salad cream on a couple of slices of rubbery wholemeal bread (I was always sure to buy wholemeal bread; sliced white with my salad cream might have been nutritionally inadequate).

As with most males of that age, I was a culinary imbecile. And in this, for once, I was in tune with my new homeland. If there is a country in the world more beef-witted about food than the United Kingdom, then I've yet to visit it or hear of it.

The soul of almost any nation lies in its cuisine. But to assume this is true of Britain would be to damn the place. Despite the claims of celebrity chefs, who have branded an adaptation of French cooking 'modern British cuisine', Britain has no cuisine *per se*; and if that premise were followed, could be said to have no soul. I don't believe this to be so, although I know people who do.

Why Britain has no cuisine is a matter of conjecture. It used to have one, so historians of the subject claim. Britain saw the world's first industrial revolution, uprooting millions from the land upon which a cuisine is founded. Still, the rest of Europe's nations subsequently underwent the same upheaval without forsaking their gustatory identities, so that seems an unlikely culprit. More plausible is the tribulation of enduring two world wars within three decades, on an island subject to barricade and potential starvation. Maybe rationing, combined with an agricultural policy geared towards self-sufficiency at any cost, served to de-nature the British palate so absolutely that it would thereafter be content with a poverty of provender unreplicated in any other wealthy nation. Including Germany, where finding any repast that does not arrive beneath half a pound of melted cheese is a constant challenge to the visiting diner.

By poverty, I don't mean shortage. As the obesity statistics indicate only too well, there's plenty of food to be had in Britain. I mean poverty of quality, of imagination, of flavour, of flair, of spirit.

At eighteen, when I too lacked not only those attributes, but also the ability to recognise any of them should they have tap-danced over my epiglottis to the accompaniment of Cab Calloway's 'Everybody Eats When They Come to My House', this wasn't a problem. Here was a land where not just teenage numbskulls but the majority of the population fed itself upon suspect matter frozen and shrouded in breadcrumbs. The British would consume anything so long as they couldn't tell where it came from. Was it chicken? Fish? Meat? Did it matter? It had been ground into slurry and wrapped up in batter, it took three minutes to heat and it served as a vehicle for ketchup. That was all you needed to know.

Inevitably, I found my way to Bejam.

Children, being children, are contrary little beggars. I was raised in a country where the produce, for those who could afford it, was of the highest standard, and so fresh that if you put your ear to a sirloin you could hear it lowing. So nothing excited me more than trips to Europe and the Americas, where I could visit McDonald's. I recall that my stepmother once grilled salmon steaks and put mine, at my insistence, in a bun. I told her that it was 'nearly as good as a Fillet o' Fish', although I didn't mean it; I was just trying to be polite. As you may gather, I had a lot to learn not only about food but about civility.

Put me in a country where McDonald's all but qualified as haute cuisine, and this, if nothing else, saw me in my element. When it came to my meals, I was a serial monophagist. I would latch onto an indelicacy and eat nothing else for weeks. I started off on tinned ravioli from the Students Union grocers – salt and sugar packed into a glutinous compound that gave off a half-familiar smell I couldn't quite identify, until I went home on holiday and was asked to give the dogs their dinner.

Even the ravioli was classy grub compared to the stuff I brought home from Bejam. Lined with freezers emitting a sinister hum, and invariably depopulated save for a refugee from the House of Usher decomposing mutely by the till, this was a morgue of a shop, tucked into an obscure corner of Brighton town centre's Churchill Square.

Just as all the oceans' shipwrecks were once held by sailing legend to inch along the marine bed until they came to rest in the Sargasso Sea, so an entire country's prandial ignorance and bad eating habits appeared to have eddied to a standstill in this one outlet. Hungry for acceptance, I adopted those bad eating habits myself. I bought and gobbled down meat pies: compact, elasticated pastry capsules filled with a dark, feculent ooze. Then came bacon offcuts, gummed together into fat, misshapen slabs sweating greasy water. And at last, inevitably, I sank low enough to uncover the nation's lowest common comestible, the uber-victual of the British diet, exemplifying all the traits – processed beyond recognition, leeched of nourishment and savour, de-textured, frozen, crispy-crumb-coated – that united into a monolithic, unthinking contempt for the pleasures of the table: the fish finger.

I was lucky. Having been brought up on good food, once I had glutted myself on Britain's quasi-infantile staples, I was ready to start feeding properly again. And even when my standards were at their lowest, I remained shockable. The first time I saw a tin labelled 'Mushy Peas' on a supermarket shelf, I took it to be a situationist jape at the expense of the British diet, and marvelled at the creditable accuracy with which the perpetrators had reproduced the store's own branding. I held it up, pointed at it and laughed. Rob, who had accompanied me on the shopping trip, gave me that look – slightly worried, a little indulgent and altogether uncomprehending – with which I was swiftly becoming familiar. It was the look I received whenever I pointed out, in wonder, something that everyone around me took to be mundane and universal. A generation earlier, my parents, also newly arrived from Africa (whence they eventually returned), had experienced similar confusion over 'fresh' fruit salad that was unmistakably canned, and most startling of all, mince pies, which were as different from their description as anything edible could be.

After a while, I began to pretend that nothing struck me as unusual, which is why I later allowed a toaster to catch fire in the hall of residence kitchen, while I fixed myself a bowl of cereal.

'Couldn't you smell the smoke? Why didn't you do anything?' said the aggrieved owner of the toaster.

'I thought you liked it that way,' I said.

The more I learned, the less I knew.

There is a story which has been told and re-told against different targets (generally Labour politicians of a metropolitan stripe), wherein the protagonist walks into a chip shop and mistakes the mushy peas for guacamole. Once again, I find myself siding with the gag's presumptive foil. Why should we taunt someone for the cheerful supposition that the dish he was faced with might be fresh and appetising rather than factory-processed into something slightly less enticing than its already off-putting name would suggest? Anywhere else in the world, the joke would be on the chip shop. Although where else in the world would you find a shop that based its entire *raison d'être* on chips?

You might find one in Belgium, if you want to be pedantic. But I defy anyone to chow down a cone of Belgian *frites* (which are usually crisped to swift perfection in clean oil) and then announce a preference for the clammy, half-mashed output of a typical British chippy circa chucking-out time. Then again, I expect I'm being over-optimistic. I have known several girls whose biological clocks alert them not to babies but to soggy chips; at 11.45 p.m. precisely, an internal alarm rings, triggering in turn a mechanism that propels them, instinctively and ineluctably, to the nearest vat of bubbling fat. Most of these girls hailed from northern England or western Scotland; no doubt there's a reason for that, but I'll leave readers to decide what it is.

The apocryphal tale of the guacamole that never was exemplifies a crucial feature of British eating – a dietary class divide unique in Europe, if not the globe. A friend I met at college, Helena (a sweet and improbably posh girl who existed at three removes from everyday reality, and whom I suspected might have escaped from an early work by Evelyn Waugh), once remarked, with the lofty compassion of Catherine the Great -

'I do feel awfully sorry for poor people, having to eat beans all the time.'

Helena was prone to such jaw-dropping utterances, and we'll hear more from her later. With that particular show-stopper she managed to simultaneously make and miss a serious point. It is a crying shame that anybody should subsist on baked beans, but thinkingly or not, people do so out of choice, not need. Pointing this out does not equate to sneering at their poverty. In most aspects of their lives, the British, like anybody else, enjoy the best they can afford. Food is the glaring exception.

In almost any other reasonably wealthy European country, the rich may eat better than the poor, but the poor do not eat badly. Money buys you fancier meals and more luxurious ingredients, but a lack of money does not condemn you to fish fingers or micro-chips. Expensive food is a privilege; good food is not. In Britain, not only is good food a privilege, but it's a privilege sneered at and dismissed as vaguely effete by those who do not possess it. Hence the contempt directed at the guacamole fancier: 'Mushy peas not good enough for you, eh? Well, they're good enough for us, so who do you think you are, coming round here for our votes?'

If you like to eat out, this is an inescapable problem. Outside of London, restaurants and cafés tend either to be cheap and dreary, outrageously expensive or driven by aspirations they cannot possibly live up to. How often have you seen a menu that offers something along the lines of 'Guinea Fowl Membranes in a Pharyngeal Jus, Piddled with Hasidic Vinegar'? A tip: the chef has probably never set foot outside Darlington. Have the boiled eggs.

My subsequent travels around Britain would take me to the chicest chophouse in a Welsh port, where the 'Mexican' specialties (each of which encompassed every form of starch known to chemistry) were distinguished not by any variation in flavour or ingredients, but solely by the pseudo-tortilla which encased them. To a hotel in St Helens, where the tuna, salmon and chicken sandwiches were marked on the menu with an asterisk; a footnote explained that these were the 'vegetarian options'. ('Well, we're bloody trying,' you could all but hear an exasperated catering manager exclaim.) To a restaurant in Brighton called Greetaly ('Greek and Italian cooking combined on one menu!'), which I visited out of morbid curiosity, and which turned out to be even worse than I expected – not only did it fall between two very tall stools, it then pulled them down on top of itself and clattered headlong down the stairs into a squalid basement of oil-slicked alimentary distress. True, I never ran into anything quite as discouraging (or as wacky) as the restaurant in Copenhagen which served me a steak and Béarnaise sauce garnished with chopped banana. But I think that was a deliberate wind-up. A Danish friend tells me he has never heard of such a thing before or since. Whereas anyone who has traversed the UK will very likely have had experiences similar to mine.

If it's true that you have to hit rock bottom before you can begin to climb back up again, then the nadir of my self-inflicted dining misadventures came about in the small hours of one munchie-ridden night. Having failed to stock my own mini-larder, and lacking even 20p for the Kit Kat machine (installed in the foyer of Brassic House by cunning confectionery pushers) that swallowed up about a third of my stipend as quickly as I could swallow up its contents, I knocked on Rob's door.

Rob wasn't pleased to see me. To be fair, it was 2.30 a.m., and only two days previously, also at 2.30 a.m., he had blearily swung back that same door to find me and Stephen goggling at him like a pair of unusually incoherent circus chimps. So wide were our smiles you could almost hear us grinning, in stereo. We had wanted Rob to get up, get dressed, walk to his car with us and drive us the five miles into Brighton town centre so we could buy doner kebabs from a suppurating, malodorous health-and-safety violation that closed at three o'clock. It had been a week since Stephen had introduced me to doner kebabs. So far I had eaten ten. Its supposed near Eastern origins notwithstanding, the doner kebab is so definitively British an offence against both the tastebuds and the digestive system that you could mount it on the foreground of the Union Jack without causing widespread dissent among the kind of people who think about that flag in any context other than sport.

Rob hadn't been pleased to see me then, either. 'You're smiling,' he said sternly to Stephen and me, 'because you actually think I'm going to do this.' We broadened our grins to face-splitting dimensions and nodded happily. The truth was we were smiling because we were hopped up on a consignment of Red Leb hashish so potent that to stop us smiling would have required a team of neuro-surgeons equipped with sandblasters. But we weren't going to argue. Gripped as we were by primeval kebab lust, and with rational thought and intelligible speech being likelier to evolve in the aforementioned circus chimps before returning to our own grasp, we weren't going to say much at all. If we just grinned and nodded for long enough, kebabs would be ours.

We were right. Rob drove us to the kebab shop. 'I don't know why I'm doing this,' he kept repeating, over the wheezing and hiccuping of his dilapidated Audi. We didn't either. Nor less did we care. We had duodena to ravage.

So when, forty-eight hours later, Rob found me at his threshold doing a solo repeat of that earlier turn, he glared at me as if he wished to shrivel me to ashes, miraculously reconstitute me, then reduce me to powder again.

'I'm not –' he began.

'I don't want a kebab,' I said quickly, which was a lie. There had not been a minute of my waking life since I tasted my first kebab that I did not want a kebab. Even when I was bolting down a kebab, I wanted a kebab. I had dreamed about kebabs, dreams in which I was surrounded by kebabs and disposed of them one after another. You didn't have to be Sigmund Freud to decipher the meaning of this phantasmagoria: I wanted a kebab.

I knew, however, that Rob had that day taken delivery of a care package from home, a cardboard box full of tins and packets – Ambrosia custard, spaghetti hoops and the like. I knew because he had cheerfully showed it to me as he itemised the contents and stowed it in his wardrobe. It hadn't contained anything I liked the look of (and bear in mind, I was a man who wanted a kebab) but that was at 3 p.m. It was now 2.30 a.m. again, and I would have settled for anything, anything at all, from that box. A statement proven beyond doubt when Rob rolled his eyes, ducked back inside his room and returned holding a can of hot dog sausages in brine, which he thrust at me with all the irritable contempt his sleepy form could muster.

I have eaten bad things in my life. I have eaten burnt tapioca. I have eaten luncheon meat so cheap and spongy I would have been better off consuming the wrapper it came in. I have eaten stomach-turning freezer shop merchandise unworthy of the description 'foodstuff'. There was even a time, let's not forget, when I wanted a kebab. These were terrible moments in the personal history of my palate. But none of them can match the all-round, eyelid-creasing, tastebud-trashing, tooth-insulting awfulness of that tin of hot dog sausages. Swallowing the contents, I was seized by the type of self-loathing described by lechers who seek the company of women they would otherwise abhor. If I ever again let anything half that foul pass my uvula and reach my oesophagus, it will happen only because the sole alternative is a lingering demise by starvation. I don't think forcing it on me at gunpoint would work – at the decisive moment, swift oblivion might yet seem preferable to another one of those repellent tubes of *unterfleisch*.

After this Damascene episode, my former haunts – the shelves and counters and freezers piled with processed muck – became anathema to me. I shuddered at the sight of faggots in gravy, of chicken slurry fashioned into drumstick shapes, of anything (fish balls, beef balls, pork balls) with the word 'balls' in its name; I feared – with some justification – this might be all too accurate a description of its contents. What was more, I no longer wanted a kebab. I haven't eaten a doner since, and I fully expect – should both the opportunity and the subject arise – to be in a position to repeat that statement on my deathbed. I am, I admit, hoping to have something more substantial to report about my time on earth. But I'm not counting on it. It's always good to have something to fall back on.

If laziness and satisfactory food were incompatible – and it seemed that they were – then I was going to have to cook. This led to another set of problems. All the people around me who cooked for themselves were vegetarians. Back in Kenya, the only vegetarians I had known were Indians who had inherited the practice along with their religion – and who were capable of contriving such delectable fare that the question of whether or not it contained meat seemed irrelevant. In Britain, vegetarianism was a personal lifestyle choice, an increasingly popular one at that, although it struck me more as an affliction.

Carrying a batch of raw ingredients into a kitchen shared with vegetarians was a test of nerve. The effect can be duplicated by wandering into an assembly of the Jesus Army looking for somewhere to sit down for a minute. I was immediately marked as conversion fodder. I wanted no part of it, but short of picking up a dining chair and laying about my persecutors with it in the style of Samson, there was not much I could do. If only, like Samson, I had had at my disposal the jawbone of an ass. They'd have fled from that in an instant, crying, 'Animal product! Animal product!'

'You're not using beef mince, are you?' one of the vegetarians would say. She could not have sounded more disapproving had I sauntered in with my belt wrapped around my upper arm and a bloodied hypodermic depending from a vein.

'No, lamb. I find beef doesn't carry the flavours so well.'

'But why use either,' she would ask, now in the gently chiding manner of one setting a misguided child upon the correct path, 'when you could use soy mince?'

'Because the soy mince tastes as if somebody else has already eaten it.'

'But there are so many alternatives to meat –'

'Each more horrible than the last. If you want meat, eat meat. If you don't, eat vegetables. Either way, leave me out of it.'

What flummoxed me most was not that anyone should

elect to become a vegetarian in the first place; after all, there is any number of excellent, flesh-free dishes from around the world to be sampled and savoured. It was the misery they insisted on heaping upon themselves, by means of all manner of specialised products that existed only to fill the void evidently gaping in lives bereft of meat. Bean burgers, nut cutlets, tofu turkeys, mushroom pâté, 'veggie' sausages – these ersatz commodities invariably held the allure of damp cardboard, and I would not have been surprised if their nutritional value were demonstrated to be much the same.

One girl I met in those days, a staunch omnivore and epicure as well as a remarkable beauty, told of how a suitor had wooed her with a romantic dinner of something called 'Beanfeast', which was sold dry, in a packet, like certain varieties of pet food. (I once knew a woman who fed her pack of German Shepherds on something similar, and similarly meatless; whenever her name was mentioned, I always expected to hear that the dogs had, at last and understandably, devoured her.)

The gauche lothario emptied out the box into a saucepan of tepid water with a flourish, as if he were Escoffier perfecting a sublime creation for the Empress Josephine, and with a wooden spoon stirred it into a noxious brown mulch. The poor wretch might as well have tried to trap a bird of paradise with no better bait than a plastic cuttlefish bone.

Brighton was a haven for these vegetarian masochists. In the days before such enterprises were common throughout the country, it boasted (if boasted is not too robust a word) a 'wholefood' collective, Eternity Foods. If by 'wholefood', they meant foods that were wholly unpalatable, I could not argue with that description.

I occasionally visited Eternity in search of fresh ginger, which was then obtainable nowhere in town – not even in Eternity Foods. What they did have – skulking in a spice cabinet full of tiny drawers which mimicked the appearance of a dusty zoological exhibit or faintly sinister medical specimen repository – was old ginger. Ginger so wizened and stringy that one felt more inclined to hold open the door for it and help it across the road than to be so disrespectful as to peel it. Perhaps the name of the store was intended to reflect the amount of time they kept hold of their stock.

I noted also that even their smallest loaf of bread was of sufficient mass to generate its own gravitational field, and that they did not stock herbal cigarettes. This was a disappointment; I thought the pale, frail, wicker-thin clientele and the perpetually nonplussed personnel looked like just the sort of people who used herbal cigarettes. This was a mistaken preconception on my part; *I* was the sort of person who used herbal cigarettes. I used them because tobacco made me feel ill. My previous attempt to buy them had ended in ignominy. I went into a branch of a chain which dealt in vitamins, soy products and so forth, and asked the very straitlaced middle-aged lady at the register if herbal cigarettes were available.

'Cigarettes?' she repeated. (Think Lady Bracknell intoning, 'A handbag?') She contemplated me with an expression of untrammelled disgust. 'This,' she thundered, 'is a health shop.'

I fled, cowering.

It was a relief when the long summer holiday arrived, and I could go back to Nairobi, where things were simple. 'If it moves,' as our family friend Hans Glass was fond of saying, usually at one of his celebrated *brais*, where we would tear into barbecued steak, chops and giant beef ribs, 'shoot it and make it into biltong.'

When I returned in the autumn, I was surprised to find Rob waiting at the Heathrow arrivals gate to offer me a lift to Brighton. He was standing among the cabbies and limo drivers with their signs and placards bearing passengers' surnames. He was holding just such a board himself. On it he had inscribed, in marker pen and block capitals, 'BNNNNVN'.

CHAPTER FOUR

DOG DAYS

I HAD DREADLOCKS. I may as well come out and admit it right now. In 1987, I did what no white man should ever do, and had my hair plaited into long, narrow braids. There are many reasons that might be put forward as to why no white man should ever do this. Cultural misappropriation. Black wannabe-ism. Implicit trivialisation of another's religious beliefs. But not by me. I believe no white man should ever do this because it looks unutterably stupid. Your blanched scalp bares itself in strips where the hair is tugged away. You appear to have unsuccessfully attempted an imprudent and overly complex multiple reverse-comb over. The cliché about small children pointing at you in the street and laughing comes true. Or at least partially true. One wide-eyed tyke keened, 'Mummy, look at him,' and burst into tears before being pulled away by his embarrassed parent.

Then again, this sort of thing happened to me even
when I sported my naturally occurring proto-Afro.
Another nipper pursued me through my local park, joy-
fully squawking, 'It's Michael Jackson! Michael Jackson
when he was little.' Had he stopped to think for a
moment, he might have spotted the flaw in this pro-
nouncement. Leaving aside the troublesome issue of time
travel, my complexion, fading in the wan British light
after years of African sun, was already much closer to
that of Michael Jackson when he was big and scary.

Much nearer to the mark were the gang of teenage scal-
lies at a music festival who, evidently put in mind of Art
Garfunkel, serenaded me in passing with a couplet from
'Bridge Over Troubled Water', concluding:

'I will cut youuuuur hair . . .'

In defence of my dreadlocks – a doomed effort, I grant
you – I can say that they were of genuine African origin,
having been woven and sealed with great skill by a lady
from Ethiopia while I was back in Nairobi on holiday. My
mother took me to have them done, at my request, and
even paid the hairdresser's exorbitant fee quite happily.
This may have had something to do with the fact that my
stepmother, Joan, for whom my father had left my mother
ten years previously, was very concerned about appearances, and had recently refused to be seen with me in
public unless I 'did something about my hair'.

I couldn't do anything about my hair. It was hopeless to
try. My hair was constructed of elements unknown to the
periodic table. Peculiarly, it had properties in common
both with an aquatic bird's plumage (water slipped off
the surface, leaving the mass beneath dry as tinder) and

with wire wool (springiness, abrasive potential, electrical conductivity).

Brushes and combs would become inextricably tangled and eventually lost in it. Retrieving them was a task on a par with Stanley's search for Livingstone. Dreadlocks, I reasoned, would remove these problems at a stroke.

My mother drove me home, and insisted on accompanying me inside; usually, she would have dropped me off and left.

'I wouldn't want to miss this,' she said.

We walked through to the patio. My father was sitting in a folding canvas chair, with a towel tucked into his collar, while Joan trimmed his beard with a pair of nail scissors.

'Hi, Davie,' said Joan. Then she looked up and saw my hairstyle. 'Oh my God!' she gurgled, and nearly severed my father's left earlobe.

'Ow!' yelped my father. Joan dashed back into the house for cotton wool and antiseptic.

My mother beamed, kissed me goodbye and left.

In Nairobi, people grinned at me on the streets – amicably, rather than with scorn – and called me 'Bob Marley' and 'Rastaman'. When I came back to the UK, I found things were very different. For a start, my timing could not have been worse. Dreadlocks were beginning to sprout on white heads wherever you looked. And these were not white heads with which I wanted my own to be associated.

Returning to college that autumn, I found that far from pioneering a new look, I had plenty of company. And while I was relieved not to stand out as much as I had expected, I remained the only white, dreadlocked individual in the south-east who didn't smell like a flatulent sheepdog's favourite blanket left out overnight in a summer thunderstorm. I was guilty by association, having unwittingly enlisted myself in the ranks – the truly rank ranks, let me emphasise – of a very British breed: the crusties.

Initially, my friends and I referred to them as 'anarchos': as rumour had it they were anarchists, or at least they thought they were. Then they were 'ropies' – short for 'dog on a rope', but also because 'ropey' summed up what you might describe, for lack of a more scathing term, as their style. Finally, they became known as 'crusties', on the basis that, however apposite 'ropey' might be, in terms of accuracy 'crusty' knocked it into a cocked felt hat. You really could see the crust on a crusty – a gnarled, knobbly patina of dust, grime and surly disaffection.

When I moved to Brighton, the crusty seemed to be no more than an occasional summertime phenomenon. Every so often I would spot one blinking in the daylight as he was gently tugged along the pavement by some mange-ridden mutt at the end of a frayed cord. At first I assumed this was the result of a well-intentioned but hard-up charitable scheme to provide guide dogs for the befuddled.

By the time I had dreadlocks of my own, the crusties had made their way onto the University of Sussex campus, in search of fresh pickings. Like the hippies before them, the crusties were, in their own inept way, both mercenary and entrepreneurial. Perhaps they were gathering funds to topple the state. But I doubt it. More likely they were gathering funds to topple themselves, via the application of Scrumpy Jack. You could distinguish between a crusty and a traditional tramp – although why you would want to is entirely your affair – by their choice of tipple. Tramps favoured Special Brew or, if they came from up north, Super T, perhaps preceded by an aperitif of Thunderbird fortified wine or 'Mad Dog 20/20'.

The standard crusty technique to obtain money was to demand it. 'Got any spare change?' they would moan. In Kenya, where most people were poor, begging was nonetheless a last, desperate resort, and I took it that in a wealthy country like Britain, the same would apply, only more so. I was already familiar with such Brighton characters as 'The 10p Man', a local celebrity in a small way. A stout, bearded gentleman of the road who roved a beat between Elm Grove and the Pavilion, The 10p Man resembled an everyday dosser in all respects bar one. The two-bob pieces he collected were hoarded towards the purchase of ever fancier pairs of stonewashed blue jeans, which made for an implausibly antiseptic intersection between his discoloured shirts and battered, yawning brogues – as if the tract twixt waistband and ankle had been transposed, in an experiment conducted by some high-street Frankenstein, with the matching expanse of a Status Quo fan.

The 10p Man was patently a crank, maybe even a genuine Status Quo fan himself. I reasoned that he must therefore be an exception to the rule that begging signalled genuine distress. I acted on the premise that if anyone in Britain were to ask me for money (and it's remarkable that, after taking one look at me, anyone in Britain bothered), then surely they must need it very badly indeed. And they surely did. You simply couldn't get stoned and plastered every night of the week on what the Department of Health and Social Security gave you in Income Support. After I graduated, I found this out for myself. My solution was to not get stoned and plastered every night. A crusty's solution was to beg for more money from the people who were already paying for the dole – and even, in my case, those who were also relying on it: 'Oi! Dreads! Got any change?'

Eventually I wised up to the truth that crusties were grasping rather than destitute. I decided that if anybody was going to spend my money on liquor and drugs, it would be me. A typical exchange on a Brighton pavement now ran like this.

> CRUSTY: 'Spare any change?'
> ME: 'Eat your dog. Then we'll talk.'
> CRUSTY: 'Fascist.'

The crusties who journeyed onto campus did so with a plan. One of them may have had a brainwave, although that would suggest he was bright enough not to be a crusty, so in all likelihood he got the idea from somewhere else. The plan was this: to take over the TV room in a hall of residence, screen videos all night and charge a £2 admission fee. I wandered down with my neighbour Matt, the sardonic Liverpudlian. Between us we had £3.97. At a table by the door, a waxen, skeletal crusty with pinprick eyes crouched over a cashbox. He resembled a bedraggled giant albino rat which had recently, and by the narrowest of margins, won a battle to defend its nest from a half-starved alley cat. He was, in his way, an exemplary specimen of his type.

'This is only three pounds ninety-seven,' said the albino rat.

'It's three pounds ninety-seven more than you'll have if you don't take it,' said Matt.

'Two pounds each,' said the rat. 'Four pounds.'

'What are you, Marks and bloody Sparks?' said Matt. 'Are you going to give us a receipt? Put it on your VAT return? It's three fucking pee. Now let us in.'

'Four pounds,' said the rat, and went back to what he was doing; that is, huddling over the cashbox and sucking phlegm up his nose every six seconds with a sound like maracas rattling in a bowl of raw egg whites.

'Did you see if Chris was in?' I asked Matt.

Chris, the gangly, amiable engineering student, was still trying to live down letting slip that his father was a high-ranking police officer in Surrey. He did this by endeavouring not to look shocked at all the petty misdemeanours that went on around him. It wasn't easy, as he was genuinely shocked by all of them.

'I think I saw him in the kitchen,' said Matt. 'With a plate of –'

'Baked beans. Yup.'

We went back to our floor and found Chris eating dinner in his room.

'Have you still got that coin jar, Chris?'

'Mm-hm.'

'Can we borrow four quid?'

'I'll lend you four quid. Here –'

'Thanks, but I mean, can we borrow four quid in cop-pers?'

Chris had by now learned not to ask the reasons for things. No doubt we required small change for some arcane and possibly drug-related purpose that would, all the same, be obvious to anyone in the know. And Chris didn't want to sound as if he wasn't in the know.

Chris's coin jar weighed about one-fifth of a hundred-weight. We emptied it out onto his bed and counted out four pounds exactly, most of it in ha'pennies. We scooped it into a bag, replaced the remainder in the jar, and head-ed back to the TV room. If Ratman recognised us, he gave no sign. He had the bearing of one whose short-term memory had long since blown a set of crucial fuses.

'Four pounds,' sniffled Ratman.

'Here you go,' I said, and emptied the bag of change onto the table. It took a while. Ratman stared at the money, a dull horror seeping into his lifeless little eyes. You could almost hear the few remaining ganglions in his cerebral cortex popping like kernels of corn and pinging off the interior of his skull. Then he started to count it.

'Fifteen . . . sixteen . . . urrr . . . and a half . . . fifteen . . . no, nineteen,' he mumbled, dragging coins to and fro across the tabletop with blackened fingernails. 'Seventy-four . . . ninety . . . fuck.' Every so often he would give up and start again. Matt and I leaned against the wall, arms folded, and watched. This was easily four pounds' worth of entertainment, and we hadn't even seen the films yet.

After ten minutes, Ratman gave up the struggle and

waved us in. 'Hold on,' he coughed as we walked by. He scooped out an arbitrary portion of currency and pushed it across the table to us with a soiled palm. 'Your change,' he said.

'We'll have to boil it now,' said Matt.

We watched three movies, culminating in *The Hitcher*, a demented, nihilistic and very superior slasher picture, steeped in menace, cruelty and gore. It was insane and quite brilliant. As Rutger Hauer perpetrated an especially grotesque act of aimless carnage, Matt leaned over to me, agog with delight.

'This-film-is-off-its-*head!*' he hissed.

It was. When we walked out, with senses rattled and sensibilities brutalised, the first thing we saw was Ratman, still sifting obsessively through the giant pile of coins and muttering random numbers to himself. I recognised his expression. It wasn't the one Matt and I could see on each other's face. It was the one – dazed, fearful, frozen, uncomprehending – that flitted across the features of the Hitcher's victims in the seconds before their ghastly snuffing out. Ratman had been wearing it for five hours straight.

Within a year of this episode, I recall looking around and thinking to myself that Ratman, obeying the instincts of his animal alter ego, had taken to raising abundant litters of identical Ratboys. It wasn't just in Brighton, although Brighton did feel like the epicentre of the plague. Suddenly, crusties were everywhere. When you went up to London, you found the boroughs of Camden, Hackney and

Islington swarming with them. They ranged across the north and up as far as Glasgow. They colonised Britain faster than the grey squirrel.

It turned out that they'd been breeding in the more affluent parts of the Home Counties, then changing their names to rough-hewn, short-form monikers which evoked smells and slops, like Spog, Spam, Stig and Swampy. Basically anything beginning with S. And Raz; presumably because the more literate among them figured this was close enough.

Crusties had evolved, if that's the right word, out of a bizarre union between punk rock and the English folk tradition. Crusty was a chalk and cheese sandwich on mouldering bread. From punk they took shredded clothing, sneering and the circled 'A' motif. From English folk they took fiddles, cider and a romantic view of the pre-industrial past – along with a footling, fuddy-duddy preciousness, reminiscent of chunky jerseys and pewter tankards, or of librarians gathering to play long-defunct madrigals.

Crusty icons included anarcho-punk band Crass, and the leader of the Peasants' Revolt, Wat Tyler. In their song 'Do They Owe Us a Living?', Crass had all but set forth a crusty manifesto, which answered the question in the title with an emphatic and indignant 'yes'. The song was crude, repetitive, self-important, self-righteous and any idiot could understand it. In other words, it was perfect. Here was a howl of protest against a nightmare future in which the most appalling outlook was not a lack of employment but the prospect of it.

From woolly-minded it was but a short step to

woolly-headed. To my chagrin, more and more crusties began to sprout dreadlocks. And not the relatively tidy dreadlocks I had been at pains to obtain, but bobtails, the white man's grisly version. Thick, fetid tubes of matted hair in shades of mouse or ginger, which could be tied back tightly to expose the lines of pasty skin between them. This explains why another early nickname for crusties was 'Crasstafarians'.

Crass also pioneered the use of symbols in circles. In addition to the circled 'A', crusties loved to decorate the backs and, more worryingly, the sleeves of their combat jackets with red or black stars, or Crass's own pseudo-Swastika. At best they resembled a bunch of bedraggled *Wehrmacht* after a Russian winter and a drubbing at the hands of the Red Army. At worst they seemed to be advocating some recondite brand of totalitarianism. In a sense they were. The original wave of crusties would never have become organised enough to actually impose their Year Zero eco-claptrap on anyone. All the same, the jackets were a handy reminder of what might happen if they ever got hold of enough spare change to buy a tank.

Fashion industry nabobs are always keen to remind us that the best ideas about clothes, from Mary Quant through Vivienne Westwood to Jean-Paul Gaultier, come from British street culture and pop movements. What they neglect to mention is that so too do the worst fashion ideas. Excluding skinheads, who in their early days at least looked crisp, crusty is arguably the most execrable pop-inspired street fashion in the history of clothes.

Early on, a crusty needed only the following: unkempt hair; loose, dirty, ripped clobber, preferably army surplus, in green, grey or black; big boots; dog. No girl-about-town ten years later would value her Prada bag the way a crusty did his dog on a string. Nor would she go about with two or three of them; but then crusties were and are simple-minded folk, and to them the equation remains plain. Dog equals status: more dogs equal more status. Like a Maasai herdsman parading his cattle, the many-mongrelled crusty is a man of substance in his world. Top dog, as it were. Cider and crusty girls shall be his for the taking.

In the late 1980s, another element was added to the mix by the followers of New Model Army, a rock band made up of gap-toothed goths who had since reinvented themselves as clog-wearing defenders of Olde English peasant ways. For a while these cloggies ran parallel to the crusties before being subsumed. Their main legacy would be a stylistic one: runic designs of Celtic origin, which began to appear as jewellery, tattoos, T-shirt designs and so forth. It was apparent even to me that this had as much to do with the English folk tradition as, say, Viking helmets, but the crusties, as ever, saw no contradiction.

At the end of the 1980s, the crusty movement was in full swing. As with any self-appointed underclass, crusties unwittingly insulted those with whom they wished to show solidarity. They mistook the outward signs of penury for badges of honour. No one born poor would ever put on old, shabby or slovenly clothes out of choice; only the well-off can afford to dress down.

Like all fashion statements, crusty garb sent a message to the world, a message which the crusties were only too happy to put into words as well. They did this in a unique crusty accent. Inevitably, the crusties' native Received Pronunciation was deemed inappropriate by these reborn Ranters and Diggers. But rather than adopt the cheerful, all-purpose estuary intonation on which the rest of us in the south rely, crusties spoke as one with a cod-plebeian cockney whine of entitlement, unheard in any other context.

The message was this: I am an outlaw. A nonconformist. I need nothing from your bloated capitalist society. I stand outside it. Give us 50p, my giro's late.

Eventually my dreadlocks grew out. Had I possessed the sense I was born with, I would have cut them off and bidden them good riddance. Instead, I chose to have them redone.

This time, there was no graceful Ethiopian lady to weave my hair into a semblance of a quasi-respectable style. Instead, in one of those decisions that you know to be doomed even as you make it, I took down a telephone number from a flier stuck to a Brighton lamp post: 'Locks! Hair extensions! Call Julia after 5 p.m.'

Julia wasn't in, but a very proper-sounding woman, whom I took to be Julia's mother, passed on my message. A week later, I found myself sitting in a flea-ridden squat a few hundred feet from the Palace Pier. Of what had once been a flat on the second storey of a fine late-Regency townhouse, the living room and kitchen alone remained habitable – and then only to the extent that both were equipped with a floor. The remaining rooms had lost this feature when a squatter – a member, it so happened, of a band popular among crusties – fell asleep with a lighted spliff between his gummy fingers and set fire to it. He continued to doss down in his burnt-out boudoir, balanced on the few remaining floorboards, despite the fact that just one nocturnal rotation in his sleeping bag would have sent him plummeting a good ten feet to the storey below, breaking most of the bones in his body and sparking celebrations among music lovers across the country.

Julia was a teenager, the girlfriend of an older alpha crusty, Soggy, who lorded it over the squat, his station confirmed by the number of dogs he owned (three) and by the patronage of Sacheverell, the floor-torching bandsman.

The advent of teenage crusties startled me. I was amazed that anyone could greet the onrush of adolescent hormones by adopting a lifestyle and appearance guaranteed to repulse all but the most desperate members of the opposite sex. That they did so was an indication of the movement's counter-cultural supremacy in the wake of the acid house explosion and the popularity of outdoor raves. A government-sponsored recruitment drive offering free, unlimited, cider-flavoured heroin could not have done more to swell the crusty legions.

From around the country, the children of comfortable homes turned up to dance and stumbled upon the perfect outlet for their adolescent opposition to everything other than dope, drinking and soap-dodging. The acid house fans who started up these illegal jamborees viewed the arrival of dreadlocked hordes with distaste. Where were their trainers and clean white T-shirts?

Come the 1990s, teenage crusties were omnipresent;

perched on shop doorsteps with the family spaniel in tow; demanding change from passers-by whose entire outfits cost less than the beggars' own army boots.

These were boom times for crusty. Like punk before it, everyone had got in on the act. The hardcore crusty element – the self-proclaimed Travellers who even today continue to induce apoplexy among country dwellers – linked up with like-minded DJs to form rave collectives such as Spiral Tribe. They dreamed of an anarchist, agrarian Albion, safe from the ravages of industry, where somehow their turntables, generators, mobile phones and fleets of old buses would continue to function as before.

At the Glastonbury festival, the flagrantly misnamed Peace Convoy assaulted well-wisher Michael Eavis, the event's organiser. Biting the hand that feeds them has always been a favourite crusty trick, one they may have picked up from their dogs.

Meanwhile, design and drama school types transformed themselves into living works of art, albeit not very good ones. Brighton, naturally, was a haven for this sort of thing. I only had to go for a walk on a sunny day to see it going on, in the parks and squares where Cyberpunk met Cider Punk amid a frenzy of piercings, mohicans, body paint and – always crusty's common denominator – bloody big boots. Aiming for Mad Max and Max Headroom, they generally landed closer to Max Wall.

It seemed as if everyone who didn't actually have a job was a crusty. Schoolgirls and students. Doleys and dossers. Hippies. Dopers. Bright-eyed young ideologues. Old punks. Old lags. Hatchet-faced scag addicts. If you watch footage of London's poll tax riot with the volume muted, it resembles nothing so much as a police raid on a Back to the Planet gig. Even the employed could join in the fun, letting their grotty hair down as weekend crusties, or shaving their bonces in a slaphead-crusty crossover look that is still in favour at the time of writing (although it was then important to wear the correct ear or nose-rings, so no one would mistake you for a skinhead.)

Julia, poor thing, was out of her depth, although she would have been out her depth in a jelly mould. Julia also looked, and moved, as if she had been created in a jelly mould. She was gifted with what the Cavalier poet Robert Herrick choicely described as 'that brave vibration each way free'. But whereas Herrick's Julia went in silks, Soggy's Julia opted for lumpy sackcloth shmutter in shades of charcoal and mud, which still couldn't disguise her endowments.

Whenever Soggy took his dogs out and roamed his fiefdom, Sacheverell would amuse himself by grasping Julia from behind and groping her. After the third time I witnessed this, she burst into tears as soon as he left the room. 'I wish he wouldn't do that,' she sobbed to her best friend, a fourteen-year-old truant and would-be tough nut who spent her school hours at Julia's side, chain-smoking, while Julia was busy fashioning my head into a spectacle that Heinrich Hoffmann, creator of *Der Struwwelpeter*, would have excised from his book as far too distressing.

'Why don't you tell Soggy?' said the friend.

'I can't,' Julia wept. 'He'll never take my side against Sacheverell.'

At that moment, through the window, we heard the sound of a car engine and a flurry of barks.

'Hello, Simon,' said the very proper voice I had heard over the telephone.

'Hello, Mrs Travers,' said Soggy.

'My mum's here,' sniffled Julia. We all moved to the window. Julia's mother, a thin, tweedy countrywoman, was loading Soggy's dogs into the back of a Volvo estate. 'She's taking them to the vet for their jabs.'

Fighting back an impulse to remark that it was a shame Mrs Travers didn't do the same with Soggy – and have Sacheverell neutered while she was about it – I returned to my seat. Julia resumed her apathetic yanking and plaiting of my hair. The fleas went back to feeding on my ankles.

Julia did a terrible job on my barnet. Bits of it fell out. Other bits fused and tangled, creating amorphous and frightening shapes which called to mind the mutant, prey-agglomerating spaceman Victor Carroon of *The Quatermass Experiment*. My earliest motive for acquiring the style – hair which would be tidy without half-an-hour's painful brushing – had long since gone by the board.

'Why,' I was one day asked by a colleague on the music paper where I had become a contributor, 'if you hate crusties so much, do you look like one?'

I couldn't answer that. I had the locks cut off the next day. No tonsorial professional would have taken on the job without danger money. It was lucky for me – not just lucky, now I think of it, but a triumph over ostensibly insurmountable odds – that I had by now found a full-time girlfriend. The Girlfriend did the cutting for me, grimacing and turning her face away all the while. It was a labour of love, all right. Had I ever doubted the commitment of a woman who could fall for me when I looked the way I looked, those doubts would surely have been stifled by such an act of devotion.

By the 1990s, when I was once again fit to be received in respectable company, the crusty wave had broken and ebbed. You might argue it had become a victim of its own success. Admittedly, success is not a word or even a concept that readily associates itself with crustydom, but there is no denying that it was the biggest counter-culture movement of its day. And this was its problem. It was too broad too keep whatever focus it might have once had – although by mid-afternoon, your average crusty was usually too addled by hotknives and Scrumpy to focus on his own hand in front of his face.

Riddled with hierarchies, snobbery and unspoken dress codes, crusty was now more conservative and conformist than the society it lived off and affected to despise. The weekenders were lost to newer trends. The teenagers grew up and obtained degrees and jobs. As a political movement it made about as much sense as Fleas Against the Dog. As a fashion it was, despite its prophetic espousal of combat trousers, obsolete.

I said as much while reviewing an album by the best-known crusty band, The Levellers. It puzzled me that the Major government, then in power, should have dedicated so much time and trouble to attacking all the things (free festivals, nomadism, tribal techno raves) with which crusty was associated. Why should one set of dull, humbug-ridden throwbacks so alarm another? That review got me barred from the Kensington, the favoured watering hole of the Brighton crusty rearguard. Had a stout rope been tied around my legs and then harnessed to a team of pit ponies, which in turn was driven into the Kensington's saloon by a muleteer equipped with a bull-whip, I might conceivably have been persuaded to pay the pub a visit in the first place. I decided the ban was something I could live with.

Unable to cope with an entire worldview, the more committed crusties are now single-issue crusaders on behalf of creatures even dumber and furrier than themselves; or they have joined the more scrubbed-up movement against large corporations. They battle security forces at G8 conferences, and 'reclaim the streets' across Britain – although from what, exactly, it is far from clear. These neo-crusties are now to be found loafing, wheedling and rioting from Parliament Square and the capitals of Europe to remote parts of the globe: the Greek islands; the Antipodes; the Indian subcontinent. For a bunch of people so vehemently opposed to any notion of globalisation, they seem to be having a fair crack at it themselves. Alas, what crusties have exported is nothing so desirable or seductive as trainers, personal stereos or giant dual-door aluminium refrigerators. Rather it is a singularly obnoxious brand of Luddite arrogance.

Of the crusty movement proper, only a rather hapless rump remains, identifiable by their taste for multi-coloured garments coarsely woven from hemp, which tend to look like a pair of Paraguayan carpets sewn together at the edges.

As with prune-faced, moth-eaten Teddy Boys, or mohawk punks posing with guardsmen for postcards outside Buckingham Palace, there's something almost quaint and comforting about crusties now. They're relics of a bygone era, nostalgic throwbacks to the Thatcher/Major years. It's sweet, really, that they can still be bothered to avoid making the effort.

Looking back, crusty was a wonderful mass exercise in missing the point. It never occurred to its followers just why English rebels such as Wat Tyler and The Levellers, the men they named their bands after, had rebelled in the first place. It was so they wouldn't have to wear filthy, ragged clothing, beg for money, dwell in hovels and live like – and furthermore, among – animals.

I once lived a muddy field's breadth from the slums of Kibera, on the outskirts of Nairobi. There, thousands of unhappy souls struggled for survival under such conditions, without any choice in the matter. I've often thought that a fortnight in Kibera would be just the thing to introduce a little perspective into the crusty mindset.

Had I possessed any such insight myself back in 1987, I might never have had those locks woven into my hair in the first place. Bad hairstyles constitute a rite of passage for any youngster, but I had managed to choose mine without the slightest understanding of what it might represent in my new homeland. I was nothing if not consistent – consistently clueless. A hairstyle does much to tell the world who you are. Mine lied, or at least equivocated. It correctly identified me as an idiot, but of the wrong variety.

As I boarded the top deck of a bus one afternoon, late

that year, a gentleman from Birmingham (his accent was so strong that even I had no trouble placing him) confronted me and demanded,

'Arrryu un Englushmun?'

I had to think about that one. I would have liked to reply, 'Not English, specifically; still, I consider myself, if not British, then certainly attempting to become so.' But this didn't look a good moment to go into the niceties of the question. My interlocutor closely resembled the talking ape Dr Zeus in a very ugly jacket, and he looked aggrieved to the point of violence.

'Yes,' I said.

'Thun woy uv yu got drudlocks?' he said, incensed.

I should have asked myself the same question a great deal sooner than he did, and saved myself all sorts of trouble.

CHAPTER FIVE

A HOUSE IS NOT A HOME

IN OCTOBER 1987, my year's allotment of campus housing was up. I moved out of Brassic House and into Brighton proper. Rob and I had met a chap called Stan when we accompanied Sally on a night out and Stan made a successful bid to pick her up. Stan was very much a ladies' man. He was also a doctorate student in philosophy, a trader in handicrafts, an audiophile and the part-owner of a house on Brighton's outskirts. He was about to become the owner of this house in full, as the one-time girlfriend with whom he had bought the property was moving to America. He had a mortgage that had suddenly doubled, three empty bedrooms and several student acquaintances. The solution was not long in coming to him.

I had never seen Stan's house. While I was back in Nairobi for the summer, Rob wrote to suggest we take up tenancy with Stan in the new academic year. This was easier than going out and looking for accommodation, so I agreed.

Driving through Brighton with Rob one day a few months before, I had launched into a snooty broadside about British residences – 'All those tiny houses, shoulder to shoulder, with postage-stamp gardens' etc.

'You'd better to learn to like them,' said Rob. 'You'll be living in one next year.'

With the arrogance of one accustomed to room – Kenya is a spacious country, and our family home stood on five acres of it – I'd failed to perceive that the British lived in small houses not because they preferred to, but because in a small country, small houses are more or less obligatory.

Rob was right, of course. On returning to college in the autumn, I found out that Stan's own house was an unre-markable late-Victorian end-of-terrace near the top of a long hill, on Orton Street, and that Rob had bagged the best available bedroom – upstairs, next to Stan's own.

'Where am I?' I said – for once with the emphasis on the 'I' instead of the 'am'.

'You,' said Rob, 'are on the lower ground floor.'

By which he meant the basement. I hauled my suitcase down the creaking, shadowy stairs and pushed it through a doorway into what looked, at first glance, like a dank utility room and, upon further inspection, was a dank utility room. I was too weary from the flight to query any of this. 'Just tell me where the shower is,' I sighed.

'Shower?' said Rob, amused.

British plumbing arrangements have long been a mystery to the remainder of the self-professedly civilised world. What, visitors wonder, is the point of cleaning yourself off and then stewing in a tub full of the resulting effluent? Why the aversion to mixer taps, a mechanism so obviously and elementarily beneficial that it demands a consciously perverse decision to fit anything else? Was the plastic hose attachment for bath faucets devised in his own service by a dedicated masochist, or by an unusually ingenious sadist for the torment of others? (Unerringly, one or other of the cups will discreetly detach itself from its corresponding tap. The unfortunate bather is focused, to no avail, on de-lathering his pelt with the insolent dribble exuding from the nozzle; suddenly, a highly localised sensation of being either poached or frozen assails him. At this moment, he yelps, reflexively jerks backwards and cracks his head on the tiles, which are invariably coloured a queasy shade of aquamarine adorned with a dismaying splash motif.)

All these – on the face of it – incomprehensible and unrelated ablutory preferences can be traced to a common source: a deep, perhaps pathological antipathy to running water. Each could have been and probably was contrived to discourage bathers from leaving a tap open any longer than absolutely necessary. In a country so frequently waterlogged as Britain, where the notion of a drought is characterised not (as it was for me) by parched, cracked riverbeds dotted with the skeletons of livestock, but by an embargo upon rinsing your car with a hosepipe, this seems symptomatic of an underlying puritan meanness.

That trait, arguably ingrained by a long era of austerity, has discernibly waned in the time I've lived here (and it may be no coincidence that adequate plumbing has become more common, too.) But in the late 1980s it remained embedded in generations of Britons for whom the thrifty and the niggardly were synonymous. It is telling, incidentally, that hosepipe bans always appeared to cause more anguish than restrictions upon the use of water in a Briton's own bathroom. Washing yourself was already taken to be an odious chore, and letting water stream away while you did so a sinful waste; but to be forbidden the use of gallons in sluicing down your car or irrigating your lawn? Tyranny!

My room featured a single, west-facing window, and three chilly walls, which formed an ineffectual barrier between the open air and my perpetually goose-pimpled flesh. I kept the curtain permanently drawn, by way of meagre insulation. Light was a problem. Ventilation was not. A relentless nor'easter wind whipped in from the Ural mountains, unimpeded until it struck my bed-chamber, within which it created its own cyclonic system of cold fronts, updraughts and icy clouds of vapour. The large *batik* wall hanging that I suspended over my bed to remind me of home and induce some colour and cheer into an environment dismally deficient in both, flapped furiously about as if it were alive and intent upon escape. Just about anything alive, other than me, would have been intent upon escape from that room, as I discovered on the infrequent occasions I was able to induce girls to visit me there.

Next door to mine was something best described as

less a room, more a cupboard with pretensions. It contained a bed, a shelf and a gap sufficiently wide to slide a half-empty pack of cigarette papers between them. Fortunately for the occupant, the bed, shelf and cigarette papers were all he required for a full and happy existence. Martin was a chipper Brummie whose shaggy ginger ringlets and wire-rimmed spectacles identified him as the heavy metal fan he unequivocally wasn't. Martin liked marijuana, dub reggae bootlegs and long evenings involving the two, along with whatever congenial company he could summon.

Rob and I didn't need much encouragement to join him. Stan was less enthusiastic; in addition to being fifteen years our senior, he preferred his music mixed by direct metal pressing and thereafter reproduced on a floating-bearing turntable via a twin-valve amplifier and external pre-amp connected with minimum-impedance coaxial copper cable to speakers hand-made in a converted Suffolk barn by audio engineers sworn to celibacy until they perfected the upper amplitude output range of the tweeter, or met a woman.

'This is an LP by Dulles Dischworter,' Stan would declare, waving a record sleeve upon which a bearded fellow appeared to be using a handheld synthesiser to fend off a giant man-eating dove. 'It's a limited edition of two thousand copies. The sound quality is extraordinary.' He was right. In the near-absolute absence of crackle or distortion, and with almost flawless warmth and clarity, you could hear perfectly how dreary and soulless the music itself was.

On a typical evening, from Stan's room would emanate

the sounds of the ECM Records catalogue: swooning harps; coffee-table jazz trumpets; and various other insipid but sonically immaculate confections. Meanwhile, his three lodgers would crouch in Martin's tiny lair, as a C90 cassette tape recording of a London pirate radio station croaked intermittently through a clapped-out ghetto blaster. Martin tended to react satirically to types of music other than dub, but it was worth putting them on for this very reason. To The Beatles' 'Across The Universe', he would sing along in deadpan nasal mock-Scouse, then begin to improvise:

> Uhp the Bootle, dowun the Mersey, on into the gruhbby ohshun
> Calling and coarruhpting little fishees from thurr fishee dens
> Three-ee-ee buhckets of muhshroom teeeeea – ommmmm

Once when I put on a Leonard Cohen album, he listened as far as the opening line of the first song –

> They sentenced me to twenty years of boredom

– then, reaching for the stop button, snapped, 'You got off light, mate.'

At Brassic House, I might have dwelt pressed up against a hillside, but at least my room allowed daylight to sneak in through the window. The troglodyte existence I now adopted bleached the last of my equatorial tan from my skin and induced in me a hollow-eyed pallor reminiscent of the denizens of Dis. Everything I had feared about life in Britain was coming to pass, but I didn't have the strength of mind to do anything about it – such as looking for another place to live.

Brighton in 1987 was still very much the Brighton of Graham Greene, picturesque but seedy, fur coat and no knickers, eking out a living on faded glories. The kind of town that, if you bought it a pint and a chaser, would recount by rote its well-worn stories until the glasses ran dry. Out where I was billeted, it was sedate and seemly enough. Head closer to the centre, where most of my friends had sought lodgings, and you swiftly found your-self in louche environs. Cramped backstreets, but also deceptively grand terraces and squares packed with bed-sitters, housing winos, drug dealers, drug addicts, dodgy traders in dodgy antiques, semi-criminals, petty crim-inals, out-and-out gangsters, forgotten thespians, dere-licts, bohemians, tarts, rent boys, rough trade of every stripe and standard.

Matt and Catherine had taken a second-floor flat near the seafront in China Way, an aptly named back alley. Too short and narrow to qualify for the designation 'road' or 'street', it had more than a whiff of pre-communist Shanghai about it – not to mention the aroma from the ever-present skip, in which skewered corpses turned up at an average rate of two per year. The pub across the way was a hard gay boozer (pagoda lanterns over the light bulbs, blood-stains of varying vintage on the Chinese patterned carpet) of a type to be found all over Brighton, before every watering hole in the vicinity went on to be scoured of its former identity and invested with the uniformity of stripped floorboards, pine tables and easy-listening electronica on the sound system.

This pub made me nervous. Not because I was one of those heterosexual men who persist in the delusion that – despite their manifest physical shortcomings, as demonstrated by their lack of appeal to women – they are nevertheless gay catnip. It made me nervous for the same reason that so many of Brighton's (and Britain's) non-gay pubs made me nervous: trouble never felt more than a sideways glance away.

There's a reason why British pubs are referred to as 'locals'. Often, if you don't match that description yourself, you shouldn't risk going inside. In all my time in Kenya, despite being as flagrantly and recognisably alien as a person could be, not once had I wandered into a tavern of any kind, anywhere – whitewashed beach bars on the coast, tin-roofed shacks in the Rift Valley – and been made to feel unwelcome.

When I lived on the university campus, I noticed that students almost never ventured into the nearby village of Falmer. My friend Stephen and I discovered why, when we stopped by for a jar at the Scythe and Cyclops. The customary malevolent hush (as definitively portrayed in a celebrated scene from the movie *An American Werewolf in London*) settled instantly across the entire saloon. The salted peanuts ceased their rustling in the packets and the beer froze in the taps on its way to the glasses below. General conversation did not resume until the pair of us had walked the icy ten-foot mile that lay between door and bar, and equipped ourselves with halves of something brewed from hops, yeast and dead field mice. We had gone in for a pint, but that would have taken longer.

'At least they're talking again,' I said.

'They're trying to work out whether anybody saw us come in,' said Stephen.

I was to learn how a selection system operates in many British pubs that matches for severity any gentlemen's club in London – although a regular opposed to your entry, rather than availing himself of the black ball, may prefer to use the pool cue beside it. As with White's or the Garrick, one can only become a regular by being nominated; that is, introduced by an existing regular, who implicitly vouches that you meet the membership criteria.

In some pubs you will be ostracised or worse for appearing in any way gay; I was once loudly denounced as a raving homosexual by my neighbour at the counter for ordering a bottled beer. In others, the problem may be that you aren't gay enough. On a stroll through Brighton's North Laines in the late 1980s, a girl by the name of Anita, with a hankering for bourbon liqueur, unwittingly dragged me into one of these hostelries, doubling its occupancy at a stroke. A youthful barman and a middle-aged roughneck in a leather jacket – literally, a tough customer – were absorbed in wordlessly ignoring each other. You could have cut the atmosphere with childproof scissors, and our arrival didn't do much to improve it.

Anita settled at a table and despatched me to the bar. The tender regarded me quizzically.

'Southern Comfort, please –'

'We don't have Southern Comfort,' he said, very deliberately, and in direct contradiction of bottled evidence on the rack behind him.

'No Southern Comfort,' I called over to the oblivious Anita. 'Why don't we try somewhere else?'

'Why don't you?' agreed the barman. I smelled whisky breath at my shoulder. The roughneck had sidled up to me and now occupied more of my personal space than I did.

'I like your hat,' he growled, in a mordant tone that suggested he liked nothing about me whatsoever, and that my hat was the thing he took the greatest exception to.

'Get me a Jack Daniels, then,' Anita sang out cheerfully.

'And a gin and slimline tonic,' I added.

'No. Slimline. Tonic,' enunciated the barman, without moving his teeth.

'I like your shoes,' the roughneck exhaled into my ear, singeing the lobe.

'No slimline tonic,' I called back to Anita. 'Maybe we should try somewhere else.'

'Maybe you should try somewhere else,' repeated the barman, nodding slowly and insistently.

'I like your belt,' rasped the fellow beside me, from half an inch away. 'Do you want me to show you my belt?'

'Never mind. Thanks anyway. Bye!' I said, and pulled Anita out through the doorway by her arm.

'What a lovely pub,' she observed, brightly. 'Nice and empty. Shame they didn't have any drinks we like.'

Most such places are gone now from Brighton; the 'gay pub' as a concept has lost much of its currency, as an influx of metropolitans, sharing broadly similar tastes regardless of sexuality, has crowded out both the bigots and the hard-bitten queens. The few establishments that remain at the time of writing are far more hospitable – the Black Horse, for example, also known as the Pink Pony. I once stopped in there for a refresher with a different and slightly dizzy young lady who, after sizing up the room for a few minutes, said to me, 'This is very much a *man's* pub, isn't it?' I could only agree with her.

None of my early encounters with British girls were particularly encouraging, even when they took place outside Britain. I had not long since returned from a sponsored student fancy-dress hitch-hike to Paris. Consider the phrase 'sponsored student fancy-dress hitch-hike'. It contains four separate elements, any one of which spells no good. Combined, they promise certain disaster. You could throw in the words 'self-mutilation' and 'heroin' without significantly adding to the awfulness of the concept.

When asked if I wanted to go, I agreed to it like a shot. I would probably have agreed like a shot to being shot, had anyone offered. Even by the prevailing standards among teenage college boys, I remained dangerously naive and suggestible.

Limited in the dressing-up department by the wardrobe I had brought from Africa, I took to the road in a dark-blue suit, of the kind worn by small boys to weddings, with a solitary scarlet sock protruding handkerchief-style from the breast pocket. I couldn't tell you what I was meant to be. But I looked no more ridiculous than all the other nitwits, as we gathered by the side of the A270.

Of course, there is no spectacle quite so winning as a

clutch of students disporting themselves in wacky garb. A few passing motorists acknowledged us with derisory toots of the horn, while most indicated their enthusiasm for our jape by disdainfully ignoring us altogether. It took me a mere three hours to pick up a ride from Brighton to Newhaven, where we boarded a ferry, and another four hours outside Dieppe – in a thunderstorm – to bag a lift to Paris.

Our party had agreed to re-group at a fast food restaurant on the Champs-Elysées at 10 p.m. I turned up on the dot, sodden and steaming like a carthorse, with a half-eaten baguette and a plastic lemonade bottle bulging in my jacket. Nobody else had arrived. I alone had adjusted my watch to local time. When I tried to use the toilets, the manager took me for a junkie and turfed me into the street.

An hour after that ejection I was back inside with the other travellers, surreptitiously downing cheap red wine that tasted of sour cream cheese. An hour and three minutes after that ejection, I had been kicked out again, along with everyone else.

We started thinking about shelter. A more robust element (the ones who had supplied the *vin imbuvable*) professed a willingness to spend the night chugging down the dregs on a park bench. It was autumn, and I reasoned that it was too late in the year and too early in my life to take up the habits of a tramp. I joined up with another group and went in search of a roof.

After being turned away by a series of Gallic jobsworths who didn't like our outfits, our accents or, in one case, the fact that we had arrived seven seconds after the purported check-in cut-off, we at last found a cheap hotel which would take us in. It was now that a petite brunette collared me and informed me that I was her room-mate. Normally I would have run away. But it was either that or the park bench. She was very pretty. And extremely drunk.

'I'm Leah,' she told me, and pushed me through the door of the hotel room. She dropped her coat on the floor and pulled off her net blouse and leather mini-skirt. 'Wait there,' she instructed, and lurched off down the corridor to the communal toilet, with what I can only describe as a gamine stagger, in her underwear, suspender belt and stockings. Almost immediately, a fellow hitcher emerged from the next room and before I could say a word, walked in on her.

'Occupied,' said Leah, unworried.

'Oh, Leah, it's you,' the intruder said, cheerfully. 'Never mind. Seen it all before.'

My technique that night was largely guesswork, but it seemed effective. After a series of back-arching shudders, Leah passed out cold. I might as well have clocked her with a paperweight. In an effort to be thoughtful, I wrote my name on a scrap of paper and put it on the bedside table. I doubted she would recall it, or much else, in the morning.

She didn't. She said goodbye and fled, spurning my phone number as if it carried a far greater risk of infection than the previous night's activity. I assume she wasn't a student at Sussex, because I never saw her again.

Before returning to Britain, I succumbed to a severe stomach complaint in Dieppe. Local medics shot me full of painkillers, leaving me with tiny x's where my pupils should have been, then slung me in a taxi which deposited me at the terminal just in time to catch the ferry. Throughout the crossing, Matt and Catherine – who had unaccountably joined me on this farrago – plied me with glass after glass of the cheap fizz they'd bought for the journey home.

'Go on, Dave,' said Matt, sympathetically. 'This'll sort you out.'

Sort me out it did, after a fashion. At first I felt quite lively. Then I felt less than lively. After that, I felt less than alive. I could barely move. When I tried to walk, it felt as if I were inching along the floor of a dark and syrupy sea.

Back in Newhaven I was detained by a mean-faced little immigration man who, like the burger bar bouncer, suspected me of dabbling in illegal narcotics. Desperate for an excuse to keep me out of the country, he flicked through my visas and border stamps, evaluating each one for evidence of drug trafficking. At last, he gave up and handed back my passport. 'You've been around, haven't you?' he remarked superciliously. He didn't know the half of it.

When I at last made it back to Brighton – having clambered, ticketless, aboard the wrong train, and been thrown off at Gatwick – I had seldom been so pleased to see anywhere. It may have been a rundown old town, but for the first time, it really felt like home.

By the look of it, the flat that Catherine and Matt rented might have been sealed up in 1923 and re-opened only to allow them entry. It must once have been a fine apartment, with the type of broad, high-ceilinged living room often found inside Brighton townhouses, and elaborate details worked into the solid cornicing. I remember it as being suffused with brownness. The carpet and walls, I'd guess, had yellowed back in the 1960s then dimmed into a dingy tan that coated every surface and stained to the colour of Assam tea the evening sunlight that drifted in through the tall sash windows. If you chose to, you could see the flat as symbolic not just of Brighton but of the whole country at that time. It was a relic from a prosperous and confident era, now dulled and decayed, half-heartedly struggling to keep up appearances when what really needed attending to was the structure within. Alternatively, you could see it as a ratty old suite and leave it at that.

Soon after installing themselves in their new home, Catherine and Matt acquired a large grey cat, which they named Leonin, in triple acknowledgement of the Beatle, the Bolshevik and their favourite songwriter, Leonard Cohen. Strap that uncanny triptych together on a speeding whirligig and shoot it into orbit, and the result still wouldn't have been half as mad as Leonin the cat.

The febrile condition of Leonin's tiny feline brain may have had something to do with his being confined to the flat in a fog of hashish smoke. He sampled fresh air only when Catherine relented and put him out on the fire escape for a few minutes at a time. He might also have been affected by the psychological torments Matt methodically inflicted upon him: staring him out; making as if to choke him, to test his tooth-and-claw reflexes. Whatever the cause, that animal was deranged. When Catherine let him out of the bedroom, he would ricochet around the lounge for minutes at a time, bouncing off the walls so fast he was visible only as a snarling, blurred streak of bristling fur.

Where Matt was sardonic, droll and ingenious, Catherine was fervid, instinctive and, at times, alarming – not least to Matt. Matt came armed with the flick-knife cerebral menace of an interloper recognising himself to be several shades smarter than the gentlefolk whose world he has infiltrated. Catherine, five-feet-nothing, with flaming orange hair and a temperament to match, was capricious, elemental, funny and dangerous. She was also, if anything, madder than her cat.

'I didn't get up in time for work this morning,' she once told me – she had taken a part-time clerical job – 'so I called them up from a phone box and told them there was a bomb in the building. Everyone was standing outside when I arrived, and nobody noticed I was late.' She recounted this with the offhandedness anyone else might use for a story about finding a 50p coin on the pavement.

Matt and Catherine's relationship was, inevitably, tempestuous. Catherine could probably have maintained a tempestuous relationship all alone on the moon, while Matt's personality was assembled almost entirely from sharp edges. One Guy Fawkes night, some friends and I had arranged to meet the pair at their flat, before heading down to the beach to watch the fireworks. When I arrived, we caught them in the middle of a barney so fearsome it rendered the fireworks redundant. They sat, mute and fuming, at opposite ends of the room. It was the first time Helena, my giddy patrician pal, had met either of them. Her breeding kicked in, as she attempted to fill the painful silence with effervescent chatter.

'You have a beautiful cat,' said Helena, watching the maniacal Leonin rocket around the living room like an unexploded shell. 'What are you going to do with him when you go back to Liverpool?'

Catherine continued to glower speechlessly at the carpet. At last, Matt spoke up. 'I was thinking of skinning it,' he said, 'and selling what's left to the Chinkies.'

Helena didn't utter another word all night. Nor did Matt. Catherine's face was enough to make you hope she wouldn't either.

The pair of them did take the cat back to Merseyside that Christmas. Unable to afford a carrying cage, Catherine picked up the yowling feline beserker, stuffed him into a pillowcase and hauled him onto the train with the rest of her luggage. Three minutes out of Brighton, he clawed his way through the bedlinen and shot off up the aisle with a frantic burst of acceleration that would have drawn admiring glances from his distant cousin, the cheetah. Catherine and Matt pursued him up the train, until they found the passage between the front two carriages blocked by a very large Rastafarian smoking a spliff to scale.

'Wass problem?' said the Rastafarian.

'Cat . . . run . . . gone . . . seen?' panted Matt.

'No matter,' said the Rastafarian sympathetically, and handed Matt the spliff. 'Cat soon come.'

They passed the spliff around between them. The guard came by and attempted to squeeze around the giant Rastafarian.

'Tickets, please . . . Oi! You can't smoke that in here,' protested the guard.

'Instead of bothering us,' snapped Caroline, fixing the unlucky official with a stare that I could categorise from experience as terrifying, 'why don't you do something useful and find our cat?'

Chastened, the guard hurried off, returning ten minutes later with Leonin clinging by the claws to the shoulder of his coat. The familiar smell of marijuana seemed to reassure the animal, and he lay down tractably by Catherine's tiny feet while the trio finished the spliff and the guard, wisely, went off to find something else to do.

The last time I wandered past Catherine and Matt's former flat, the whole street had been smartened up. The iffy pub across the way is now a fashionable B&B. Few of Brighton's backstreets have escaped this process. The fortunes of the ruined duchess were restored in a recent property boom that saw almost every dwelling in the BN1 postcode change hands. Rumour had it that vulturine estate agents kept lists of elderly homeowners who might any day topple from their perch. When, in 1987, I moved off campus and into Brighton, I noticed that around eleven in the morning the pavements were thronged with old age pensioners. Now you rarely see anybody over the age of fifty – and if you do, they're dressed as if they're thirty. Which I suppose is fair enough, when those of us in our thirties are dressed as if we're fifteen.

As its population has become steadily more youthful, Brighton has done well out of the contemporary British obsession with home improvements. Always a good-looking town, it has recovered something of its former grace. The convex Georgian windows, the ornate Regency detailing and the august Victorian housefronts have all benefited from the arrival of prosperous and houseproud new owners. Taking a walk is like going on holiday; choosing a slightly different route each time can turn a humdrum errand into a sightseeing tour.

The threadbare venue for a million dirty weekends has become salubrious enough for even the residents of neighbouring Hove to find it tolerable – a good thing too, as a civic shotgun wedding has seen Brighton and Hove united in cityhood. Not long since, the Hoveites would have recoiled at the prospect. So keen were they to set themselves apart that their town was sarcastically referred to as 'Hove actually', and chose as its motto 'A Distinguished Resort' – distinguished, that is, from Sodom-by-Sea just along the road.

Even Churchill Square, a concrete pit from the Brutalist school of the late 1960s, has been re-built in keeping with the architectural principles which now guide British urban planning. Where it once had character – a brooding, inimical character, granted, but character nonetheless – it now corresponds to the stale anonymity of every other town centre in the country.

Across Britain, what the Luftwaffe may have started, contemptuous design and construction have been sure to complete. Bath is famously and fortuitously unscarred by any of these malignant forces, but this gives it the slightly unreal feeling of a well-kept theme park. There are those who would wish the same on Brighton, and who dismiss in the same breath Sussex Heights, a splendid white tower block in the city centre, and the Hilton West Pier, a drab, festering pile a little way to the west that sullies one of the most fetching sea views in the city.

These folk loathe with blanket prejudice all modern – and modernist – buildings. In this they echo that aesthetic dullard Prince Charles, whose stultifying influence lay heaviest at the time of my arrival in the UK. I could see it made manifest almost immediately in the raising of Trafalgar Place, below the railway station. This hefty, ponderous office complex – the city's most unsightly structure, if you ask me, which by some oversight nobody thought to do – makes as if to chime with Brighton's style by incorporating such period details as curved bays and latticed windows. It's a pointless fudge, implying either disregard for or ignorance of the role played by scale and balance in Georgian and Regency terraces, and it serves only to mock the sensibilities it aimed to placate. You might as well draft a prop forward into a chorus line by equipping him with tap shoes and mascara.

Trafalgar Place shares the look of buildings that were cropping up all over the UK at the time, and have done ever since – bland, reddish-brown, neither charmingly retrospective nor bracingly original but half-hearted and compromised. Office blocks, tenements, housing estates, all designed not to please but to avoid offence – a sure-fire formula for offending just about everybody a few years down the line.

'You're right about Trafalgar Place,' Matt said to me, not long after I met him. He was enrolled in a History of Art course, and had just spent an exasperating seminar defending the I.M. Pei glass pyramid in the courtyard of the Louvre to a coterie of fogeys, young and old, who damned it as an insolent defacement of that pedestrian palace. 'It's just the way things are going. They'd never let anyone build an equivalent of the Brighton Pavilion nowadays. Too exciting, too individual.'

I had seen the Pavilion for the first time only a few days before. 'I don't know,' I said. 'I wasn't that impressed with it. It looks like a big blue aircraft hangar.'

Matt laughed. 'Nice one,' he said.

'Huh?' I said.

'You mean you weren't kidding?' said Matt. He explained to me that the Pavilion had been covered with corrugated iron while repairs were carried out.

'Ah. I wondered what all the fuss was about.'

Brighton, like everywhere else in the UK, may be rowdy on weekends, when juiced-up wayfarers pile in from nearby boroughs such as Burgess Hill (the home, inevitably, of 'Burgess Hillbillies'). Yet it isn't ceaselessly choked by the oppressive air of incipient violence that hangs over many of Britain's towns and smaller cities. In Brighton, you need to be careless or very unlucky to meet with harm. Elsewhere, you need to be careful and very lucky not to.

A little way up the coast lies Hastings, no less fetching in appearance, but as bleak, tawdry and crime-ridden a municipality as you could hope to avoid. Unemployment, drug addiction, depression and suicide are rife. Predatory eyes track your progress along every street. Hastings greets foreigners (easily differentiated by their healthy appearance and good-humoured mien) with habitual aggression; so habitual that, in the spring of each year, Hastings police mount an operation in the vain hope of preventing attacks on overseas students, who are advised never to walk about on their own.

The first time I stopped in Hastings, I found the place more disturbing even than the putrid hamlet of Dagoretti, near my home in Nairobi. In Dagoretti, squalor and filth had made people wretched, but it hadn't made them savage. Hastings was a paradise by comparison, at least on the surface, but it had the cruel, pitiless air of a jungle about it. The African bush, where I spent much of my childhood, had never alarmed me one half so much as Hastings.

A friend, Terry, who foolishly moved to Hastings after several tranquil years in Brighton, found himself caught up in a succession of unruly episodes. The first of these involved walking down to the end of his street and stopping in at a pub, the Mottled Scar. A football match was unfolding on the television. Terry took a seat near a table of pub-goers who provided a vivid and pithy critique whenever a black player touched the ball.

'It's that fucking nigger again.'

'Nah, it's the other fucking nigger.'

'Fuck me, they take one coon off and stick another one on. Don't they have no English players no more?'

Terry considered pointing out that both of the footballers in question had been capped for England's national side. Discretion outweighing valour, he instead set down his pint, opened up a biography of Rudyard Kipling and tried to blot out the unwanted commentary. This worked passably well until the half-time whistle blew; almost instantly, the book was snatched from his eyeline, to be replaced by a knotty, empurpled tract of flesh which might once have been a face. So far as the view went, this was not an improvement.

'Hoi!' grunted the part which looked least unlike a mouth. 'This is a fucking pub, not a fucking library!'

It was a rare week that did not provide a similar incident. Terry at last gave up on Hastings after getting punched in the nose outside a convenience store where the shelves were barricaded within iron mesh and the clientele should have been, too.

'Do you know who I am?' barked his assailant, a snaggle-toothed troll whose arm bore an amateur tattoo reading 'QPR 2-47' (implying either that the tattooist had difficulty with the idiom '24-7', or that the troll had once taken a rather excessive step on the day of a late kick-off to remind himself of a Football Special train timetable). In Hastings society, he was evidently Somebody. The mayor, perhaps.

When I went to visit Terry in Hastings, the first thing I noticed was a quartet of black-clad vagrants leading a goat on a rope past the railway station, suggesting that even the town's Satanists are in an uncommonly sorry state. If the Devil himself can't get you out of Hastings, maybe you should consider hawking your soul to someone else.

At least in Hastings you're liable to be assaulted in a tasteful – if run-down – milieu. The town calls to mind an ill-starred junkie identifiable as a onetime model by her cheekbones alone. The surface may be ravaged, but the structure that underpinned the beauty is still discernible. There are plenty of other towns where you can expect to be chased by gangs of youths in tracksuits – or middle-aged delinquents with vests almost as frightening as their features – through acres of unlovely concrete onto streets lined with post-war housing so ill-favoured and shoddy it inflicts upon the spirit precisely what your antagonists intend to wreak upon your body.

I once found myself in Stevenage, on the northern outskirts of London, a 'new town' the very sight of which caused the soul to wilt and wither. I was in the company of a band who were due to play there that night. We stopped in for a sharpener at the Edward the Confessor – 'Ted the Grass', as the drummer had it – and observed what, not counting the band, passed for entertainment thereabouts: an all-in brawl between four generations of the local Jukes and Kallikaks.

It began as a handbaggy scrap between a pair of teenage boys, whose respective fathers (or current 'uncles') reeled over to pull them apart. Moments later, these paternal role models were grappling on the floor, with arms, legs, thumbs, feet and teeth all brought abundantly into play. This was the cue for the wives to scuttle up to the action, shrieking imprecations at their menfolk, each other, the publican, everybody else in the room, and various absent relatives and ancestors of the opposing clan about whom they held some emphatic opinions. Then they flew at one another like polecats. Within half a minute, all able-bodied members and associates of both families had launched themselves into the mêlée, which mimicked a Gauls-versus-Romans battle from an Asterix comic – a swirling cloud of dust, noise and commotion studded with briefly protruding limbs and orbited by loose teeth.

'Fuck 'im, Ronnie!' keened a gummy crone, gamely

stabbing at a trapped buttock with the heel of her crutch. 'Cripple the bastard!'

By this time the members of the band were standing on their chairs applauding. A short, scrawny young fellow wearing milk-bottle glasses ran up to our table, his lips flecked with spittle, and bayed, 'I'll fuckin' kill you and all! Cunts! I'll kill the fuckin' lot of you!'

'Will you bollocks, four-eyes,' sniggered a guitarist, but Four-Eyes wasn't listening. Something else had caught his attention. He scurried back to the fray and proceeded to lay out, then deliver a remorseless kicking to, a man twice his size.

'Cunt!' he spat with each connection twixt trainer and ribcage. 'Cunt! Cunt!'

At this, everybody in our corner simultaneously made for the exit at a brisk walking pace, before Four-Eyes could revert to Plan A, involving as it did fuckin' killing us and all – an assignment he had shown himself to be unmistakably well-equipped to discharge.

It was not an edifying display. For a long time I've wondered how closely linked are British town planning and the national propensity for combat – whether that hankering for mayhem stems from lives passed in surroundings of hope-crushing ugliness. It doesn't take a great leap of sympathetic imagination to imagine how an environment like Stevenage could induce you to wallop everything in sight. Yet I've never come close to seeing that Stevenage fracas repeated in any concrete purgatory encircling a continental European city – nor, for that matter, in the most deprived parts of Nairobi, where horrific 'mob justice' onslaughts on supposed criminals occur once in a while, but punch-ups are seldom launched just for the hell of it.

I have, however, seen plenty more such incidents here in the UK. I've had to conclude that it's a distinctively British spectacle. I've visited, and lived in, places where violence is commonplace and sometimes casually deadly, but Britain is the only country I know of where fighting is treated as a hobby.

If you want to know how Britain held out, against all odds, in the Second World War, and wound up on the winning side, Four-Eyes from Stevenage may provide the answer. He would have been happy to 'fight them on the beaches', no matter who They were or what They'd done. And if he'd suspected They were students, he'd probably have given Them twice the battering.

It didn't take me very long living away from campus to twig that students were not popular in Britain. Back in Kenya, students were well thought of, and this despite their habit of rioting regularly and often – sometimes because they opposed the government, sometimes because they didn't like their food, which made it hard to take the first reason seriously. All the same, to be a student was deemed admirable; you were trying to learn, to achieve something.

In Britain, to be a student was to be a walking target. At first, I tried to refrain from looking, talking or behaving like a student. If I succeeded, it was only because, despite my best efforts, I didn't look, talk or behave like anybody else in the country either. That worked, for a while. Then I came up with a better strategy to avoid being taken for a student. I graduated.

CHAPTER SIX

COR, BABY, THAT'S REALLY FREE

PEOPLE ARE NOT designed to live together. Even people who love each other find it all but impossible to get along at close quarters. So for a menage united not by affection but by expediency, dissolution can only be a matter of time. In a country as densely populated as the United Kingdom, one can only guess at how many times a day someone marches into a shared living room and, with no little relief, announces their imminent departure – as I did at Stan's place in 1989, shortly after I left university.

House-sharing may not be unique to Britain, but it does constitute so widespread a prerequisite for living anywhere at all – what with ever smaller homes and more numerous households – that I know people who have been unable to escape it well into their adulthood. It would take me years to find a home of my own, and then I only achieved this by the pure fluke of wading into the tumultuous property market at its lowest ebb. I was the Inspector Clouseau of real estate, surviving by luck where shrewder men have, with the best of judgement, been undone.

When I left Stan's house, it was to move into another shared home – this time without a resident landlord. In retrospect, I feel some sympathy with Stan. Having a res-ident landlord may be a prodigious aggravation, but being a resident landlord must be torture. I don't think Stan was temperamentally suited to the role. When you are wary by nature, and unusually protective of your pos-sessions, then renting out rooms to a trio of teenagers is probably not the smoothest route to peace of mind. If an Englishman's home truly is his castle, few prospects can rankle more than being obliged to invite the marauding Picts indoors and give them the run of the place.

As is always the way, small quarrels magnified them-selves until they loomed, ogre-like, over the conscious-ness of every person in the house. I had been raised on the dictum that you should never argue over food, but that seemed to happen every day in Orton Street. Then there was the issue of bills. Should we split them equally? I felt that was unfair, as the central heating brought no warmth at all to my windswept basement. Adding to the chill factor of three outside walls and a draughty win-dow, my own door stood adjacent to the back door of the house. So loosely did the back door hang on its frame that when I locked myself out, I could squeeze in via the gap. I was thinner then, but it's still fair to say that anything I could fit through would not present much of an obstacle to the north wind.

Britain's supposedly temperate climate feels like nothing of the sort to those raised in warmer parts. It's true that Britain doesn't experience the ferocious and potentially devastating cold of other regions on roughly the same latitude – southern Scandinavia, or Labrador, where as a ten-year-old I spent a winter getting lost in snowdrifts and falling through river ice. But those places know what's coming, and are well prepared for it. Winter, despite being on all past evidence an annual event, never fails to take Britain by surprise. Most housing is not equipped to repel it. Moderate snowfall – of a type which Norwegians, for instance, would not accord the slightest notice unless it dropped directly from their bedroom ceiling and landed on their eiderdown – brings transport across the UK slithering to halt. Britain's response to undergoing relatively clement winters is a refusal to acknowledge that winter happens at all. And as anyone from south of the Channel can tell you, even a 'mild' winter feels very, very uncomfortable when you're trying to pretend it doesn't exist.

Each year the weather eventually turns nasty enough for residents of Tyneside to don a second layer of clothing. Shocked headlines shriek about a 'Big Freeze'. News programmes despatch junior correspondents, microphone in one fist and short straw in the other, to the most exposed patch of ground in the mainland, there to keep their footing as best as they can in a raging blizzard whilst informing dumbfounded viewers that it is, indeed, cold. The hothouse flowers among the audience – that is, those of us who think it reasonable for our circulatory systems to receive a little outside help in staving off hypothermia – will by now be irately heckling the screen: 'Next: object which went up now reported on downward trajectory. Plus exclusive report – large yellow disc manifests itself in sky following period of darkness.' There's nothing like a touch of indignant sarcasm to bring a ruddy flush to the cheeks.

It was only to be expected, then, that Stan denied I had cause for complaint.

'Try wearing more clothes,' he said.

'There are times when you don't want to wear more clothes,' I found myself, against my every inclination, being forced to explain. 'There are times when you shouldn't *have* to wear more clothes.'

He pondered this and, unable to come up with an answer that would not sound prohibitively puritan, instead put forward what he must have believed to be an artful solution: if the problem couldn't be dismissed, perhaps it could be displaced.

'Why don't you and Rob swap rooms?' he suggested.

'Because,' said Rob, 'I don't fancy freezing my knackers off any more than Dave does.'

Stan's eventual answer was to lend me a heater fuelled from a portable gas cylinder – for free, he was at pains to point out, although I would have to pay for the gas. I ascertained that if I left it burning night and day, the temperature would rise to the thawing point of reptilian blood. That winter, I wound up spending more on gas than I did on rent.

Stan was never, in his own mind, clear on his role in the household. Often he wanted to be one of the boys. He would generously invite us to play our favourite records on his expensively set-up hi-fi, and they did sound wonderful. He also helped me assemble, at minimal cost, a goodish sound system of my own from the classified ads in the back of his audiophile magazines. Then he would be seized with a sudden and inappropriate impulse to act *in loco parentis*. He once huffily ordered me to tidy my room, which admittedly could have used it. I told him it was none of his business. So long as I didn't damage it, my rent payments entitled to me to keep the room in any state I damn well pleased – a piece of moral logic I thought would be self-evident to a philosophy post-graduate.

These inevitable and petty aggravations began to mount up. I wouldn't wish upon any sensible person the ordeal of living with three student slobs, but Stan was as bad as any of us. He would complain that the washing-up had not been done. When it was pointed out to him that the dirty items were his own, he replied that he had left the house at daybreak to run his business, and we should have done his dishes for him. That brought forth the response that we were lodgers, not communards. When Stan broke a glass, he swept the shards into a dustpan, and left the dustpan on the kitchen counter for a week. Finally, Martin attached a Post-it note to the offending receptacle. It read: 'Is this paying rent?'

'Erm, I really wasn't sure what to do about the glass,' said Stan. 'I thought it might be dangerous.'

'Did you think it would be safer next to the food?' said Martin.

Stan started to exhibit symptoms of paranoia. He became convinced that impish entities – namely, Rob, Martin and me – were conspiring behind his back to damage his property and defile his living space. That he could never catch us at it did nothing to alter his suspicions, which for an empiricist cannot have indicated the soundest state of mind. Maybe he surmised we had chanced upon the power to transform ourselves into invisible sprites, wreaking mischief he was helpless to prevent.

Stan was also agitated by the possibility that The Girlfriend might spend enough time in his house to qualify as a tenant. As it happened, the venues for our dalliance were seasonally balanced; in autumn and winter, we rarely spent a night at Orton Street, preferring The Girlfriend's house, where we could remove our jackets without first breaking up the icy, rigid sleeves with a blunt instrument.

One evening, as we made for the front door, we heard Stan galloping down the stairs, bent on intercepting us. He thumped onto the landing, a towel tucked around his waist, foam slathered abundantly across his chops, and a badger's-hair brush brandished aloft in his right hand. He appeared to be rehearsing an aberrant bath-time impersonation of the Statue of Liberty.

'My shaving brush is wet,' he declared, accusingly. 'Have you been using it?'

I wordlessly pointed to my face, upon which bristled a week's growth of stubble.

He turned to The Girlfriend. 'Have *you*?'

She goggled at him, open-mouthed.

'You might have done,' he contended, a defensive note now colouring his voice. 'On your . . . legs.'

'Bye, Stan,' I said, and ushered The Girlfriend out of the door. As I closed it behind me, I could hear him calling down the stairs to Martin.

'Have you been using my shaving brush?'

The Girlfriend had housing problems of her own. She had been living in a firetrap across town, halfway up Britannia Rise, an incline so sharp that when black ice coated its pavements, folk who slipped upon it would slalom half a mile downhill until they reached level ground or struck a lamp post. The house was a notorious student pit, its population shifting and amorphous, its landlord a shadowy, apocryphal figure, its tenancy agreements lost in a legal netherworld between the arcane and the imaginary. Everyone of your acquaintance lived there at one time or another; often, when you visited, they all seemed to be living there at once, even when you knew for certain that half of them lived somewhere else.

Cryptic, twilight characters of campus life moved through its rooms. There were the two Keiths, Keith Hair and Keith Leg, men who – although they were not close friends – orbited one another, as if each was trapped in the other's gravitational field. Keith Hair was so called because he possessed a remarkable mop – a two-tone hayrick of a barnet – beneath which his tuberous face and tall, stocky frame wheeled cumbersomely this way and that, like a farmer's wayward oxcart. Keith Leg's handle derived from a limb perpetually encased in plaster. He lived in the back of a tiny 1960s mobile home – or in the back of The Girlfriend's house. It was hard to tell, even, I think, for him. En route to Britannia Rise I would spot his cast protruding from the rear window of his Lilliputian van, and hear him strumming tunelessly on his guitar. When I reached the house, he would be there, too, ensconced in a mildewed armchair, guitar in lap. There can't have been two of him, and he was not, for obvious reasons, a brisk walker. It was one of those mysteries not intended for unravelling by mortal man.

A glass-fronted cabinet of collector's items also called Britannia Rise home. Violet was a dumpy exhibitionist whose misfortune it was to possess little that anyone wanted to ogle. I recall a crowded party (there was always a party at Britannia Rise, it was always crowded, and there was never anything to eat or drink) which spilled over into the bathroom. In came Violet; she ran a bath for herself, stripped naked and climbed into it, without attracting even furtive glances from the chattering throng. Eventually she climbed out and sploshed pettishly away, leaving behind a reproachful trail of wet little footprints. The next time I saw Violet, some weeks later, she was skipping through the kitchen, waving a soiled sanitary towel above her head. 'I'm having such a wonderful period,' she exulted. 'I feel so in touch with everything.'

'Except hygiene,' muttered The Girlfriend.

The attic was occupied by a tall, stick-thin fellow with the air of a professional mourner gone to seed. Austen was 6ft 5in and weighed 103lbs, half of it beard. The Girlfriend had spent several months fending off his uninvited attentions, a chore rendered that much more onerous by her sleeping arrangements. Lack of living space meant she had to bed down in the lounge, where she made not a sitting but a lying target for Austen when he slouched home after midnight.

'I'm feeling awfully sexual tonight,' he would drone, stooping over her recumbent form like a creature of nightmare sprung from the brush of Henry Fuseli, albeit longer and hairier.

'Go and feel it on your own, then,' she would say, recoiling as far as her sofabed permitted.

He would then turn and trudge upstairs, confounded as to how his silver-tongued wooing had yet again failed to yield results.

Austen was a pirate broadcaster; on campus, his bashfully monikered venture, Radio Austen, had built up a small but solid reputation for being even worse than Radio Falmer, the official student station. Rob and I had presented (if it is technically possible to present to an audience of precisely zero) a show on Radio Falmer: *Dave and Rob on Sunday Afternoon*. It went out on Tuesday nights, which we thought was rather funny. The name was certainly funnier than the show itself, on which we played Pink Floyd records and talked drivel; and the show in turn was a Diaghilev spectacular compared to the output of Radio Austen.

Radio Austen fearlessly championed freedom of the airwaves. It transmitted an unending stream of subversion and defiance to the three or four people who, when they weren't broadcasting on it themselves, listened to it. By its very nature, it offered the best argument for strict regulation of radio frequencies that you never heard.

Austen seemed convinced that it was only a matter of

time before the government, and perhaps the whole apparatus of the state, crumpled under his onslaught. It must have given him some satisfaction to know that the state was listening; or at any rate, that arm of oppression known as the Department of Trade and Industry, which despatched a platoon of coppers to arrest him on the same afternoon that The Girlfriend finally moved out of Britannia Rise.

The Girlfriend was alone in the house, waiting by her suitcase in the living room when the police rang the doorbell. She didn't hear it; it hadn't worked since the previous spring, when a spliffed-up Keith Hair pressed the button so forcefully that it stuck, leaving the bell to shrill unattended until its batteries expired. But she did hear the subsequent thumping at the door. Expecting her taxi, she was startled to find herself crushed back against the wall as a squad of heavyset CID men muscled into the corridor. Austen, without mentioning it to anyone else in the house, had moved his transmitter from the campus to his attic room – at once facilitating the task of tracking it down by a factor of approximately two hundred. In the rabbit warren of residences on the University's East Slope, the culprit could have been anyone. On a quiet terraced street peopled (as it was then) by old ladies and blue-collar families, a house thronged with a raucous, hirsute, itinerant rabble singled itself out as a credible target.

While the DTI detachment dismantled Austen's equipment and carried it out to their van, the policemen, irked at missing their quarry, inevitably turned to The Girlfriend as a surrogate. An avowed feminist, and nobody's fool, she

nonetheless instinctively took on the persona of an innocent and none-too-intelligent girlie.

'How long have you been doing the pirate radio, luv?'

'I don't have a radio. I do have a Walkman, though.'

'Is that yours, then?' (Indicating a bong on the mantel-
piece.)

'The vase? I don't know whose that is. But the card next
to it is mine.'

The card stood almost two feet high. It was festooned
with drawings of teddy bears, ribbons, balloons and
valentines, and bore the legend 'Happy Birthday to My
Wonderful Daughter'. The Girlfriend's father had the
habit of sending over-demonstrative anniversary greet-
ings. It was the only possession she hadn't packed. ('I did-
n't want that thing at my new house,' she later said, and
you could see why. The round, glassy eyes of the bears followed you around the room. After a prolonged session on
the bong, Keith Hair had become fixated on the design
and fled gurgling into the kitchen to escape its 'evil
vibes'.)

The card did the trick. Reluctantly concluding that a
charge of being Adorable After the Fact might not be
made to stick, the CID men let The Girlfriend go. She
dragged her luggage out of Britannia Rise, and into a
home where her flatmates didn't alternate the roles of
ineffectual Lothario and bungling outlaw.

What I had happened across here was Bohemia. In
Nairobi, we didn't have Bohemians. We just had weirdos –
and not enough of them to form a recognisable group. I

had grown up as one of those weirdos. My interest in matters beyond sport and White Cap lager; my embryonic awareness of politics; my unbearably snotty and, at Knollpeak Secondary School, swiftly corrected haughtiness towards those who cherished only sport and White Cap lager; these things marked me out as an anomaly. Nobody was much taken aback by that. The whole Bennun family had a reputation as rum customers. Rumour had it that our home contained several shelves of books, many of which did not bear the names Dick Francis or Wilbur Smith on the spines. Plus, my brother talked to trees, and I spent a fortnight wearing a paper tag on a piece of string around my ear for no particular reason, so the reputation may have been deserved.

When I encountered the two Keiths, Austen, Violet and all the other unorthodox folk who lurked in and around Britannia Rise, I didn't realise there was anything strange about them; or rather, I didn't realise that everybody else would see them as strange. To me, they were simply British. I had been taken aback by the behaviour, habits and language of almost everybody I met. I had no criteria for distinguishing what was and was not conventional. Brighton was a magnet for drop-outs and *soi-disant* non-conformists; it was as if the whole mainland had been shaken like a snow globe, and every last flake had settled upon the south coast. But having as yet seen little else of the mainland, I didn't know this. I thought that Brighton was normal. I thought the inhabitants of Britannia Rise were normal, which was something their own mothers would not have said about them.

In a curious way, though, I was right. These people *were*

ordinary – to a degree that they would rather not have recognised themselves. For all their avouched individualism, each of them corresponded to a recognised type. They lived by the rules and depended upon the approval of their own kind. Looking back, I'm put in mind of a cartoon by Gary Larson, creator of *The Far Side*. It depicts a colony of penguins – thousands upon thousands of identical, monochrome penguins. One penguin, as interchangeable with its fellows as any other, raises its head above the throng and sings,

Oh, I just gotta be me.

You could name that penguin 'Violet'.

Even the two Keiths, it turned out, were not as colourfully nicknamed as I had supposed. Big, bushy Keith was in fact called Keith Hare, and small, hobbled Keith's name was Keith Legg. Neat as that might be, it was also a bit of a disappointment.

It was hard to deny that the Bohemian lifestyle had appeal. It undoubtedly appealed to me. Most of these folk considered themselves to be artists of one kind or another. If they ever did anything the rest of the world would define as work, they made sure never to be caught at it. Those of them who had exhausted their student grants or never qualified for them in the first place were happy enough relying upon the Department of Health and Social Security. And if you were going to content yourself with a life on the dole, which is usually a small and constricted one, then you may as well aspire to making it a life of the mind.

That, at least, is what they must have told themselves. Being a Bohemian means making a virtue of necessity. In your head, you're F. Scott Fitzgerald. In reality, you're hunched in a government office that smells of nappies, Special Brew and sour, irremediable misery, waiting to sign on. You wear fifth-hand gladrags from charity shops. You live in a dank basement with a girl whose sole ambition is to prove herself as loopy as Zelda. So you convince yourself that penury is chic, that creativity is everything, that you are the beautiful and the damned. The truth is that you are the sallow and the asthmatic, and you've just blown your housing benefit on a lump of yellow hash which wouldn't intoxicate an uncommonly small stoat.

This hankering after destitute glamour is the art college equivalent of the style latterly known as 'ghetto fabulous' – the instinct among the impoverished to put on a display in express contradiction of everything around them, to sport flashy jewellery and expensive fashion labels. Among Bohemians the idea may not be to pose as wealthy, but it assuredly is to pose, to superimpose hackneyed fantasy on top of grubby actuality. If they put on enough of an act, then somehow – despite the absence of cameras or clapperboards or an audience that cares about anything other than its own vanity – they'll achieve a kind of cinema club immortality. People very much like them will discuss their performance and copy the way they smoke.

Still, when you're twenty years old, and willing to subsist on supermarket seconds sold off cheap in bulk from market stalls (in one week, I ate my own weight in fancy French hazelnut yoghurt for about two quid), the Bohemian way of life has plenty to recommend it. It wasn't until I graduated and applied for income support that I fully apprehended the meagreness of that existence. Eking out a DHSS stipend didn't just restrict your finances; it drew in your horizons to the point of claustrophobia. The wider world began to look as remote as the outer reaches of the solar system.

Every Thursday, I would buy the *Evening Argus* and shuffle through the employment ads, applying for entry-level clerical posts. Although I now had a degree, it wasn't a very good one – I had winged it, frankly, a thought that has shamed me ever since. Many of my college contemporaries had boasted of how little work they did; it amazed me then and amazes me now that anyone could be so purblind as to consider this a point of pride. When you grow up in a country where children will walk eight miles, barefoot, along rutted dust tracks strewn with acacia thorns, to seize the chance of the most basic education, you have to be even denser than I indubitably was not to get the point: that all of human life is a lottery, and you should make the most of a winning ticket. But even if I didn't flaunt my sluggardly attitude, in the end I was no better than those who did. Remorse over a failing doesn't excuse having lapsed in the first place. Unless, as I understand it, you're Catholic – and then you feel so guilty by default that it makes scant difference.

Each week I sent out covering letters and CVs, printed in indistinct dot matrix type via my steam-driven Amstrad computer. Each week I received . . . nothing. No replies at all. The job market was in a slump. A vacancy for an office junior would attract hundreds of replies from first-class graduates, redundant filing clerks, redundant middle-managers, redundant senior managers, former chief executives of the Banque Credite Suisse, Nobel laureates and top-level defectors from the Chinese space program.

One classified ad, for a position at an insurance broker, gave no postal address, only a phone number. For all the difference it made, I could have put my details in a blank envelope and sailed it off the Palace Pier in a model dinghy, but I took this to be a test of initiative. I called the number, and found myself speaking directly to the chief of the firm.

'I'm calling about your job advertisement,' I began.

'Oh, yes?' he replied, and then said nothing. After ten seconds of silence, I panicked and began to jabber.

'Well, I'm a recent graduate,' I said. 'I'm very good with –'

'Don't tell me over the bloody phone,' snapped the boss, who in my imagination has ever since borne the face of Prince Philip. 'Write it down, man.' He hung up before I could ask where I should direct my application, which was probably for the best. He might well have told me.

If this really was a test of initiative, I had flunked it – along with the concomitant test of nerve. My response to this setback was far from resilient. I would go so far as to say it was pathetic; I was so discouraged that I stopped applying for jobs altogether. Again, my luck was in. It wasn't as if destiny was saving me for bigger things. Destiny has other fish to fry and wouldn't have saved me for dessert. But being kept out of the conventional working world by compulsion – as manifested in the excellent judgement of potential employers throughout the East Sussex area – left me with no choice but to do something else. I was back in Bohemia whether I liked it or not. I resolved to like it.

CHAPTER SEVEN

BABYLON BY THE BUS GARAGE

A S THE 1980S TURNED into the 1990s, The Girlfriend and I were living under the same roof, in another shared house, on Green Street, across the road from a bus garage. It took me a few months to accustom myself to the nocturnal medley: the hoarse reverberation of the engines; the grinding of gears; the squeaking of wheels; the thump, clatter and pneumatic hiss of the cleaning devices and attendant impedimenta. Once I did get used to it, I found it impossible to sleep without this mechanical lullaby. At which point the garage shut down for good.

The great metal gates, which had folded back in accordion pleats when shouldered open, were now flattened across the mouth of the building, forming a solid steel sheet. This acted as an echo board for the music that blared from neighbours' open windows on warm nights and bounced back through ours, whetted with a thin, brassy vibration capable of inducing tinnitus within the span of a single R.E.M. tune. Worse yet was when they played reggae. It was always Bob Marley, an artist I once admired, but whose work had come to grate on me like a rusty chain-mail thong.

Marley was dead – to begin with. But his music lives on, despite the best efforts of buskers on the London Underground to kill it. Marley's ghost haunted me then, and it still does today, unrelentingly. It clutches at me with wispy claws in shops, pubs and cafés. If a palm tree gets so much as a second of television airtime, you'll hear his spectre skanking in the fronds. Radio summons up his dread presence with the grim inevitability of cardboard ectoplasm at a Victorian seance. Those subway buskers are possessed by him, although sadly not by his ability to hold a tune. At the foot of every escalator, his songs die the death of Prometheus – agonising, and on a daily basis. Worst abused of all by the cloth-eared strumbums is 'No Woman No Cry'; a number which, through persistent repetition, has become the reggae 'Stairway to Heaven'. Whatever qualities once infused it have been leeched away by the numbing frequency with which one is exposed to it.

Bob Marley is credited with being the first Third-World superstar. In my Nairobi days, his portrait was painted on the sides of *matatus*, the criminally hazardous minibuses that passed for a public transport system, and his songs issued from speakers in the cabs. His 'Buffalo Soldier' became the theme tune of an attempted coup in the early 1980s, played by both rebel and government forces when they in turn took and re-took Nairobi's principal radio station. To many Kenyans, Marley was an all but tangible presence. His insurrectionist battle cries, calling for a Zion in Africa, spoke directly to people whose nation had known only two decades of independence. And even if it didn't speak directly to you – if, for instance, you were me – you could still dance to it. Chances were you could dance to it better than Marley ever did. Those mistimed little sideways jigs of his, bearing no discernible relation to the rhythm behind them, were always engagingly comical.

On arriving in the UK I had found that, if Marley was esteemed in Africa, that was nothing compared to the reverence he was held in by certain Britons – almost invariably white and of a genteel background, and more often than not female. Helena adored Bob Marley and all his works. She refused to accept the possibility that anybody might differ on this point.

'But you *have* to love Bob,' she would insist. 'How can you not love Bob? He's *Bob*.'

'I can take him or leave him alone. Preferably leave him alone.'

'But you're from Africa.'

'Um, yes. And Bob Marley was from Jamaica. I'm not sure why it matters.'

'Well, he was black, wasn't he?'

'Last I heard. But I still don't follow your argument.'

'He was Bob. You *have* to love Bob.' Here she would

start singing along to 'Exodus', and I would wander off to find a hangout where nobody was playing Bob Marley records. It wasn't always easy.

What, I wondered, was it – aside from Blu-tack – that stuck Marley to the bedroom wall of every second college girl in Britain?

The clues lay not in Marley's records, but in the posters themselves. Gazing at his varied guises – the 'rasta Che', the 'giant spliff', the 'compassionate sage' – you could feel at one with the oppressed of the earth. Unless they were female. 'Woman is a coward,' Marley had once gallantly asserted. 'Man strong.'

Marley was black, but not too black, given his mixed-race lineage and his sharp, quasi-Caucasian features. Not scary, scowling, kill-Whitey black, but safe, friendly black, an organic revolutionary preaching peace 'n' love 'n' dope. So long as you didn't listen too closely to the lyrics, that is, or read up on Rastafarianism – a creed that might be genuinely dangerous if its adherents ever kept off the weed long enough to get up, stand up.

Marley was the unwitting founder and embodiment of what you might call Wholemeal Black – a musical genre popular among whites who want desperately to believe that there exists in other races an innate dignity and spirituality seemingly lacking in their own. One look at Marley's selection of tank tops and jumpers – think Woolworth's bargain bin circa 1976 – should have kicked that notion into touch. But such was his charisma that his fashion gaffes generally went unnoticed. The eye was drawn instead to the flailing dreadlocks, thick and furred as old tree roots, or to the bulging tea cosy that often contained them.

There was something of the woods about him, and something of the carpet slipper. You still see people today who have Marley's look down to a T. Most of them come from Surrey and play the didgeridoo.

Wholemeal Black, too, is very much a thriving genre, defined not by any one musical style, but by its mystical affectations and vague political leanings. It typically nods towards global harmony. Universal love. Mother nature (especially those bits of her you can smoke). The unquestionable goodness of all things African. It presents a ludicrously idealised picture of Africans that none could ever hope to live up to. It depicts them as wise and happy, grave but playful, in tune with ancient creation yet bearing a message for the modern world. It's the ideal of the noble savage come to save us from our industrial western purgatory. And when it recoils off a bus garage entryway and through your bedroom window at 3 a.m., buzzing with a high metallic whine, you would gladly see its fanbase strung up from the nearest lamp post by their own hempen trousers.

Helena had by this time moved her Bob Marley posters to second-storey lodgings not far from London Road station. There she lived with her new boyfriend, a softly spoken Scots lad named Andy, and their flatmate, Ted. Ted was a happy little stoner, so he was well suited to the routine there, which involved Helena waking up, skinning up, smoking for the rest of the day and eventually going to bed.

Like many recent graduates, myself included, Helena was at a loss as to what to do with herself. She had undertaken modelling work in the past, but was understandably reluctant to resume it, as it had coincided with a bout of anorexia which all but did her in. She still erred on the bony side, but no longer did she give the impression, painfully evident in her portfolio photographs, that she might at any second disintegrate into a heap of kindling.

Of our contemporaries, Stephen had gone straight into the job he had long ago targeted at a high-powered consultancy firm. Rob had tarried an extra year at college. Matt and Catherine, both signed up with temping agencies, were being despatched to subvert and unnerve new workplaces each week. Sally had gone to Europe to follow a band called Lederhosen, whose shows generated the atmosphere of a Munich beer hall rally staged by dubious Dadaists. And I was engaged in demonstrating to every personnel department in the wider south-east region that they would be better off hiring a vervet monkey in a Burtons suit than allowing me within fifty feet of their front door.

Helena's approach to solving her career quandary was nothing if not novel. And arguably, even taking into account its novelty, it was still nothing. She went to see her financial adviser.

'My dad's getting really grumpy,' she told him.

'I know,' said the financial adviser. 'He keeps complaining about it at our golf club.'

Helena's financial adviser kept an office in the stockbroker belt on the route between Brighton and London, conveniently located close to a number of greens.

'What should I do?' asked Helena.

'You need to make some money,' said the financial

adviser. (Nobody could accuse him of not living up to his job title.)

'Well, obviously,' said Helena, 'but how?'

'I'd recommend a job,' said the financial adviser, dryly. 'Unless you want your dad to get even grumpier.'

Helena reported this tête-à-tête to me and The Girlfriend with the same blithe detachment she brought to every conversation.

'So what are you going to do?' I said.

'Oh, I've found a job,' said Helena, airily. 'I'm going to work for my financial adviser.'

'He sounds good,' I said. 'Can I have his number?'

Helena's job didn't last long, involving as it did such exigencies as getting up before 11 a.m. and foregoing marijuana until the working day was over. Helena then went back to what she was good at – in her case, sleeping until noon, chain-smoking dope and coming out with such deathless, out-of-the-blue conversation stoppers as, 'My godfather crashed his helicopter the other day.'

'You know,' she would declare, reclining on her mattress and embellishing her remarks with the graceful wave of a jazz woodbine, while Andy washed up in the kitchen, 'I think I've really always been a communist. Perhaps I ought to be an MP. Yes, I think I really ought to be an MP.'

Helena was a sweet girl, but her understanding of Marxist precepts might fairly be summarised as, 'From each according to his ability, to me according to my needs.' She once invited me and The Girlfriend around for a late lunch of roast lamb. We arrived to find her still abed, rolling a joint.

'I really should have a wash and get dressed,' she said, slightly reproachfully – as if it were our fault she hadn't already done this, but she forgave us anyway. 'Do you think you could go out and buy the lamb while I'm doing that? I'm not sure what to do for seasoning.'

'Garlic and rosemary?' suggested The Girlfriend.

'Oh, please, that too – if it's what people use. In fact, maybe you'd like to cook it. You seem to know how it's done.'

What Helena didn't know about communism could fill a compendious series of very large books, and indeed has done. As an ideology, I suspect, she understood it to consist of being nice to poor people, and maybe passing on to them last year's frocks. In terms of its relevance to her daily life, it must have ranked somewhere between advances in particle accelerator technology and the cultivation of kumquats.

Communism may have been crumbling throughout Eastern Europe, but that fact showed no sign of impinging upon Helena's consciousness. This was very likely the only attribute she shared with actual communists, such as the Radical Marxist Union, an organisation that had been conspicuously active at Sussex University during my time there. So far as I could make out, the RMU nourished itself upon the cult-like fervour of a small but vigorous bloc of adherents, and was structured along similar lines to a double-glazing sales centre.

The RMU's recruiting approach echoed that of the Scientologists, who do not, of course, comprise a cult, as their lawyers are always keen to make clear, but a bona fide religion. The Scientologists favoured sending representatives to buttonhole passers-by in the street. I had been nabbed by their agents now and then myself. Initially, out of courtesy, I answered the questions ('What do you want most in life?'; 'What would make you truly happy?'), but declined an invitation back to the group's Brighton headquarters to discuss the matter further. On the second occasion, I told my glassy-eyed interlocutor that my life was perfect and complete in every way and that true happiness was already mine on a daily basis. Stymied, she said, 'Oh, good', and gave up. After that, it occurred to me that being clever at the expense of Scientologists was as much a waste of my own time as being polite to them, and I ignored them.

If only Sally had done the same with the RMU's evangelists, she wouldn't have spent the bulk of her time at college hawking the group's publication, *Permanent Revolution*, bickering with her comrades over who had or hadn't shifted their quota, and trying to cajole me into attending workshops.

'There's no point. I'm useless with my hands.'

'It's not that kind of workshop, and you know it. We discuss things.'

'I already have something like that. They're called seminars. If I go to enough of them, I get a degree.'

'Yes, but our workshops aren't pre-defined by ingrained capitalist ideology.'

'The ingrained capitalist ideology's my favourite part.'

And so on, until her fellow communists came to call and I took my leave.

Judging by the turnover of visitors, the RMU's membership was pretty fluent. I seldom saw the same faces for more than a few months. Either they became disillusioned, or they gave up on the objective of sleeping with Sally, or they slept with Sally and then became disillusioned – I didn't keep track. But Sally herself was a stalwart of the cause. So too was Alessandra, a pint-sized Milanese doctrinarian who unaccountably developed the hots for me, and vied for our union with the unbending tenacity of a true believer in historical inevitability. In this, as in the dictatorship of the proletariat, she was to be disappointed. It wasn't that I didn't find her attractive; it was that her implacable pursuit so unsettled me that I didn't even stop to consider whether I found her attractive or not.

Alessandra was the only person I knew, or knew of, who had managed to get herself ejected from an Amsterdam nightclub for unruly behaviour. That trumped being turfed out of a library for excessive hush. With her head full of acid, she had stripped off on the dancefloor – an action reserved for those on the venue's stage, presumably – and then punched out the bouncers (or at least delivered some vicious haymakers to their knees) when they remonstrated with her in a tolerant, Dutch sort of way. Instinct warned me that Alessandra was not to be tangled with, however importunate her urge to tangle with me.

'When are you going to make my dreams come true?' she demanded one night, as a group of us hunkered on the pebbles of Brighton Beach.

'I thought your dream was of world anarchy,' I said.

'Anarchism,' she corrected. 'But I can bring anarchy to your world first,' she added, suggestively.

'That,' I said, 'is what I'm afraid of.'

I had known only a single party state when I grew up in

Kenya. I'd seen people queuing at the polls in Nairobi, before the introduction of the secret ballot, to choose between nominees for what was then the sole legal party, KANU. They lined up behind their favoured candidate, so that the winner and all his partisans could see who had opposed him. They were willing to risk dangerous disfavour, and in some cases serious violence, to exercise a choice that was really no choice at all.

After moving to Britain, I continually met citizens who dismissed free and fair elections as unworthy of their attention. The childish conceit of it made my blood boil. 'I'm too clever to vote,' the argument effectively ran. 'They've fooled everybody else, but they won't fool me.'

'Don't vote,' I would hear somebody say, as if they'd just thought of the epigram themselves, 'it only encourages them, hur-hur-hur.'

'So do you think that if you don't vote, there'll be fewer politicians?'

'But whoever you vote for, the government gets in, hur-hur-hur.'

'And who gets in if you don't?'

'I hate politicians. They're all the same.'

'What gives you the right to complain, if you don't vote?'

Refusing to vote because you didn't like politicians made as much sense to me as refusing to eat because you didn't like farmers. You'd suffer much more, and much sooner, than they would.

I knew I was becoming a shrill, old-fashioned mother figure, admonishing recalcitrant tykes for not finishing their greens when little children in Africa are starving.

But I couldn't help it. I found it quite marvellous that in the UK, not only could you vote for any political party that took your fancy, but if you didn't find one to take your fancy, you could start your own. And, even more remarkably, persuade other people to join it.

The Radical Marxist Union had sprung not from the grassroots of working-class activism, but fully-formed from the brow of a toiler in academe – a professor, to be specific. No group better illustrated that wonderful knack of the far left, when faced with a choice between two evils, to unfailingly plump for the greater. It supported the IRA in Northern Ireland (calling for 'Troops Out Now!', as if the troops were having a whale of a time there, basking in their own wickedness); it backed the Serbs in the break-up of Yugoslavia; associates of *Permanent Revolution* took it upon themselves to defend the genocidal Hutus in Rwanda. Bizarrely, the RMU would wind up being labelled a front for far-right interests by rival leftists and other groups of self-proclaimed dissidents. That would have come as a shock to Sally and Alessandra. Or to Sally, at any rate. I'm not sure what it might have taken to shock Alessandra, and whatever it was, I wouldn't want to see it myself.

To be fair to the lady, a headbanger she might be, but she was nobody's fool. Once I took up with The Girlfriend, even Alessandra, who was not given to nuance, took that particular hint and let well enough alone.

I had chosen my new home because The Girlfriend lived in it. Had she been living under a rock, I'd have bought myself a robust hat and some galoshes and joined her there. Had she been living under a rock, it would still have constituted an improvement on her previous Brighton domiciles: Britannia Rise, and prior to that, a brief stint in the home of a sexagenarian sex-pest, who spent most of her stay importuning her to eat various kinds of fruit while he watched.

'I'd love to see you eat a peach,' he would drool. 'Or a banana. Would you like a banana? Off to bed already, eh? Want some company?'

It was thanks to the old sod's bothersome satyriasis that The Girlfriend wound up riding the sofabed in Britannia Rise, grateful just to get away. Now at last she had a room of her own. It was little more than a boxroom, a tiny square space tucked between the kitchen and lounge, but it had a large sash window that opened onto the dinky patio and overlooked a mildewed knock-off of a classical statue. As she rose up the pecking order and inherited a bigger room upstairs, I moved into the box-room.

'You don't have a resident landlord?' I asked her.

'No, no, you're perfectly safe there,' she said.

It was true. The landlord, George, didn't live there. He lived next door. He seemed a decent sort, but he had the disconcerting habit of letting himself in unannounced at any hour of the night or day to undertake odd jobs. You might be woken by drilling at six-thirty in the morning, or by footsteps on the landing in the wee hours, as George stole up the steps to the attic door that he kept locked at all times. One night, when I stumbled downstairs for a drink of water, he materialised from the shower room at the far end of the kitchen – equipped with pink rubber gloves, a large screwdriver and an unnaturally broad grin – and scared me silly.

'Just unblocking the drain,' he said merrily, holding up a monstrous clump of hair clotted with matter I'd prefer not to think about, his stance calling to mind Perseus wielding the head of Medusa. My own hair would have been standing on end, had it not still been tied back in braids, and I will swear that it was after that night that the first small knot of it turned white at the roots.

George deserves credit for caring about both his house and its occupants. If not for his disquieting and unheralded maintenance forays, he might have been a model landlord. Not knowing where or when he might pop up made it hard to relax. You could be sitting in front of the television, drifting through the placid zen eventlessness of *Inspector Morse*, at peace with the world, without a thought in your head; suddenly George would be kneeling on the carpet, ripping lengths from a roll of silver-grey gaffa tape with a noise like the fabric of the cosmos coming apart at the seams, and sticking them across a tear in the arm of the ragtag foam rubber couch, two inches from your elbow.

'Don't mind me,' he would beam. 'I was just having dinner when I remembered this, so I thought I'd attend to it while I was thinking of it.'

For George, there was no time like the present; an admirable attitude, if it hadn't precluded acknowledgement that his present was also our present, and we might have other plans for it.

Feigning concern for George's dinner didn't help. He wouldn't leave until the entire sofa could pass for a piece of set dressing from *Doctor Who*. (Not that I would have been able, then, to identify a piece of set dressing from *Doctor Who*. That was yet another generational touchstone which I never had the chance to accord its due childhood worship – with the result that, when I did finally catch up with it, I could straightaway recognise it for the otiose, tuppeny-ha'penny tat it was.)

George represented my first encounter with a singularly – perhaps uniquely – British phenomenon: the DIY zealot. No doubt every country has citizens who centre their existence around tinkering with their habitat. And no doubt those citizens are thought of as being rather odd. Only in Britain is it normal, bordering on obligatory, to devote your spare time to DIY. Or failing that, devote it to watching the astonishing volume of TV broadcasts on the subject, which now has its own dedicated channel, known as BBC One.

My own view is that, of all life's simple pleasures, there is nothing to match the stolid contentment of standing back after a hard day's work, arms folded, surveying your well-fitted new bookcase or freshly plastered ceiling, and murmuring to yourself with quiet satisfaction, 'I didn't do that.'

DIY perplexes me. It is an aspect of British life I have never got to grips with. When you work as a writer, you become accustomed to having everybody you meet assume that they could do your job as well as you can, if not better. This may be irritating, but there's no point arguing about it. It's impossible to prove them wrong, and presumptuous to try.

ACQUAINTANCE: 'When are you
next going on holiday?'
WRITER: 'Don't know – depends on
work.'
ACQUAINTANCE: 'Can I fill in for
you while you're away?'
WRITER: 'But you're a Geography
teacher.'

How much more infuriating must it be for a skilled
painter and decorator, who watches the entire nation take
his duties for a cakewalk – and make an indisputable
hash of them. His only consolation is that he will be
called upon to patch up the resulting mess.

The division of labour is a hallmark of progress.
Back when the phrase 'handyman' meant anybody with
opposable thumbs, you wouldn't go looking for one. He'd
probably hit you with a femur – which was the only skill
he'd developed, so he did it a lot. You can understand why
DIY was all the rage then. Nobody else was going to turn
a ready supply of Yeti dung and spittle into a surpris-
ingly spacious open-plan living space on your behalf.

Then came civilisation, and with it, perhaps the
most significant philosophical leap mankind has ever effect-
ed: an idea that might be summed up as YDI, or You Do It.

The earliest flowerings of enlightenment, whether in
North Africa, East Asia or Central America, had one thing
in common. They caused things to get built. And you can
be certain that the chap whose idea it was to build them
didn't find himself pushing a wheelbarrow full of bricks
around. Even the most ardent Egyptologist has yet to

track down a hieroglyphic of a Pharaoh atop a rickety pyramid, balancing a spirit level on the apex and adjusting a few rivets accordingly.

But what the ancients lacked in power tools, they made up for in slaves. These days it's the other way round. We have gizmos aplenty, but no free labour. We have to pay artisans large sums of money – much more, usually, than we can earn in the same amount of time ourselves – to come and work on our homes. And it's worth every penny, because the alternative is so much worse. To put it bluntly, the British are very, very bad at DIY. The evidence is everywhere, inside and out.

At the time of writing, news has just come in of a Christopher Pendery from Loughborough, who was convicted of criminal damage after he wreaked almost £15,000 worth of damage upon his home, sawing through timbers that held up the roof and lining the attic with chipboard so feeble it would not have sustained the weight of a portly hamster. 'The most serious aspect,' the trial judge told him, 'is the risk you placed innocent people in by your thoughtless actions.' Which may well be true, but as the house was rented, its owner could probably have offered a more concise appraisal of the matter.

The truth is that Mr Pendery's behaviour is exceptional only in its degree, not in its essence. Most of us might as well trash our homes as commit DIY upon them. It would be a lot more fun, the outcome would be the same, and we'd still have to pay to get them fixed.

The first step to overcoming a problem, as any reformed alcoholic will tell you, is recognising you have a problem in the first place. I maintained my own delusions of competence, right up to the point where The Girlfriend and I moved into the flat we currently occupy. It was here that I uncovered my talent for coaxing disaster from the most innocent of household chores. In this instance, bleeding the bedroom radiators.

After a chain of action and reaction, which both shame and decorum prohibit me from recounting, I managed to drain the entire contents of the gas boiler onto the kitchen floor. The resulting burlesque saw me bobbing about the lino in a baking tray, wielding bath towels and a pint glass, mistakenly trying to bail with the former and mop with the latter, and all the while bellowing at The Girlfriend to run downstairs and shut off the water main.

'Why?' she asked, from the next room, with that unhurried, childlike inquisitiveness all womenfolk display at moments of extreme emergency.

'Never mind bloody why, just do it!' I howled back.

'Well, if you're going to be like that . . .' she said, and returned to watching *EastEnders*.

Eventually I tracked down the problem to its source, which was about quarter of an inch long and shiny, and temporarily plugged up the gusher.

'See,' I crowed. 'I'm actually a pretty good troubleshooter.'

'Yes,' The Girlfriend replied. 'It's just that it's you who causes all the trouble in the first place.'

I couldn't argue. And now if I so much as reach for a screwdriver, she clutches my shirt-front in her fists and begs me to put it down again. Who can blame her? Lord knows what would happen if I actually tried to repair or, worse yet, construct something. I'd rather call in the professionals. I know my place. And I don't want it ruined.

Why I can see the light, but the rest of Britain's population – female as much as male, lately – cannot, I can only conjecture. The compulsion towards DIY may sink its roots from infanthood, thanks to homemade mobiles dangling over tumbledown, shed-built cribs. It seems to me blindingly obvious that when it comes to home improvements, we don't know what to do, we don't know how to do it and we don't know what we're doing even as we do it. That's the reason we don't do it for a living and double our incomes at a stroke.

With DIY, we risk ruining not only our own living quarters but other people's into the bargain. A few streets away from my flat stands a secluded terrace of immaculate Regency houses. When the coastal sunlight bathes these buildings, simply looking at them serves to calm the spirit and nourish the soul. Until, that is, one's gaze is snagged by the thick, lopsided bands of black paint crudely daubed across the front of one property in crass imitation of Tudor beams. There you have DIY in a nutshell – by which I mean a hell created by a nut, and inflicted upon his neighbours.

My own flat is located in a conservation area, so I can't put up so much as a satellite dish, but that's probably for the best. I might have done something terrible to it by now – stone-clad it, maybe, then pebble-dashed the cladding. People like me (and the British public in general) need to be protected from themselves. Official warnings on DIY-related products, like those on cigarette packets, would be a start:

Government Taste Warning: For Professional Use Only

Government Taste Warning: Dear God, Woman, Think What You're Doing

Government Taste Warning: Will Make Your Bedroom Resemble A Kosovan Cathouse Knocked Together By Psychotic Militiamen With a Grudge Against What Remains of Their Society

We could learn from the Americans here. The sale of paint should be regulated by controls similar to those governing gun purchases in certain US states; that is, a mandatory, week-long 'cooling-off' period between ordering and receiving any colour other than white. How many heartbroken victims are even now crouching numbly within walls resembling those of an abattoir; a day-glo crèche; a little-missed local nightclub from the 1980s called the Pink Coconut; a combination of all three?

There are useful parallels in our drug laws, too. Certain items should be categorised as 'prescription only', including cordless drills, socket sets and grout. Others must be prohibited altogether. I recommend two levels of classification: 'Class B', where possession is met with an on-the-spot police caution, would cover decals, glitter, posters purchased at Athena and seashells, to discourage young people from experimenting. 'Class A' – the hard stuff – would include crazy paving, and fashionable, casually used, but highly addictive multi-coloured tiles. The trade in such materials is tearing British communities apart, then gluing them back together in a profoundly unsightly fashion. Civil liberties are all very well, but dammit, there are limits.

In the interests of full disclosure, I should admit that I have no taste of my own. Really. None. Not when it comes to the rooms I inhabit. In my current home, the walls remain as bare as they were when I moved in. That's how I prefer them. My furniture is plain, wooden, minimal and of muted tones. My front room looks like an undusted corner of Ikea, the only splashes of colour provided by records, books and so forth, which came that way.

But although I have no taste, I have at least attained discernment. I know what I don't like and don't want around me; although for a long time I couldn't tell until I'd already lugged it home from the shop. And I know whose advice I trust. I follow the counsel of those people, not to fool the rest of the world that I can choose wisely when it comes to carpets and sofas, but because I know from experience that the results make me comfortable. With this in mind, I find it hard to disapprove of anyone who has genuine taste of their own, however visibly rank it may be.

'To understand bad taste,' the film director John Waters famously instructed, 'one must have very good taste.' Waters, sadly, was mistaken. That may have been his own avenue to bad taste, but few others take such a scenic route. The popularity of kitsch, for example, has grown enormously since I arrived in Britain (although the two things are not, I think, related). Kitsch, in the current understanding of the word, began as a form of amused contempt among high-culture buffs for the tastes of the wider public. Now, in the UK, it's the wider public that sneers at the tastes of the wider public.

Increasingly difficult to avoid, kitsch functions mainly as an excuse for those with no judgement of their own to laugh at the judgement of others. Bad taste mocked by no taste. I've met a remarkably high number of younger Britons who deliberately surround themselves with trashy objects. Their lives are dominated by a gaudy aesthetic for which they have no instinctive liking. A 25-year-old man who collects ceramic cats does so in a drearily sarcastic way. His grandmother may have the same hobby, but at least she takes uncontrived pleasure from it.

Kitsch styles itself as the enemy of Middlebrow, the house style of Middle England. Middlebrow, so runs the script, insecurely tags along with received notions of good taste, furnishing its small brown nest with mock-Restoration furniture, drab reproduction oils and CDs of the better-known classical composers. Then Kitsch, a superhero nemesis in hot pants and a feather-boa, flies in its face, waving banners adorned with all the schlocky gubbins Middlebrow is so desperate to leave behind, and blowing raspberries thirteen to the dozen.

The devotees of tat would like to believe that Kitsch is a celebration of everything bright, colourful and alive in a dun-coloured world. An expression of rampant, kooky individuality, which sneers at the discernment of the world at large while simultaneously adopting it. A version, palatable to straights, of the camp by which some gays ceremonially flaunt their opposition to a humdrum society.

From my own interloper's perspective, Kitsch is merely the flipside of Middlebrow, a blindly unimaginative response to a perceived enemy's blindly unimaginative preferences, born out of vanity rather than Middlebrow's anxiety. Kitsch yodels with hilarity at the idea that somebody actually takes this nonsense seriously. It believes that it is better, smarter and more refined than that somebody, even though it lumbers itself with exactly the same rubbish. To deride someone else's lifestyle paraphernalia, and at the same time crave it, denotes a corkscrew snobbery that could almost make one nostalgic for the old-fashioned, straightforward snobbery more usually associated with these islands. What a heroic level of insufferable conceit it must take to assume that, while others admire junk out of some long-standing pandemic of mass cretinism, you cherish it because you are a subtle and cunning sophisticate.

Not only does a kitsch sensibility mendaciously turn junk into treasure, it also mistakes treasure for junk. It has no conception of value. It knows only sniggering, uppity disdain. Kitsch is an elbow forever jabbing into pop culture's ribcage. It drags colourful and brilliant work of real worth down to its own level. It claims not only the designer Philippe Starck for its own, but also Walt Disney, Aubrey Beardsley and Roy Lichtenstein. In pop music, Kitsch mistakenly surmises that Pulp, one of the finest and least cynical pop groups of the 1990s, belongs to it, and that the Pet Shop Boys' career is one long self-satisfied snicker.

The first, relatively mild instance that came to my attention was the habit among my student housemates of rising, as the saying went, at the crack of *Neighbours*. This meagre Aussie sudser has been broadcast after *The One O'Clock News* for as long as I can remember; and for as long as I can remember, it's been dreadful.

'But it's so bad, it's good,' a housemate would protest.

Which would have explained viewing it once for five minutes, but not for half an hour every weekday.

'I can't believe how stupid it is,' ran the other rationalisation, although this didn't reflect very well on them for watching it. I began to wonder if the adult audience for *Neighbours* consisted entirely of people watching it because it amused them to think that everybody else was taking it seriously.

In due course, I acquired a bigger room and a newer tenant took the boxroom. His name was Gordon and he was American.

It's a fact of British life that anti-American sentiment is either bubbling just beneath the surface, or boiling over it. The British left seems to harbour a petulant revulsion towards the USA and all its works, whatever they may be, while the rest of the country views America with amused disdain. This doesn't dissuade the rest of the country from wearing American clothes, buying American music, watching American films, eating American food and taking its holidays in Florida.

Having grown up in an environment that was no less influenced by America than by Britain, I don't share the widespread British contempt for America, and initially I couldn't make sense of it. I now believe it to be something akin to sibling rivalry – a combination of jealousy and silent, grudging admiration. America is the golden boy: successful, attractive, outwardly confident, widely emulated. Britain – more in its own eyes than anyone else's – is the scrawny, nerdy brother, coveting America's self-assurance, its flashy gear, its fascination among the girls, and consoling itself with the belief that it, Britain, is the more intelligent and cultured. Typically, the British over-estimate their supposed rivals – although the idea that Britain might be the USA's rival in the first place would be the source of much American hilarity were it widely known over there. One thing that it is fair to say about most Americans is that their interest in the outside world doesn't extend that far.

The British feel impelled to dismiss Americans as loud, brash, obnoxious, arrogant, asinine, over-indulged, pushy, fatuous, ignorant and oblivious. I've always thought this to be an unjust stereotype. A pity, then, that it applied in its entirety to Gordon. And more of a pity that I had to live with him.

Gordon was also gay, allotting him a second demographic to which he could give a bad name. It's no coincidence that Brighton hosts the largest gay community, proportionately speaking, in the country; the city has a deserved reputation for accepting those who might be excluded elsewhere. But it didn't accept Gordon, and nor did the gay community. The gay community, or at least that part of it with which I was acquainted, considered him both an embarrassment and a nuisance, and wanted no part of him. Like the tenants at Green Street, alas, the gay community couldn't get rid of him.

'For God's sake,' grumbled one friend, a college lecturer who – to his chagrin – had been unable to prevent Gordon signing up for his Gay Studies course, 'why can't he shut up about being gay? It's as if he's got something to prove. I find myself wanting to tell him, "Look, Gordon, we believe you. You're gay. You're the gayest gay who ever was gay. You're gayer than all the rest of us gays put together. Now put a Pierre Cardin sock in it, will you?"'

Persuading Gordon to stop talking, whatever the subject, was all but impossible. He was the only American I have ever met who actually emitted that peculiar, hateful whine favoured by Britons attempting a generic American accent. It became the defining sound of our household, occasionally augmented by the dull arrhythmia of George attacking some doomed fragment of the superstructure with a claw hammer. Gordon talked across conversations. He talked across the television. He talked across your meals, and frequently contrived to eat a fair bit of them while he was doing so.

When you came home, you could tell if Gordon was in or out by whether or not you could hear him. He hardly ever went out, unless it was to annoy his fellow scholars or the gay community.

A theory arose about Gordon: that he wasn't really gay at all. At least, not by inclination. But that, as an able-bodied, well-educated white American of affluent stock, he had grabbed hold of the only ticket to oppression he could find. If this were true, then his dedication to that objective was almost admirable, in an odd way. He was, after all, willing to have sex with men in order to realise it. Not that this proved a drawback in practice, as men were utterly unwilling to have sex with Gordon. On the solitary occasion we noticed him entice a fellow back to his room, he spent most of the night honking and blaring his inane opinions into the ether and keeping the rest of us awake until the small hours.

'Can you keep it down a bit next time, Gordon?' I said to him when, bleary-eyed, I encountered him in the kitchen the following morning.

'Sorry,' he simpered. 'Were we kind of loud? We just couldn't keep our hands off each other.'

'Not that,' snapped The Girlfriend, who was much less patient with Gordon than I was. 'The talking. Not everybody needs to know how wonderful you think Toni Morrison is. Not at half-past two in the morning.'

Morrison, the much-admired novelist, was one of Gordon's pet causes. When he spoke of her, it was as if the garlands of the Nobel and Pulitzer committees had served merely as preludes to the accolade that really mattered: his own. Morrison's work concerned itself with black American history. To hear Gordon tell it, it might have been his own roots that Morrison so deftly and powerfully fictionalised. He seemed to genuinely believe, firstly, that being gay secured him access to a notional fellowship of the subjugated; and secondly, that this was something to be desired.

'Toni Morrison used to work in the daytime to support her family, and write at night,' he told us. I was impressed. I thought of this fine writer hefting a mop from floor to floor, or taking orders in a seedy diner, all so that she might gift her creations to the world.

'What did she do?' I asked.

'She was an editor at Random House.'

Gordon's personality was irritating enough on its own. Combined with the assumption that his sexuality translated into moral capital, it made him unbearable. When he joined a Gay Rights procession on Brighton Beach, it tried to march away from him. A clutch of scabby minors flung a few desultory pebbles towards the activists and half-heartedly bleated, 'Homos!' They were ignored by everybody except Gordon, who scuttled up and down the line squawking, 'Oh my Gawd! Rawks, everybody! They're throwing rawks! Call the police!'

'The police are right over there, Gordon,' said one of the marchers, spotting an opportunity to shake him off.

Gordon ran up to the pair of bored coppers tasked with keeping half an eye on proceedings.

'Why,' he spluttered, 'don't you do something about this . . . this . . . *hate crime*?'

'Would you like to make a statement, sir?' sighed the senior policeman.

Gordon glanced around to see the column making its escape up the steps to the promenade. The stone-throwing brats had disappeared.

'Never mind,' he said, and scampered off in pursuit. 'Hey! Wait up!'

Gordon probably did more than any of his compatriots, with the possible exception of the late Ronald Reagan, to sour British–American relations at what was already a low point in their history. Reagan tended to go for grand gestures: using British airfields as a base for bombing Libya; suggesting that Europe might serve quite nicely as a Cold War nuclear battlefield. Gordon, chronologically Reagan's successor in the task of alienating the British, adopted a grassroots strategy, repulsing hearts and minds one Limey at a time. I sometimes ponder whether, if Saddam Hussein hadn't invaded Kuwait, uniting most of the Western world against Iraq, Gordon might not have single-handedly brought about the withdrawal of the UK from NATO.

Gordon may only have stayed in Britain for a year, but for those around him, it felt so very much longer. His ability to slow time defied Newtonian physics, and lent weight to the theories of Einstein. In Gordon's company, time bent back upon itself, as if nearing the rim of a black hole.

At last Gordon concluded his stint in Britain and went back to the United States (where they had probably seized the opportunity to change the locks while he was gone); although not before The Girlfriend, in revenge for an exceptionally inflammatory provocation, the details of which escape me, used his Christian Dior facecloth to clean under the rim of the toilet bowl, then replaced the textile on its customary peg. It was then that I made a mental note that I would sooner cross the Cosa Nostra on a narcotics deal than get on her bad side. To this day, people ask me why I'm so jumpy.

With Gordon's departure, a welcome hush settled upon the house, interrupted only by the intermittent rasp of George scraping mildew from the bathroom walls with sandpaper clasped in a monkey wrench. Compared to Gordon's voice, this was a siren song of deep and limpid sweetness. I made a further resolution never again to gripe about George's DIY. Inevitably, I broke it within a fortnight, at around 6 a.m., when George smashed the banister rail while re-tacking the stairwell carpet directly outside my door.

CHAPTER EIGHT

LEARN TO SPEAK IMPROPER

'YOU WILL, EVENTUALLY, get a job,' said the man in front of the blackboard. 'I don't know anybody who has never had a job.'

It was 1991. There was a recession on. It was now two years since I had left university, and I had yet to obtain a job interview, let alone a job. I didn't share the confidence of the man in front of the blackboard, nor his belief that my future employment was a matter of inevitability.

I knew that there were people in the country who truly would never work again, and that I didn't fall into the same category. I didn't come from a mining or steelworking community. I hadn't been swept into an industrial dustpan by the cruel brush-head of monetarist reform. I was schooled in the ways of the white-collar world. I also, apparently, remained the nearest thing to Kryptonite that employers had ever confronted.

The man in front of the blackboard was not referring exclusively to my own prospects. There were a dozen of us there, attending a seminar for jobless graduates. It is indeed an ill wind that blows nobody any good; our enforced idleness meant an earning opportunity for the man in front of the blackboard.

I was given to understand that the government was paying for this seminar, which was thoughtful of it. In return, it was allowed to strike me, along with the rest of that day's unwaged audience, from the unemployment figures. It had done the same when I joined the Enterprise Allowance Scheme – a slightly upscale variation on the notorious YTS (Youth Training Scheme) that would, reputedly, take anybody. I was living proof that this reputation was justified. There were barnacles clinging to rocks along Brighton Beach that possessed more spirit of enterprise than I did.

This latest wheeze was conducted in central London, and the permitted travelling expenses were minimal. The train was out of the question. That meant getting on a coach shortly after 6 a.m. and travelling for two-and-a-half hours from Brighton via Gatwick airport. The skills I was supposedly attaining – mainly in writing CVs and management training – did not add much to my shallow reservoir of ability. If there was one thing I was good at by this point (and I'm not going to insist that there was), it was writing a CV. As for the management training, that was as hopelessly over-optimistic as instructing a circus seal in the niceties of diplomatic protocol.

Before the course ended, and not to my credit, I stopped going. After a week, I received a letter from the organisers informing me that my registration had been terminated, my participation was over and I was not to return. Two weeks after that, I received a certificate affirming that I had completed the course, passed with flying colours and was now accredited management material. Perhaps I deserved it. My own standards of thoroughness and professionalism were more or less on a par with the company's own.

I didn't get a job. But I did get taken on as a stringer by a weekly music paper, *Harmony Fiddler*. This magazine's old-fangled name harked back to its origins in the 1920s, as the publication of choice for the British jazz and popular song fraternity. Since then it had survived successive stylistic revolutions – rock 'n' roll, the blues boom, psychedelia, punk and so on – by cannily surfing each wave as it swelled.

Perhaps a more apposite way to put it is that the *Fiddler*, as it was affectionately known, acted as an antenna, poised to detect the earliest, tiniest vibration of a forthcoming musical trend. While the *Fiddler* was far from infallible, it was right often enough to make it seem indispensable and indestructible. Then it hired me. Within eight years, it would close.

I can't take the credit for finishing off the *Fiddler*; I was long gone by the time it shut up shop. While I may not have been the author of its misfortune, I feel that I was its harbinger. My subsequent record on newspapers, magazines and supplements would show me up as the journalistic equivalent of that creature from Celtic folklore, the Sluagh, whose black wings brushing against a darkened window signified grim tidings for those within.

Joining the *Fiddler* gave me something to do with my time, aside from shouting at the television. The hours and days spent on this habit had not, as it turned out, been wasted. It formed the basis for what a charitable onlooker might call my career. Instead of heckling *The ITV Chart Show* on a Saturday morning, I would channel my seething indignation onto a word processor. Moreover, the *Fiddler* would pay me for it. Just.

The Lightarians, devotees of the antipodean guru Jamusheen – a woman who reportedly once claimed to have survived for several months on nothing but solar rays and 'the occasional Hobnob' – might have been able to subsist on what the *Fiddler* paid (although their unfortunate habit of keeling over from self-inflicted starvation suggests not). I couldn't duplicate the Lightarians' frugal practices. Spoiled as I was by five years of First-World life, I simply would not forgo such fripperies as meals, shoes and toothpaste.

Control over what little payment did seep out from the *Fiddler*, like blood oozing from a painful graze, lay in the hands of a woman called Cecilia. I have since discovered that every office has a Cecilia – an individual, usually in a relatively lowly berth, who dominates the place by combining volume, intimidation and access to some or other necessity into a weapon of control. Hailing from south London, Cecilia was no more than four feet high, with a voice like the keening of a rabid seagull, and – to my mind – gave every indication of being as mad as a revolving footstool.

I once watched Cecilia at work, calculating freelance payments. She didn't add up the words; she simply measured the length of the printed columns with a ruler, and estimated the word count from that. That some columns were narrower than others did not influence her sums.

'Why don't you measure them across, as well?' I asked.

'Takes too much time, dunnit?' she squawked. 'Rikki Lake's starting in a minute.'

The afternoon talk shows, which Cecilia watched on a TV set in the reviews room, provided the only respite from Cecilia's radio. Although the paper was devoted to new and alternative music, the office resounded each day to the screeching and blathering of a station that broadcast the same seven unendurable hit records on heavy rotation all week. None of the freelance contributors dared to say anything. If Cecilia were to capriciously lop a few pounds off our paycheques, our incomes could be halved. Trying to reclaim the rightfully due sum would mean dealing with the accounts department, a chore that might be unfavourably compared with constructing a pontoon bridge out of wet tagliatelle.

Staff members who were not in thrall to Cecilia's wayward disbursements were more forthcoming about the radio, but it didn't help. At the first hint of protest, she would advise the dissenter to 'fuck right off, wankah'. She was a rare and delicate blossom, was Cecilia. She was also black, which would have held no relevance to anything had I not been issued with the desk directly behind hers, marking me out as a target for her singular style of conversation.

'Oi! Bennun!' she would caw, as the paint visibly withered

and peeled from the wall beside her. 'You're from Africa, innit? An' you've got the curly 'air. 'Ave you got any of that niggah blood in ya, then?'

Cecilia was by no means the oddest individual in the *Fiddler* office. The paper was written and put out by a bevy of anthropological curios. It was a haven for me. I had spent years trying to pass for whatever passed for normal at any given moment in Britain. My efforts were invariably doomed by my ingrained foreignness. Now I was working with people who, although British born and bred themselves, could probably not have passed for normal in their own living rooms. We might have been spared by benevolent fortune the physical traits of Tod Browning's *Freaks*, but we were all the same a clan of outcasts. If new arrivals were not greeted with the chant,

> One of us! One of us! Gooble, gobble,
> gooble, gobble

it was probably through an administrative oversight.

What welcomed new arrivals was startling enough. The offices of the *Fiddler* stood high above the Thames, commanding an impressive view across London. On the floors directly above and below were housed *Huntin' & Shootin'*, *Shropshire Squire* and *Dry Fly*. The gentlefolk in the hire of these titles avoided the *Fiddler*'s floor as if it were the Bronx. If you met them in the stairwell en route to the coffee machine, they cringed and clutched their hand-tooled carry-alls closer to their tweedy chests. I don't know why they were worried; statistically speaking, they were the ones more likely to own a gun.

When HQD (House of Quality Distribution), the publishing giant that ran the show, organised a 'clean up our building campaign', chivvying its employees into neatness, the only desks to remain untouched were those at the *Fiddler*, where few hirelings dared venture. It would have taken a demolition team to clear that office. Dusty towers of paper, plastic and other detritus loomed and listed over every surface, each a reverse chronology of duty derelicted and work undone. Peeking out from the foot of these mesas were the corners of yellowing documents dating from the jazz age.

The first time I was invited to an editorial meeting, I sat in the crowded reviews room, a newly fetched-up dreg amid the general rabble, and incredulously tried to take in the exchanges between the editor and one of his senior contributors.

The editor, who shared his name with the celebrated pop artist Peter Blake, was inevitably known as Blakey, although he bore not the scantest likeness to the inspector from 1970s sitcom *On the Buses*. Even I was aware of this; back in Nairobi, as a child, I had watched this show on the national television channel, Voice of Kenya – along with other mystifying imports such as *Mind Your Language* and *Love Thy Neighbour*.

Had I understood these programmes at all, I might have concluded that I was headed for a grey, surly country populated by sexually repressed and sartorially backward casual racists (and there remain enough places in Britain which fit this description today as accurately as they no doubt did in 1975). But I didn't understand those programmes. I thought that the ideas they represented and the situations they portrayed were as fictional as the scripts themselves. All the same, who knows what they added to the delusional impression of the UK that I would later bring here with me?

The only screen character Blakey physically resembled was Bert Lahr's in *The Wizard of Oz*, which led one colleauge, Errol, to dub him 'The Cowardly Lion' – an unfair sobriquet, and one I would never have dared to use myself. Throughout my time at the *Fiddler*, Blakey was nothing but genial and supportive towards me, but he was not a man to be trifled with in his more choleric moments.

Drawing the meeting to a close, Blakey asked if there was any other business. He didn't put it quite like that, naturally. His actual words were, 'Right, anything else, or can we go down to the Wothorpe?' At the foot of the building sat the Wothorpe Arms, also known as 'the office', and inside it, more often than not, sat the *Fiddler*'s staff. It was a mystery how the paper ever came out. I think gnomes snuck in at night and assembled it.

Chairs began to scrape back from the table. Then came a noise from somewhere near the door. Its origin was obscured. The press of bodies shifted to reveal a red mouth, set below a pair of wide red eyes, in a red face, beneath a close-shaven crop of red hair. The effect suggested a balloon effigy of a football hooligan's head lowered onto a sparsely filled shirt. As this ensemble was propped up against its neighbour – a gaunt, taller figure whose thicket of greying hair shadowed menacingly sculpted features – I thought for a moment that it might be a Guy Fawkes dummy brought in by the latter for a lark. If so, the taller figure was an admirably skilled ventriloquist. The Guy again emitted a noise, and this time I saw the mouth move in time to its slurred output.

'Yeah,' it said. 'Yeah. I reckon, yeah, we should do a feature on this band The Druggy Chancers. Because they're brilliant, yeah? They're the future of rock 'n' roll.'

'Really?' said Blakey, moon-eyed in mock amazement. 'I suppose we'd better, then.'

'Yeah. Yeah. We need to. It's important because ... they're ... I haven't heard them yet, but little Ron' – here the Guy indicated the *Fiddler*'s intern, a shaven-headed youth and avowed dance music fanatic – 'told me all about how great they are.'

'Well, that clinches it,' crooned Blakey. 'Let's get them in the paper straight away.'

Even the unmistakably inebriated Guy could tell from Blakey's tone that something wasn't quite right.

'Are you taking the piss, yeah?' he said.

'No, no,' soothed Blakey. 'As if I would.'

'Are you taking the piss?' repeated the Guy. 'Because if you are ...' This gave him pause. He knew he was against the piss being taken, as a matter of principle; but he was, temporarily at least, stymied as to the practical remedies.

'Tell you what, Barney,' said Blakey. 'We'll not only run a story on them, but who knows? If you're lucky, we might even print a nice little picture of them, too. Meeting over.'

This was my first sighting of the *Fiddler*'s *enfants terribles*, the Flint Twins, Barney and Frederick. They weren't brothers, let alone twins, and neither of their names was

Flint; but they did work as a duo, terrorising interview-ees, famous or not, with a bad cop/worse cop routine that regularly delivered the *Fiddler*'s best material.

Having returned from a debilitating assignment in the Netherlands, during which they had sampled much of what Amsterdam had to offer, the Flints had stayed up through the previous night, reviewing the week's single releases. At dawn, they had liberated a bottle of Polish vodka from Blakey's office. Barney had swallowed the last of it seconds before he stumbled into the meeting at its conclusion.

The Flints followed their colleagues down to the Wothorpe, but didn't join the table. They had an appoint-ment with a pair of teenage girls from Liverpool. These girls had recorded and pressed onto vinyl a self-penned song that reflected their own sunny innocence. The Flints had heard it, liked it, and invited the pair down for an interview. Having spent all their money on the record, the girls hitch-hiked to London. Now they waited, shy and nervous, at the back of the pub, for their big break to arrive.

'I'm Frederick,' said Frederick, with unusual cordiality, setting a tape recorder down upon the table, 'and this is my writing partner, Barney.'

'Hello, girls,' said Barney, and passed out, his skull striking an ashtray with a glassy *ding*. Frederick, ignor-ing this entirely, drew a notebook from his bag and began gently to question the gobsmacked lasses.

As the interview was ending, Barney abruptly jerked upright as if he had been injected with adrenaline. He looked about himself and – patently convinced he was still in Amsterdam – began to harangue the girls across the table.

'You fucking Dutch!' he railed. 'You think you're so fucking clever, with your fucking clogs and your fucking cheese and your fucking tulips! Where the fuck were you when the skies were black with Dorniers?' With that he collapsed again, his snores bubbling through a small beer slick that had formed beneath his cheek.

Drinking and swearing. These are undertakings for which the British possess a peculiar genius. There are nations which drink more heavily, particularly in Eastern Europe and Scandinavia. In Sweden, where there are only three off-licences – all of them owned by the government and, in an effort to put people off, grievously overpriced and located north of the Arctic Circle – the citizenry still manages to guzzle itself into a stupor each weekend. Iceland is by all accounts a never-ending bender on a very big volcano. But nobody drinks quite like the British.

The Russians drink doggedly and sombrely, seeking insensibility. The Swedes drink furiously, perhaps as a last, faint echo of their Viking past. The British drink by default. They steep themselves in booze, as if it's their natural element. Hence the unique institution that is the pub, a social arena devoted exclusively to libation. A pub is very different to a bar. One goes out to a bar; one goes down to the pub. The first is something of an occasion, the second is as unremarkable as staying home.

In continental Europe, food and drink are seldom far apart. In the British pub – so-called gastro-pubs notwithstanding – food is an afterthought, purely functional, to permit the customers to soak up yet more alcohol. That, I've concluded, is the key to understanding how the British drink. Other nations drink for fun, or to get drunk, or to forget. The British drink for the sake of drinking. They drink because they can. They drink until they can't. They drink because it's there.

Working for the *Fiddler* was an education in many matters, and British drinking culture stood, albeit unsteadily, in the front rank. Not everyone at the *Fiddler* drank the way the Flints did. The female contributors were a tad more circumspect, although a few of them could match the hardest-headed male pint for pint when they chose to. But the Flints were more the rule than the exception. Sitting outside the Wothorpe one sunny day (and that was a foolish proposition in itself as the pavement was narrow and abutted a major thoroughfare; juggernauts roared past your ear and diesel fumes percolated through your lager), I watched a senior staffer approach the nearby zebra crossing at a medium-paced stagger, then traverse it while holding up his company pass card for the scrutiny of waiting lorry drivers. This was at 2 p.m.

Barney Flint, a south Londoner, was himself in awe of the drinking prowess he had recently witnessed on a trip to Leeds. He had joined a pal, Pugsley, along with Pugsley's father and Pugsley's father's friends, in their local. Here, a pint of ale was not something to be quaffed, or even gulped. It was something to be shipped, in one or two swallows. Barney tried to keep up, but glasses kept appearing by his elbow; at one stage, there were seven or eight lined up like skittles. After that, he remembered nothing until he awoke the next morning in the Pugsley home and stumbled down to breakfast. Pugsley the elder was engaged in conversation with Mrs Pugsley.

'You were stinking last night,' said Mrs Pugsley, evenly. 'You were rotten.'

'Aye,' admitted Pugsley Sr. 'An' Pugsley an' all. You were all right though,' he added, looking at Barney. 'You must have knocked over half a dozen of yours when you fell onto the table.' Barney was not, as a rule, a predictable chap; but there were certain facets of his behaviour you could set your watch by.

Pugsley Sr was a man of few words, but he made good use of them. A supporter of Leeds United Football Club, he had not long before taken the train south, to see them play away to a London side. The result was not to his liking. Before returning home, he stopped into a pub at King's Cross station, attempting without success to improve his mood. A couple of hours later, he got up to catch his train, only to be barred from the platform by a guard.

'Ticket, please,' said the guard, in an Aberdeen accent.

Pugsley Sr felt in his pockets and realised that, to his even greater chagrin, he had lost his ticket.

'I'll buy one on the train,' he said.

'Sorry, sir,' said the guard. 'You need to buy a ticket in advance, or I can't let you on.'

He would not be persuaded otherwise; Pugsley Sr was still remonstrating with him when the train pulled out. He retraced his steps to the pub, muttering under his breath, and spent a further stretch drinking and formulating the decisive comeback with which he would silence the guard. The next train departed, and the one after that;

still Pugsley Sr sat fulminating and plotting his revenge. At last, having settled upon a suitably cutting riposte, he rose and lumbered back to the platform.

'Ticket, please,' said the same guard.

'Fuck off, you Scottish cunt,' said Pugsley Sr, with feeling; and barging past his tormentor, he boarded the buffet car.

Which brings us back to the British talent for swearing. Bad language could be considered a form of folk art in Britain. Those who dislike swearing complain that it betrays a lack of imagination. Anyone who has been trapped next to a congenital halfwit on public transport, and forced to hear him eff and blind at tedious length, might have some sympathy for this view. But it ignores the precise impact of a judiciously applied curse, and the cumulative effect of well-tuned, foul-mouthed rant. The Salford poet John Cooper Clarke illustrated this beautifully in his masterpiece, 'Evidently Chickentown':

> the fucking view is fucking vile
> for fucking miles and fucking miles
> the fucking babies fucking cry
> the fucking flowers fucking die
> the fucking food is fucking muck
> the fucking drains are fucking fucked
> the colour scheme is fucking brown
> everywhere in chickentown . . .

the fucking train is fucking late
you fucking wait you fucking wait
you're fucking lost and fucking found
stuck in fucking chickentown

The sense of futility and exasperation – immaculately conveyed in the final stanza, which is repeated throughout the rest of the poem, neatly mimicking the rhythm of the longed-for train – would not be so effective without the use of 'fucking'. Even if you substituted the milder 'bloody', you would end up with something that sounded merely a tad grumpy. For emphasis, for vehemence, for bathos, for shock value, you can't beat a good dirty word. Swearing is as much an outlet for the imagination as a cover for its absence, and the British are masters of it.

English is such a marvellous language for swearing that I have even heard native Welsh speakers break into it at crucial junctures. To my monoglot ear, it sounds something like: '*Rhubarbliverwurstgogandmagoglochness* fucking*syllabubglockenspiel?* Bloody hell! *Sugarbaby goggleboxbrentcross*bastard*gigglemuffin.*'

American English doesn't come close; 'ass', for instance, rings feeble when set beside the rough-hewn, rasping syllable that is 'arse' – an exemplary slab of Anglo-Saxon.

After I left the *Fiddler*, I worked for a while at a socially conscious publication where, rumour had it, a tally was kept of all the swear words in each edition, with figures monitored and scrutinised at the end of the month. Upon hearing this, I made a point of smuggling an 'arse' into every piece of copy I wrote, in the hope that it would create an inexplicable spike in the graphs pored over by confused executives.

FIRST EXECUTIVE: 'There seems
to be an awful lot of arse in the
paper of late.'
SECOND EXECUTIVE: 'Yes, up forty-
three per cent year on year. But on a
positive note, the cock count is way
down.'

My run lasted six months, and if you think it took no
imagination to come up with a novel context for 'arse'
twenty-six weeks running, let me set you straight. It was
quite a challenge.

Foul language is so bound up with British life that,
among men, it is the standard means for expressing
friendship and affection. I knew a handful of Britons who
moved to New York to launch a magazine. The American
staff they took on – thoughtful, clever, well-mannered
folk one and all – were deeply dismayed to overhear conversations between the Brits such as:

'Where's that print-out, y'cunt?'
'Fuck off, wanker – get it yerself.'

The Americans were understandably convinced that their
bosses despised one another, and that the whole enterprise was therefore doomed. It took months before they
discerned, to their relief, that this is how British men
converse when they like each other. Although, as British
men also converse this way when they don't like each
other, it's worth attuning your ear to tones of voice.

The British talent for swearing feeds a matching gift for slang, which over the years has been lovingly collated by lexicographers as diverse as the great Eric Partridge and the editors of *Viz* comic. I would happily put one of my associates from the *Fiddler* up against the best of them.

Teddy Sheener, the *Fiddler*'s chief photographer, was an outstanding exponent of Cockney rhyming slang. A stocky London Irishman possessed of an uncommon roguish charm, Teddy conducted most of his highly entertaining conversation in this dialect. Going on assignment with Teddy was always a joy.

'Hoi,' he would hiss theatrically, as he spotted a pair of bright yellow flares striding across a departure lounge. 'Clock the geezer in the lemon Lionels.'

I once stepped onto the streets of Tokyo with Teddy, on a balmy summer's evening. The city lay before us, with its myriad possibilities, a shining, futuristic adventure waiting to unfold. A thousand neon signposts beckoned, their ideograms flashing with unintelligible blandishments. Teddy's eye went straight to one in the middle distance, which spelled out, in English lettering, the word 'Tandoori'.

'Ooh,' salivated Teddy. 'I couldn't half fancy a Ruby Murray. Maybe a few Frankie Vaughans and a watering can.'

'Teddy,' I griped, 'I haven't come halfway across the bloody world to eat takeaway prawn korma.'

'All right, all right,' said Teddy, defensively. 'Who shag-piled your Hampton? Don't mighty-white my loaf off.'

Part of the fun with Teddy's rhyming slang was that he

made up a good deal of it as he went along. Even pooling their resources, a pubload of jellied eel fanciers from the Isle of Dogs would have been hard pressed to keep up.

Another of Teddy's quirks was what I can only describe as his comedy homophobia. A veteran in showbiz photography, he would have found a genuine loathing for gays too great a handicap in the pursuit of his vocation. And, family man though he may have been, he was by no means deficient in camp mannerisms of his own.

'Come on, chaps, throw some shapes,' he would urge, directing his lens at a sullen quartet of throwbacks whose haircuts appeared to have fallen on them from out of a tree. 'That's lovely, m'dears. That's right, sweetheart – you there, with the bumfluff – give it some.'

Yet whenever the subject arose, Teddy was eager to stress the degree to which all matters gay were 'not my game, old son'. This was bound to backfire on him. The Flints, in a fit of malevolent inspiration, recorded a birthday tribute to Teddy whereby they merged his twin fixations – rhyming slang and homosexuality – into a pastiche of The Ramones' song 'Sheena is a Punk Rocker'. The opening line, snarled out over the top of a cacophonous guitar, set the tone:

Sheener is a big queer!

Then:

Well he's a ginge, ginge, ginger beer
A rich, rich, Richard Gere
Well he's a right, right, a right roarer
A back, back, a back doorer . . .

It rattled along in this vein for three minutes straight, before climaxing with a single, bellowed line of justification for this litany of invective:

He puts ice cubes in his beer!

'It's the bloody Wothorpe, isn't it?' protested Teddy, when the laughter finally died away. 'They served me up a peasy pig's ear. So I stuck a bit of Vincent Price in there – that doesn't make me a Perry Como.'

Much of British slang is at best derogatory, and at worst, ocean-going, high-tonnage filth. But to close your eyes and ears to it on this account would be to deprive yourself of real pleasure. Happily, there was no danger of this happening at the *Fiddler*, where argot and obscenity fused into a rich mélange, both on the page and off it. On the page, there was a tendency towards delirious exaggeration studded with asterisk-laden qualifiers, as each successive clutch of slack-jawed simians just evolved enough to work a guitar strap was acclaimed as the very breath of heaven. Off the page, the mixture took on an earthier flavour.

'Another glowing write-up of The Dismals by Archibald Verity, I see,' Blakey would note, scanning that week's proofs. 'All screaming peacocks and lighthouses at dawn.'

'Yeah,' the reviews editor would concur. 'Old Archibald was ejaculating like a stallion when I handed the album over to him.'

The reviews editor was an Australian prodigy by the unlikely name of Sandy Miller, although he was more commonly referred to as 'our teenage *Sturmbannführer*'.

Sandy was the one who had brought me on board at the *Fiddler*, at the time unaware that I was, in his words, 'a fellow colonial'. His relationship to Britain paralleled my own; a long-distance love affair with an ideal, followed by close-up bafflement with the reality. Sandy had to contend with the added impediment of manic depression. He would later make this public knowledge, but initially many at the *Fiddler* simply assumed he was a rude, grouchy git.

This was not an obstacle to advancement. When I joined the paper, a man called Ned Coco occupied the post of features editor; he left a couple of years after I arrived, having acknowledged my existence on one occasion only. I was typing up some copy when he lobbed a half-eaten sandwich at my head and trumpeted: 'David Bennun, you've got a nose on you like a policeman's knob.' Then he went back to his work, and I went back to mine.

I came to realise that, in this secluded corner of journalism, exhibiting the symptoms of a psychological disorder, whether you had one or not, was *de rigueur*. I would go on to work at another magazine where many of the staff were genuinely and clinically certifiable, while the rest of them took the opportunity to act like it. Had you pooled the prescription medication to be found in that office at any given moment, you would have garnered the pharmaceutical firepower to take out the globe's remaining population of the blue whale.

At the *Fiddler*, we were, on the whole, oddballs rather than viable candidates for the booby hatch. It required a specific personality defect to care so obsessively about the minutiae of pop music in the first place, and we all had that. This in turn often associated itself with other drawbacks, chief among which was hypersensitivity. Of all the afflictions that might beset you in such an office, this had to be the most disadvantageous. If you couldn't withstand banter, mockery and browbeating, then working at the *Fiddler* was not for you.

I was lucky, in this respect, having grown up in a family where sarcasm and ridicule were freely dispensed. I could both dish it out and take it. At any rate, I could while I was at the *Fiddler*. Later on, I would find myself marooned in harsher conditions, after I moved across the street to another of HQD's titles, *Blasted*.

Blasted was the definitive men's magazine of its time. Its name denoted a generation of cheerfully hedonistic youngsters. It was decried across a broad spectrum of bluenoses and moral panic-mongers, who mistook its brazen humour for – depending on the pitch of their hysteria – anything between oafishness and an omen of the apocalypse.

When I reported for my first day at work, I had to squeeze past a long line of glamour models trailing down the narrow stairway and out the entrance to the building. Then I couldn't get through reception for half an hour because the editor, Bob Bird, was engaged in a Subbuteo match on the corridor carpet with a shaggy-haired subordinate, and refused to be interrupted. The desk behind mine was occupied by a hefty, hungover fellow drifting in and out of consciousness. Affixed to his shirt-back by an unknown japester was a sticker retrieved from an airline seat pocket. It read, 'Please wake me for meals'. This was the deputy editor. As I headed for my chair, a light-fitting moulded in the form of an outsized ice-tray dislodged itself from the low ceiling and landed squarely upon my head.

A typical week began with the art director, Tom Bond, a man with a peculiar and highly original mind, walking over to my desk. He did this not to speak to me, but to load onto the adjacent stereo an album of techno favourites re-recorded by an award-winning brass band. Having set the volume to a level that vaporised passing birdlife, he then returned to his own desk in the far corner, nodding in time to the tuba part with placid satisfaction.

This was the cue for the 'nerds' – responsible for *Blasted*'s website offshoot – to begin pelting the art department with junk, triggering an all-out debris battle. Computer disks, tape boxes, gym bags, disposable coffee cups, books about drug-taking on the Balearic islands, promotional video cassettes for hopeful, large-breasted, boot-faced models, and the stuffed monkey identified in the magazine's pages as its senior reviewer, flew back and forth across the partition separating the two camps. The writers now joined in, using the urban warfare tactic of drive-by shooting – in this instance, one would pass the combat zone at high speed pushing a wheel-mounted swivel chair in which another sat, firing rounds from a specially modified elastic band gun.

Two individuals remained heedless of the barrage: Tom Bond himself; and a designer called Seb, a preposterously good-looking and perpetually anxious young man. He would usually be inspecting some part of his body – toes, elbows, navel – for signs of gangrene, ringworm or dry rot, while frowning and sucking in air through his teeth. Plastic, cardboard and rubber ricocheted off his shoulders. Stray flecks of monkey kapok dotted his blond locks. But nothing distracted him from his fretful inquest.

Tom was no less fixed upon his own business – inflicting unspeakably cruel and comical computerised mutations upon celebrity photographs (a commonplace practice now, but one he pioneered). He didn't so much as look up until a used teabag smacked into the centre of his screen at cannonball velocity. Even then, Tom didn't flinch or jump. He gazed for a while at the brown, sodden lump sliding down his monitor. Unhurriedly, and without a word, he slid his chair back. He stood and picked up a bulky potted plant from the window sill. He strolled to the partition, and heaved the plant pot over it, upside down. Then he returned to his desk, abstractedly brushing off his hands.

The silence and the stillness were instantaneous, absolute and brief. Then they were supplanted by wails of incredulous horror.

'Oh my God. Oh my God.'

'You nutter, Tom. You fucking nutter. That fucking nutter went nuclear on us.'

Tom had, indeed, pressed the red button. War was over, because he wanted it.

Tom was a vandal, but he was a vandal of genius. Only he would have had both the imagination and the daring to set fire to Bob Bird's paper hat moments before the inaugural *Blasted* editorial meeting. Until I introduced them there were no editorial meetings. I quickly saw why. Tom's other contribution was to give an impromptu presentation, complete with flash-cards he had illustrated himself during the conference, on why editorial meetings were a bad idea. He had me convinced.

I didn't last long at *Blasted*. Opinion became divided as

to my proficiency at my job. Some were of the unshake-able view that I was worse than useless. Others defended me, arguing that I was definitely as good as useless. My competence was not, I think, the real issue. The real issue was compatibility. I was a Walter Softie in an office pop-ulated by Dennis the Menaces. My failure to fit in there was attributed by one HQD executive to 'a clash of cul-tures'. I don't think he knew how right he was. He meant that I was a big girl's blouse with no instinct for laddish-ness, and while that may have been true, the problem ran much deeper. My colleagues were deeply, innately British, and I was putting it on. I had, unsurprisingly, been found out.

Even so, I might have carried off the bluff had I been less obtuse. My greatest blunder was in failing to notice something that could not have been made more obvious or literal at *Blasted*: the British workplace is a near-perfect replica of the British playground. The cliques and rivalries, the joshing and sundry shades of bullying, the critical necessity of keeping up a front, the pack instinct that sees a mob coalesce at the first whiff of blood – you ignore these, as I did, at your peril.

There were very few women in the *Blasted* office, which – allied to the nature of the magazine itself – allowed the elemental nature of the British workplace to run ram-pant, red in tooth and claw. But the difference between that workplace and any other in the country was merely, so my later experiences suggest, a matter of degree. You might think that women would have a civilising influ-ence, but they do not. They have a masking effect, which is not the same thing. Again, the playground archetype applies. The girls scheme amongst themselves and against each other, while competing for the favour of their preferred boys.

At the *Fiddler*, I managed to overlook the blatant reality that I was back in the feral world of break-time, because I never wound up on the sharp end of it. But if the *Fiddler* offered a relatively gentle grammar school environment, then *Blasted* was a rough-and-ready comprehensive, and the sharp end swivelled in my direction swiftly and decisively.

In Britain, you never leave school. Wherever you go, however old you may be, you'll find it takes two Britons to make a gang, and three for that gang to have someone to pick on. The trick is to ensure you're part of the gang. It's a trick I never mastered, and this omission didn't come about through any innate decency on my part. There were times at the *Fiddler* when I joined the persecutors almost by accident – and my behaviour made my subsequent misfortune at *Blasted* take on the aspect of karmic retribution. One episode in particular skulks, unexorcised, in the guilty corridors of my memory. It revolved around a lad called Howard.

Howard made the mistake of baring his soul both in print and in the pub. It did not go well for him.

He penned a record review for the *Fiddler* that was, in effect, a love letter to a South American girl with whom he was smitten, Lulu. He described how he and Lulu had listened to the record in question in the wee hours, after a night on the town, while he gazed adoringly into her eyes and thought – here I quote – 'You're so wonderful, you're so wonderful.' Somehow this mash note masquerading as critique slipped through into the paper. Maybe the gnomes were in a spiteful mood that night.

Howard's problem – let me rephrase that, one of Howard's problems – was the altogether unrequited nature of his feelings. Lulu was playing him for a chump. Although she had made it clear as daylight that he had not the ghost of a chance with her, she encouraged him to hang around her, not as a suitor, but as a courtier. Under the delusion that proximity might bolster his magnetism, Howard compounded his own misery by inviting Lulu to share his flat. She moved in and, inevitably, began to bring home other men.

Soon after Howard's *cri de coeur* in the *Fiddler* hit the news stands, he was to be found in the Wothorpe, choking back tears and confiding his heartbreak to Blakey, whom he considered his mentor. Whether Blakey shared this view is moot. Errol – whose benevolence of spirit may be inferred from his status as a former warlock, and who lived by the maxim that if you couldn't say anything nice about someone, you were probably Errol – had once described Howard as 'the son Blakey never wanted'.

'She brought this South African surfer back last night,' snuffled Howard. 'A big, muscular, blond guy.' Howard himself did not meet any of these criteria. 'I had to listen to them going at it all night in the next room. I thought it would never end . . . the stamina . . . why is she doing this to me?'

Blakey nodded sympathetically, wearing the serious, slightly surprised expression that signalled he was stifling a powerful urge to laugh.

'You mustn't tell anyone about this,' said Howard, as they ascended in the lift to the *Fiddler*'s office. Blakey nodded again, solemnly, the significance of which would have been evident to anyone but Howard. Only getting picked up as the lead item on the BBC's evening news bulletin would ensure Howard's quandary a wider circulation than divulging it to Blakey.

The day proceeded as normal. Which is to say, languidly, save for the occasional flurry of excitement when the deputy editor, Sid Shelby – a man who displayed a much remarked-upon similarity, both in manner and appearance, to Benito Mussolini – launched a verbal blast at some passing writer.

Come five o'clock, diverted from his sorrows by both the tasks at hand and Sid's denunciations, Howard had regained what little composure he possessed. He headed for the door, with something not far off from a spring in his step, and had just about made it into the corridor when Errol shuffled by, nonchalantly intoning one of The Beach Boys' early hits, 'Surfer Girl'. Howard froze. Then he swung around and his gaze swept across a roomful of grinning faces. 'You *bastards*!' he howled, with the primal fury of a wounded animal, and fled the building.

'Excellent,' smirked Errol. 'Quick, padlock the doors.'

Worse was to come. When Howard opened the next issue of the paper he discovered that Barney and I, one drunken night, had concocted a missive commiserating with his plight, affixed to it the name of an imaginary retired colonel, and submitted it to the readers' letters page, where it duly appeared.

I too have been smitten with a young lady,

it ran,

> and she too has informed me that it will be a frosty
> evening at Beelzebub Mansions before I come
> within touching distance of her. But never say die,
> what? I propose a small wager – a crate of cham-
> pers from the loser for the first man to have his
> way. I mean, of course, with our respective pop-
> sies. Otherwise the bet would be rather unsport-
> ing. I did have the pleasure of entertaining your
> young lady when she was a regular visitor to our
> regimental barracks.

Nobody saw Howard for quite a while after that. In his
absence, both the review and the letter occupied pride of
place on the *Fiddler* noticeboard – just as the pelt of a
coyote may be nailed to a fencepost to warn off other
varmints. In time they were replaced by a picture of
Mussolini with Sid Shelby's head superimposed on top,
and Howard discreetly returned to work. I'll say this for
Howard – he was a quicker learner than I was.

CHAPTER NINE

CLOTHES UNMAKETH THE MAN

THE SUIT WAS A black Hugo Boss knock-off that I bought from a shop on Brighton's North Street in early 1993. It wasn't the first suit I had owned. But it was the first one that was worth owning.

After graduating, I had lashed out a hundred pounds on a silver-grey, synthetic, bulging, vast-shouldered item. When the reflective fabric caught the sunlight, spy satellites orbiting overhead went onto yellow alert. It gave me the air of an incompetent trainee spiv at a shady used Jaguar dealership.

I had intended to wear this hideous item to job interviews. With hindsight, I can imagine the effect it might have had on the panel. They were surely accustomed to seeing ill-fitting numbers plucked from the rack at Burtons, but this was something else again. There are only two methods of discouraging employers that might conceivably have been more effective. One was to don a sandwich board bearing the inscription 'I don't know what I'm doing'. The other, to have the phrase 'kiLL kaptilist SCUM' tattooed on my forehead with a rusty nail and Biro ink. Fortunately, as I was not summoned to a single job interview, that suit didn't make much difference to my prospects.

My new suit was passable, and it had the distinction of being purchased out of choice rather than necessity. It's always preferable to put on a suit because you want to, and not because you have to. I was not required to wear a suit to the *Fiddler*. The office livery, which could well have been handed out to recruits like an army uniform, consisted of: faded black promotional band T-shirt bearing picture or motif of luckless unknowns; sagging black denim jeans; Doctor Martens boots, cheap copy of same, or dirty trainers; gunny sack worn as a jacket (optional).

There were a few scribes who flouted the dress code. The Flints, for instance. Barney went for a snappy, neo-Mod look, while Frederick favoured 1970s New York punk rocker couture. As they invariably travelled in tandem, they formed an unlikely and somewhat menacing duo, and stood out wherever they went. Nowhere more so than at HQD, where few of the more conventionally garbed staff would hazard sharing a lift with them. One notable exception was the managing director, who in the spirit of corporate camaraderie introduced himself on the long ride up.

'I'm Peter Charlemagne,' he said, with the forced good humour of a field marshal essaying banter with a pair of squaddies. 'Who are you chaps? From the way you're dressed, I can tell you don't work on my floor, ahahaha.'

'I'm Barney,' said Barney, unaware of who Peter Charlemagne might be. 'That's Frederick.' Frederick, well aware of who Peter Charlemagne was, said nothing.

'And what do you do here?'

'We're at the *Fiddler*.'

'Really? Jolly good. I'm the company MD.'

'Glad I ran into you,' said Barney, ignoring the series of kicks delivered to his shin by Frederick. 'I've got this terrible cough, and my knee's been well dicky lately. When can I stop in and see you?'

The *Fiddler*'s most notable nonconformist in matters of apparel was Paul Worth, a Welsh lad with the build of a prop forward and the tastes of a *Rocky Horror Show* devotee. As one of our senior writers so neatly put it, 'It takes balls to dress as if you haven't got any.' It certainly did if you worked at the *Fiddler*. Paul could wander around London, on and off tube trains, past building sites and bus queues, clad in bondage gear and a leather skirt, without attracting a single comment, derisive or otherwise. On arriving at the *Fiddler* office, he would have to brace himself for a day's worth of jibes at his expense.

Paul's doggedly outré accoutrements were not for me, nor was the Flints' hoodlum chic. So I did the most rock 'n' roll thing I could think of under the circumstances, which was to dress in the most un-rock 'n' roll way I could think of. I bought my new suit.

It was the beginning of a compulsion. Not long afterwards, I found myself at the Paul Smith shop in London's
Covent Garden, an emporium well beyond my means,
determined to upgrade my suit selection. After a good two
hours' worth of wandering around like a dandelion in a
light breeze, I had narrowed the choice down to two: a
sober, elegant, slimline two-piece in midnight blue wool;
and a lurid neon-green polyester number embossed with
garish paisley swirls.

Naturally I favoured the paisley job, lending me as it
did the appearance of an ill-stuffed duvet in a peacock-
feather coverlet. I stared at myself in the craftily lit mirror, still undecided. Then, in a rare moment of insight, I
fled the premises, vowing not to return unless accompanied by The Girlfriend. I subsequently opted for the dark-
blue whistle. It made me look as smart as I ever will. As
for the green-dyed monster, I later saw it clinging mock-
ingly to some hapless minor pop star at the foot of the
society pages. There, but for fortune, went I.

There are worse-dressed nations than Britain, but most
of them have reasonable excuses. The former Soviet satellite countries, for example, had no choice but to wear dismal and shapeless garments for half a century, and it
takes a while to recover from something like that. Britain,
conversely, has a reputation for fine tailoring, and a rich
history of dandyism. Americans still seem to think of the
British as debonair – or at least, those Americans who
have never visited Britain do. If they were to come here,
they would very likely be dismayed to see just how avidly
a small but highly visible segment of British society now
dresses in poor imitation of American ghetto style, a look

that has little to recommend it. What might induce in them greater disillusion still is how ineptly the broader (and I use the word advisedly) mass of British men choose their clothes.

British men who buy their own clothes are easy to identify. They are either arrogant, single or gay. Of these, only the gay have any clue how to dress (a fact that has long been evident to photo shoot stylists, and has since entered folklore via the medium of television). The arrogant are the ones who don't have the good sense to listen to their womenfolk. Single men, obviously, don't get the chance.

The headstrong can be identified by their inappropriate clobber. Summer sees them at their most shameful, with obnoxiously bright shirts worn over trousers distinguished by their complete lack of suitability for any occasion whatsoever – except, perhaps, a karaoke gong show.

The most extreme cases, unable to discriminate between class and flash, aim for Italian Playboy territory but land smack in the heartland of Haitian Pimp Made Good. They are attracted to shop displays created by a window dresser who, as a child, ran away from the circus in search of something more vivid. In they go, to demand the most expensive suit in the establishment – usually some grievous double-breasted sub-Versace confection with a Nehru collar, huge rococo buttons, five pockets down the side and quite possibly piping or epaulettes on the shoulders. As a result, they automatically repel any woman with two opinions to rub together. It's nature's way.

As for the unattached males, they look as forlorn as they feel. Each is a living jumble sale of ill-fitting and mismatched garments. No matter how much money they spend, they cannot shake off the effect of having haphazardly rifled the bargain bins at Primark. Their strides, bulky and amorphous, are belted too tightly around their flaccid waists. In profile their casual shirts assume a staunch A-line silhouette, like a tarpaulin in a stiff breeze. Come evening, they don shapeless jumpers so ridden with holes they could serve as a miniature golf course for moths.

These unfortunates are trapped in a vicious circle of loneliness and sartorial inadequacy. Without a woman to help them smarten up their act, they haven't a chance in hell of attracting a woman. Even if they don't go about in shell-suits and tramps' trainers held together with string, they might as well. Their only hope is to meet a woman suffused with either pity or masochism.

I know this only too well. Before The Girlfriend came along, I numbered among them. As usual, I managed to single myself out, with regard to something the British do very badly, by doing it worse myself. Because I had no idea of what else to do, I dressed in black. It felt like the safest option. And it worked to the extent that The Girlfriend permitted herself to be seen with me, which was magnanimous of her.

Hubris inevitably followed. With my confidence boosted, I began to experiment. At the time, I still wore my hair in dreadlocks, the former style of the pop singer Lenny Kravitz. An apt comparison because, like Kravitz, I swiftly acquired the wardrobe of a colourblind wino run riot in Oxfam. Skin-tight, long-sleeved T-shirts with silvered slogans. Weird second-hand canvas drain-pipes. Shoes that belonged on cartoon donkeys. I wore them all.

It humbles me now to think of how patient The Girlfriend was about this. For a start, she sensibly ignored my suggestions for her own wardrobe (micro-skirts, fluffy bra-tops, Chinese dresses). Then she calmly showed me what I ought to be wearing. Gradually, I was transformed from a figure of fun into someone who looked as if he might be able to tie his own laces. I knew then that I should never again select so much as a pair of socks without the go-ahead from the missus.

There are many other British men who share the malaise I once suffered. The solution is at hand for them, as it was for me, and you'd think they would be grateful. But no. Every Saturday you can see them being dragged like whining children through the high streets of Britain. In dressing rooms, they are sighingly instructed to forget about the canary-yellow denim shirt by women whose forbearance, sorely tested, will one day snap. Then they will take their revenge. They will maliciously guide their male charges into vile velvet cummerbunds and out-landish jumpsuits in shades of puce and meringue. And those men won't know anything's amiss until the clown-catchers come with their nets and lock them up, down at the Bozo pound.

You can spot the men to whom this is about to happen. They're the ones in late-Raj-style baggy knee-shorts – a kind of warning shot across the bow. Asinine enough in Jaipur, they are nothing short of humiliating in Portobello Market. Readers with long memories may recall William Hague's infamous bare-knees-and-baseball-cap get-up at the Notting Hill Carnival (readers with shorter memories may need reminding that William Hague was, briefly, leader of the Conservative Party). I'm not saying that's what lost him the subsequent election. But all else being equal, it could have done, on its own. He must have done something that his wife found exceptionally annoying.

During my tenure at the *Fiddler*, I never went to the Notting Hill Carnival. Helena, of course, was a regular. It helped that she had friends whose gracious houses featured balconies overlooking the parade route. The last I heard of Helena, she had changed her name to Winston and moved to Ladbroke Grove to pursue a career as an 'urban' DJ. Were it possible to measure these things, I would have said that Helena was the least black person I had ever met. If there is a racial approximation of transsexuality, then Helena surely fell into that category. She genuinely felt that she was a black man trapped in a white woman's body. I knew plenty of other white women who made it their business to have a black man trapped in their body as often as possible. And who, moreover, believed that by doing so they were proving themselves the moral heirs of Martin Luther King Jr. But Helena's fixation was not, to be fair, triggered by any such motives.

The reason I never went to the carnival was that it coincided with festival season, and festival season made up part of my duties. There were, at that time, an unsustainable number of music festivals. Britain's promoters had vowed they would not rest easy until every man, woman and child in the country had their own music festival. And the *Fiddler* tried to cover them all. There was little point. With the exception of Glastonbury itself, which remains singularly gruelling, you could have been airlifted into any festival, anywhere in Britain, and have no idea which one it was. The stages played host to the same acts, stopping off on summer-long European festival tours. There were the same dance and comedy tents. The same rows of stalls selling tie-dye tat and suspect food at risibly high prices. The same granite-faced drug dealers peddling the same low-grade carpet fluff to the same blistered and dazed children of suburbia.

The most entertaining part of attending festivals wasn't listening to the bands or watching the punters. It was observing my colleagues. At Glastonbury, after two hours of preparation in his hotel room, Paul Worth arrived at the site in a studded dog collar, black mesh singlet, skin-tight PVC shorts and bovver boots. His entire head – which was clean shaven but for a horn-shaped tuft of hair above each temple – was plastered with half an inch of pancake slap. A film star of the silent movie era would have balked at the amount of mascara he had used.

I was in no position to remark upon Paul's unusual get-up, as I was wearing a linen suit acquired for the purpose of festival-going.

'Why?' I was asked, again and again.

'Somebody has to set an example to the kids,' I would reply.

It was a very hot afternoon. Rivulets of blackened sweat soon began to stream down via Paul's eyelids and carve dark valleys through the make-up on his cheeks.

'Paul,' I murmured, discreetly, 'I think I should tell you that your mascara's running.'

'Is it?' he said. 'Thanks – all day I've been wondering why people were looking at me funny.'

It was three o'clock, and Paul was on his fourth Malibu and Coke of the afternoon. He teetered off to find a mirror. I didn't see him again until late in the evening. I was chatting to Sandy Miller when a very solemn American PR lady picked her way towards us through an obstacle course of litter and small, pungent fires.

'Are you the reviews editor for the *Harmony Fiddler*?' she asked Sandy.

'I am until the horse gets back from holiday,' said Sandy, cryptically. He was fairly drunk, and swaying slightly.

The American PR lady paused, then thought better of following that line of enquiry.

'I'm Aurora Fiddlesticks, from Desperate Records,' she said. 'Our band, The Gutless Wretches, is appearing on the second stage in fifteen minutes. Could you tell me which of your writers is assigned to cover that stage?'

'That would be Paul Worth,' said Sandy.

'Thank you,' said Aurora Fiddlesticks. 'And where would I find Mr Worth?'

'That's him over there,' Sandy replied, indicating a motionless, bulky and distinctively clad figure lying face down in a nearby drainage culvert.

'*That*,' said Ms Fiddlesticks, 'is your designated reporter?'

'Absolutely,' said Sandy. 'He's doing an excellent job.'

We were then distracted by the arrival of a Pat Buckeridge, another hired hand on the *Fiddler*. He was a bloodhound-faced Cornishman whose trail was unfailingly dogged, footprint for footprint, by imps of misfortune. If the notion of bad luck struck you as fanciful, a few minutes in Pat's company would change your mind. A few minutes in Pat's company would also leave you with fixed dilated pupils, a plummeting body temperature and no discernible pulse. There was no malice in Pat, but he did have a talent for tedium – perhaps even a genius for it.

Pat's favoured anecdote, about the historic occasion he witnessed a long and justly forgotten indie band from Barnsley split up onstage, didn't merely seem longer every time you heard it (twice a week, on average); it genuinely was. With each re-telling, he dredged up new and ever less intriguing details: 'As I'm sure you remember, the singer was Arthur Drabness. He was the one who went on to start up The Monotones. I once spent a satis-factory long weekend in Pevensey with them. They were touring in support of their amusing album, *Sold Our Souls For Sausage Rolls*. There was some confusion at a shellfish stall over their order. They said they'd asked for cockles. The stallholder insisted it was whelks. But that's another story. One I will arrive at in due course. Now apparently, Arthur was already in a peevish mood that day owing to a loose corn plaster. His mother had insisted he keep it on from the night before . . .'

Pat's yarn had transmogrified into an epic of *ennui* to rival any Icelandic saga or Red Chinese opera. Spying him by the lifts at the end of the day, *Fiddler* staffers would take any excuse to linger by the reception desk until he had gone. When, as often happened, the lift was delayed, a large crowd would build up, rhubarbing uncomfortably to itself and casting surreptitious glances into the corridor. The *ding* of the arriving elevator would prompt a stifled hubbub of anticipation; followed, as the doors slid shut, by a stampede to catch the next one.

In a Wiltshire field, there was no opportunity to execute such a manoeuvre. We could only watch Pat approach and wonder to ourselves how long it would take before he began to relate the break-up story to Ms Fiddlesticks and we could slip away. But Pat, we found, had something else on his mind.

'I was wondering if you had, by any apparent possible chance, seen Imogen, perhaps?' asked Pat, mournfully.

Imogen was Pat's German girlfriend, a towering Valkyrie with a Vulcan Death Grip for a handshake. Their dalliance was only a fortnight old, but as Pat was not always in a position to show off a girlfriend, he had proudly introduced her to his cowering workmates at every opportunity. Having gained entry to the festival through Pat, Imogen had vanished within minutes.

'Apparently, she was seen in this general vicinity,' said Pat. 'I was hoping that I would be able to effect a reunion. But apparently this information is either incorrect or outdated. I think it might be best to make my way back to the hotel and wait for her there.'

Pat trudged to the car park, where he happened across Sid Shelby climbing into the driver's seat of a sporty hatchback.

'Ah, Sid,' said Pat. 'I notice that you are apparently preparing to leave the festival site, and I presume that you are heading back to the hotel. Also, apparently, you have a spare seat available, and I was wondering if –'

'No,' said Sid, slammed his door shut, and drove away.

Pat began the long, slow walk to the city of Wells,

where the *Fiddler* contingent had its hotel rooms. The country lane was narrow, and bordered by high hedges. The night was quiet, save for the distant, low hubbub of the festival, and dark. So it is a mystery how he could have had no hint as to the approach of Deviant Refuse Collective.

Deviant Refuse Collective, a performance art group, had built themselves a monster of a truck, all zebra stripes and rhino horns; an outlandish behemoth in which they rode around the country at a slow trundle in case bits fell off. You could see them coming two miles away, and hear them three miles before that. Unless, that is, you were Pat. The truck bounced him smartly into the hedgerow. Bruised but not broken, he clambered out via a bed of nettles and plodded back to the hotel, where he found a note from Imogen waiting for him at reception. She had encountered a band of hippy space-rockers and run off with their lighting roadie.

It took me a while to admit to myself that I didn't like music festivals. It went against the grain to allow that something pivotal to my trade could hold so little import for me. It happened, at last, in a park on the outskirts of Glasgow. Over the course of a long weekend I watched soft green grass turn to dust and balmy sunshine to clammy drizzle. I wandered from tent to tent, tripping over the prone bodies of cataleptic teenagers clubbed into insensibility by cider and sunstroke.

It came to me in one of those flashes of self-revelation that all I wanted was to leave. So leave I did, trudging past a small contingent of ticketless locals by the exit. They were dispiritedly lobbing insults and beercans at a few bored coppers. You could tell that none of us had our hearts in it.

I went to music festivals because I was paid to. And I'll go again if someone offers me a great deal more money than they used to. That, to my mind, is the only good reason to go. There is nothing I can do at a festival that I cannot do with more enthusiasm, in greater comfort and in better company somewhere else.

Some might think that I'm jaded. They could argue that, not having been required to pay my way, I've never fully appreciated the essence of festivals. I'll give them that one. I've found festivals irksome, miserable, unhealthy, dirty and cramped. If I'd ever actually forked out upwards of £100 for the experience, I'd have found them downright satanic. I could get myself whipped to hamburger by a strapping bulldyke for less, and I'm sure it would be no more of an ordeal.

Festivals are little more than jamborees for masochists devised either by zealots or by profiteers. I don't mind the profiteers. At least their motives are easy to follow. And – come to that – share. As for why every other Tom, Hilary and Tarquin gets involved, the reasons are more complicated and even less savoury.

Music festivals are very revealing about two particular aspects of British life: the British relationship to nature; and the British notion of mass-market fun. I found both to be completely out of kilter with any notion I had of either.

My *Fiddler* colleagues, for the most part, seized the opportunity to drink themselves silly. As they seized any opportunity to drink themselves silly, all a festival signi-fied was a change of locale. But for people whose daily occupations were of a more sober turn, a festival lived up to its name. It was a Saturnalia, an orgy with colour-coded wristbands.

Look around any music festival and you'll see people having fun, no question. Many of them are having so much fun they're passed out and completely oblivious to the fun they're having. The remainder aren't merely con-scious, they're self-conscious with it. This is particularly true of the girls. It's a curious characteristic of young British women that – as Lord Hewart might have noted – they should not only have fun, but should manifestly and undoubtedly be seen to have fun. Not fun as we might recognise it – relaxed, freewheeling enjoyment – but bois-terous, bouncing, screaming, gurning, primary-coloured, chimpanzees'-tea-party fun. Fun under duress. It paral-lels the old conundrum about a tree falling in the forest. If a British girl has a good time and there's nobody there to watch it, is she really enjoying herself?

With British men, the opposite is true. When they carouse mob-handed, they will usually be rowdy and rau-cous – not because they hope, like their female counter-parts, to draw attention; but rather because they don't care if they do. It isn't onlookers they're trying to convince; it's themselves. There is an axiom – or if there wasn't, there is now – which states that the amount of genuine pleasure to be had from any given pursuit is inversely proportional to the quantity of silly headgear involved in it. It might be ageing middle-managers wearing lampshades at parties. Or it could be twenty-year-old twits with huge patch-

work-and-felt jesters' caps. But you can be sure that anyone wearing something asinine and incongruous on their
noggin is desperate to assure himself he's having a much
better time than he really is.

Few ticket-buyers are under the illusion that festivals
are not squalid, rank, crowded, perpetually noisy and
occasionally dangerous. But still they go. Some go for the
music, but the music is only one part of it – a pretext,
almost. The underlying purpose of a festival is to make
people feel that they're part of something bigger than
themselves. A festival is effectively a fake community for
people who feel uneasy about not having joined a real
one. It's hard, in a city, to be part of a community. You may
even have to create one from scratch. It's much easier to
muck in with ready-made jollity out in the sticks.

The festival professionals know better. They are issued
with a series of passes which grant access to ever more
exclusive compounds within the site. Media and liggers
have an enclosure somewhat like a sheep pen. Beyond lies
the true 'backstage', where only bands and their lackeys
may proceed. Even here varying degrees of status apply.
The further up the bill you are, the more privacy and relative luxury you command. But wherever you rank on the
food chain, you share the same aim – to keep the hell away
from those below you. Using fences and guards, if needs
be. Thus punters avoid invaders, press avoid punters,
artists avoid press and stars avoid everybody. This is the
only aspect of festivals that genuinely reflects authentic,
day-to-day community spirit: the feeling among the elite
that if the great unwashed (literally, in this case) want to
get together en masse, the best place to be is somewhere

else. In short, the festival is a microcosm of the society from which it supposedly offers escape.

During festival season, the *Fiddler* crew doubled up in hotel rooms – officially. Unofficially, we slept four or five to a room, as those colleagues without assignments turned up anyway and demanded somewhere to doss down. Nobody minded accommodating their fellows, but limits had to be observed. A female reviewer, billeted with another woman who imbibed a few too many sherries and gave away her key, woke up to find two members of the hippy convoy copulating noisily on the next bed – a spectacle so hideous it would make a gargoyle gag.

Come the small hours, the hotel took on the air of a halfway house operated by people-smuggling racketeers. The management did their best to exclude the unwanted human traffic, by barring those without key cards, or admitting only those whose names appeared on the list of reservations. Heading out for that day's assignment, I once passed a well-oiled Barney Flint trying to talk his way in.

'I'm Matt Bishop,' he said to a receptionist with a clipboard, confusing the names of two *Fiddler* photographers.

'The only Bishop I have down here is Phil Bishop,' said the receptionist.

'Phil Bishop, yes, that's me.'

'But Mr Bishop has already checked in.'

'I mean, I'm Phil Hope. Sorry. I got mixed up.'

'We have a Mr Matt Hope . . .'

'Right. Matt. Matt Hope. I'm Matt Hope.'

'But he's already checked in, too. In fact, he's sharing a room with Mr Bishop.'

'That's why I got mixed up, you see. Because we're sharing a room. *I'm* Matt Bishop.'

'We don't have a Matt Bishop.'

Round and round this dialogue went. The last thing I heard as I strode out of earshot was Barney's indignant, inevitable assertion, 'I've been thrown out of better hotels than this one.'

Even a thronged hotel room was preferable to the alternative, which was to do as the punters did and sleep under canvas. I had grown up associating tents with the African wilderness. To me, camping was something you did so that you could get as far away from civilisation as possible. That you might choose to do it in the company of 100,000 intoxicated wingnuts was incomprehensible to me.

Bear in mind that, by the final night, most music festivals resemble the closing scenes of 1980s Armageddon movie *The Day After*. Many of those present will have consumed so much in the way of drink and drugs that they no longer care about their surroundings. That's probably for the best. A festival is an instant city, with all the drawbacks of city life and none of the benefits. The campsites at festivals are three-day slums, filthy, disease-prone and crime-ridden. They even mimic the pattern of cities, with well-off family groups settling in genteel enclaves, circling their wagons against the nightmarish shanty towns below, where they may occasionally venture to score substandard marijuana from the kind of low-lifes who shot up at Glastonbury in 1995.

Worse yet, festivals manage to stir the scummiest aspects of country life into this ugly hash. The habitual combination of suspicion and avarice that townies bring out in country folk is inevitably heightened by the presence of urbanites in their thousands. But this is nothing compared to the fake rusticism you find on the sites themselves. Every would-be child of nature looks on a festival as their God-given habitat. Packs of crusty Marie Antoinettes of both sexes, beaded, bobtailed and nose-ringed, seize the opportunity to play Back to the Land. They dance round evil-smelling campfires to variants on tribal techno (the music favoured by subsistence farmers before the invention of the steam engine, evidently), and do their damnedest to become at one with the soil.

The rural ideals that abound at festivals hark back not to pre-industrial times, but to the 1960s. Rock festivals grew directly out of the fertile mulch in which hippies cross-pollinated with entrepreneurs. Woodstock was never intended to be a free festival; it was just so hopelessly planned that in the end the organisers had no other option. Glastonbury has always charged for entry, but gives much of its proceeds to charitable causes. Once the CND was the main beneficiary. Today, appropriately, it's Greenpeace – appropriately because not even a corporate merger between the petrochemical industry and the Seven Plagues of Egypt could mimic the devastation wreaked by hordes of eco-fervent punters.

Festival-goers believe that by spending a few days hunkered down in a bivouac in the green belt, or somewhere near it, they will connect with Mother Earth. Poor old Mother Earth, our frail and ancient relative; she gets put away out of sight, tended by brusque, unsympathetic professionals, and descended upon every so often by overly hearty offspring whose guilty enthusiasm exhausts her. It will take her until next year's visit to recover.

The popularity of festivals in the mid-1990s revealed a hankering after the countryside on the part of British city-dwellers. At least the people who went to festivals had the sense to go home afterwards. More recently, that hankering has induced waves of townies to decamp to the countryside, dreaming of a pastoral idyll. Not a week goes by without a plaintive newspaper article by a metropolitan refugee bleating on about how miserable it's all turned out to be.

There's a reason for such despondency. It's a simple one. The countryside is a wretched place to live. That's why over 90 per cent of us in England and Wales prefer to occupy the six per cent of land classified as urban. It's no coincidence that the word 'civilisation' finds its root in the Latin *civis* – city dweller.

The chief factors cited by migrating urbanites are: fear of crime; noise; dirt; pollution; transport difficulties; and above all, the lack of 'community spirit'.

I spend a fair bit of time in London, and as little as possible anywhere rural. Do I fear crime? Occasionally, but I'd rather stroll through the nether regions of Peckham wearing a suit made of £5 notes than take my chances in a tiny market town full of shiftless, glue-sniffing adolescent yokels itching for an excuse to re-enact the more harrowing moments from *Straw Dogs*.

When it comes to dirt, noise and pollution, it's hard to top a tractor grinding through the gears in a newly fertilised field. Transport? Try getting around the country-side if you don't run a car. It would be quicker, cheaper and more comfortable to post yourself, second-class.

As for community spirit, yes, the countryside has it in spades. That's precisely why nobody from the city should ever move there. Accustomed to the luxury of going unno-ticed and undisturbed about your business, you'll discover that suddenly it's everybody's business. Assuming, that is, they don't hang you for a spy on your arrival.

Unlike the city, where tolerance for our neighbours is essential, the countryside is ideal for people who can't stand other people, or indeed any other warm-blooded species. Each has an average of 50 acres to himself (as against 0.02 acres per urbanite), where he can crouch, alone and brooding, over a shotgun in a darkened farm-house, in wait for underage burglars, before popping out to stab a horse or two.

Recently, an acquaintance of mine who grew up in a Somerset village was forced by a lack of funds to return to the family home for a spell. He called up after a week and complained that the monotony of life there was mak-ing him miserable. The next week, he phoned again, sounding much more chipper.

'I think things are starting to turn around for me,' he enthused. 'I doubled my money last night.'

'I thought you didn't have any money.'

'I was down to a fiver. But it's ten now.'

'How did you do it?'

'Betting on a ferret race.'

Oddly for a boy who grew up with the wonders of Africa around him, I had always cherished an image of the British countryside no less rosy or sentimental than that evoked so potently in the films of Michael Powell and Emeric Pressburger. It is telling that Pressburger was himself an emigré – perhaps, even in the 1930s, an outlander could see in Britain the tranquil sanctuary that for a native would be obscured by familiarity.

Seventy years on, that countryside is as remote to many Britons as it is to any foreigner; which may go a long way to explaining the romantic notions so widely held about it – and so easily dispelled by spending any length of time there.

The last time I did so was – and this is no coincidence – also the last time I reported on a music festival. I was interviewing a band aboard their tour bus, just after sunrise. The rain beat horizontally against a few muddy, distant, early-morning hippies as they picked their way through the mire. From the top deck of the coach I had a fine view into a nearby van with a painted eagle emblazoned on the roof. In the cab a German roadie, all paunch and body hair, was slipping into something more likely to reveal his testicles.

'I've seen a lot worse than this,' said one of the musicians, a fellow by the name of Colin. 'Years ago I had a friend who moved down from Huddersfield to Crawley, in Sussex. He said, "There's loads of jobs down here." So I came down. I'd been on the dole for three or four months. Thought I'd save a bit of money. The next day I had a job.

'There'd been a bin strike in Crawley, and they'd hired all these ex-students to clear up after them. It was disgusting. You'd get maggots falling out of the bags down your neck. We got kicked out of our flat midway through that, and we couldn't find anywhere to live, so we thought we'd camp in the woods. I used to come off work, go to the pub and get pissed every night because it was the only way I could cope with it.

'We'd end up rat-arsed, chasing each other through the woods, falling over, and one night I rolled around in a load of dogshit. I didn't have anywhere to wash, no change of clothes. I had to go to work on the bins stinking of dogshit, and they were all going, "Fuckin' hell!" and recoiling from me, all these people who were used to getting maggots down their collars. After that I slept in someone's garden for three months.'

I saw, across the pasture, one of the hippies go down. Two others struggled vainly to pluck him from the bog.

I don't doubt that Colin, and the luckless hippy, represented the British experience of nature far more accurately than anything in Powell and Pressburger's *A Canterbury Tale*. There is, to me, a corner of some English field that is forever foreign. And I plan to keep it that way.

CHAPTER TEN

MAD GIRLS AND ENGLISHMEN

I N 1993, THE *FIDDLER* brass offered me a part-time desk job as an editor. It was a touching – not to say rash – act of faith on their part, tempered only by the day-rate wage that went with it. My stipend amounted to just over half what they gave the paper's copy typist, whose abundant errors were characterised by such boldness and verve that the outcome could make for quite a bracing read in its own right. And even on a performance-related scale, the copy typist was by no means overpaid.

My new post required me to spend more time at the paper, which was just fine. Life at the *Fiddler* was a cabaret. Every day brought a new diversion. One morning,

I shared the train ride to London with Barney Flint, who had moved down to Brighton. On the walk to the office we met up with his writing partner Frederick. The Flints both looked as if they had spent the previous fortnight in the back of a Transit van, shuttling around the loucher parts of Europe and ingesting veneniferous chemicals. Unsurprisingly, that was because they had.

We arrived at the office to find the senior staff – Blakey, Sid Shelby, Ned Coco – lined up in ambush for the Flints.

'Where the fuck is our cover feature, you pair of fucking wankers?' barked Sid. It was clear right away that this wasn't the amicable kind of abuse. It was just abuse.

'You had three weeks to write it before you went away,' griped Ned.

'What do we pay you your retainer for?' Blakey wanted to know.

The Flints stood there, visibly wilting before a slow-burning furnace of denunciation and reproof. At the *Fiddler*, supervision tended to err on the side of relaxed. It was rare that late submission of copy was noticed by editors, largely because it was rare that those editors could recall what they'd commissioned in the first place. Thus carpetings were infrequent, and usually half-hearted. This one, however, was a doozy – a tag-team effort that went on and on without slackening. When one complainant lost impetus or ran out of breath, another stepped up to take his place. Frederick shrank into his jacket, and the peak of his baseball cap lowered itself over his face until it covered all but his jaw. Barney assumed the demeanour of a penitent toddler, hands behind his back and his down-cast gaze darting across the floor.

At last the triumvirate concluded their recriminations, by which time the entire staff, a few passing freelancers and a notoriously frugal photographer by the name of Tony Sugar, who had stopped by to collect some unused prints, were gathered together to witness the disgracing of the Flints. Frederick had almost entirely sunk into his clothing, which maintained the illusion of standing up of its own volition. Barney, with nowhere to hide, continued to stare at his feet, his face scarlet with shame.

'Ned, you're right,' he mumbled contritely, shifting his scrutiny from his own shoes to Ned's. 'You're right, and all I can honestly say is' – he cleared his throat, as if to stifle a sob – 'the truth is . . . I'd really like to fuck your wife.'

If not the truth Ned had hoped for, this was undeniably *a* truth (I had never met Ned's wife myself, but I was assured that she was a toothsome morsel). By the time Blakey, Sid and the watching throng had stopped laughing – and Ned had forced himself to start laughing – Barney and Frederick were stepping up to the bar in the Wothorpe.

On another occasion I arrived for work to find the main part of the office deserted. Everybody was in the reviews room, watching a Swedish hardcore pornography video that one of production team had brought in. As I opened the door I heard moaning and panting, and a voice declared, in a strong Scandinavian accent,

'Ah, *ja*, I like a tight cunt.'

Without missing a beat, Sandy Miller retorted, 'You should try going on assignment with Tony Sugar then.'

Travelling between London and Brighton as often as I

did, I was conscripted as a porn mule by the office filth aficionados, principal among whom were Barney and the production department's Errol. As the working day drew to a close, Errol would surreptitiously shuffle over to my desk, hand me a Sainsbury's carrier bag full of VHS cassettes, and mutter, in conspiratorial fashion, 'Could you get these to Barney?' Why he bothered with the air of secrecy, I could only guess; everyone knew what he was up to, and nobody cared.

Inevitably, there was an interval between my bringing the tapes to Brighton and Barney stopping by to collect them. Inevitably, I wound up watching them. Leave a man alone in a room with pornography and you can't expect him to ignore it.

To say that Errol and Barney's selection made for an eye-opener is not strictly accurate. Much of it made me squeeze my eyelids shut as tightly as I could.

In the early 1990s, pornography had attained a certain vogue. In a pointed effort to flout the country's traditional attitude to sex – that familiar compote of repression, euphemism and the singularly British quality that is naughtiness – respectable publications had taken to printing critiques of pornography. Far from defying custom, this effectively fed into it; where other countries might treat sex with a relaxed matter-of-factness, the UK's notions of obscenity meant that even confronting the matter head on required calculated – and self-congratulatory – daring. In its efforts to appear casual, the approach invariably niffed of the risqué.

Pornography might well have adopted the slogan of a soft drink advertisement of the time, and described itself as 'so misunderstood'. There were, and still are, two basic schools of thought on the subject. This is where the misunderstandings started. With thinking.

For those men who use the stuff – and I have no doubt that this will include, at one time or another, every last man Jack of us – porn involves no thought of any kind whatsoever. The whole point of porn is to sidestep the brain and set a direct course for the groin. To porn consumers, porn is neither good nor bad in any generally accepted sense, moral or aesthetic. It either works or it doesn't. Good porn is porn that helps you masturbate. Bad porn – well, that helps you masturbate, too. It just takes longer.

Here's the thing about porn. However bad it is, it's always good. And however good it is, it's never that good. But there's no point trying to explain this to either of those schools of thought. One hails porn as the vanguard of sexual liberty and free expression. The other reviles it as an attack on the female sex, preying upon the frail and the abused, and teaching men to see women as pieces of meat.

These opposing lobbies have only one thing in common. To them, porn is homogenous, a single, uniform entity. What nobody outside the sex industry sees fit to mention is that porn is as diverse as any mainstream media form. It is full of subtle variations. Granted, that's the only thing about it that could possibly be called subtle. Still, viewing those contraband tapes provided me with – among other things – schooling of a kind.

Britain's convoluted and ill-defined censorship laws meant that much of what I saw was illegal, except when it wasn't. If the BBFC couldn't be clear on the matter, then nor could I.

The films varied wildly in their frankness, quality and geographical origin. There was British-made softcore, tending towards the cheap and cheerful – happy slappers in bright surroundings and halfway out of lurid nylon knickers. Much of it possessed a tawdry, 1970s, *Confessions-of-a-Milkman* air. Other examples were not so much tawdry as grotesque. Angela Carter once wrote that pornography has a hole in it exactly the size of the user's penis, and with this literal-minded metaphor she more or less summed up softcore porn. What she didn't mention was that it can range from the enticing to the frankly gynaecological. Some of it was best approached not with manhood in hand, but a speculum.

Then there was polished, American hardcore, following in the *Playboy* tradition of soft lighting trained upon impeccably coiffed and groomed performers. These skin-flicks resembled such soap operas as *The Bold and the Beautiful*, but for the explicit sex and slightly better acting. Which style was preferable, the American or the British, depended on whether your taste leaned towards gloss or realism. I use the term 'realism' in the cinematographic sense. Porn is by nature of its very existence unrealistic. If it wasn't, we wouldn't need it.

The misguided notion of treating porn as an art form goes back to 1970s America, when the directors of movies including *The Devil in Miss Jones*, *Deep Throat* and *The Opening of Misty Beethoven* aimed to bring their work somewhere near the mainstream, or at least the cinema club, only to be thwarted by the advent of home video. In truth, most of those films displayed such insufferable avant-garde pretensions that nobody would have gone near them but for the sex. (In the UK, the same errant thinking lay behind a 1998 attempt to re-launch *Penthouse* magazine as a smutty style-sheet for the so-called chattering classes. The publishers didn't account for the possibility that the chattering classes might like their porn exactly the way everyone else does: lewd, and unencumbered by deliberation. They just don't much like to chatter about it.)

Video put hardcore where it belonged: in a room where the viewer didn't have to hunker with a pack of strangers all furtively tossing themselves off onto the unimaginably putrid carpet. Certainly, the production values suffered, but the audience didn't care. They wanted screwing, not *Brideshead Revisited*.

Some of the films I ferried to and fro took the low-budget idea to extremes. Take, for instance, the remarkable Euro production, *Greedy Cunts*, which took up houseroom in my flat for longer than I would have wished – the optimum duration being zero days. I watched it once, and only once, but it will stay with me as long as I can lay claim to both memory and conscience. The Andrea Dworkinesque theory that porn embodies a single male voice speaking to other men was literally true in this instance, for reasons more to do with economy than conspiracy. All the male protagonists had been dubbed into English by one deadpan, nasal Dutchman, who also served as the narrator.

'What Misshish Jonesh likesh,' he intoned, as the lady in question cleaned up a meths-swilling tramp by the road-side and prepared to match actions to words, 'issh a gud assh fuck. He looks like a gennel guy. Mebbe he will giwit to her.' To the surprise of nobody, giwit to her he did. 'Wurry nice,' approved our Virgil, guide to this netherworld. Everything in this opus, according to him, was 'wurry nice'. 'Go on, man,' he enthused, as if it was the most obvious thing in the world. 'Pissh on her titsh. Wurry nice.'

Far from being wurry nice, *Greedy Cunts* – starring, among others, a young woman working under the fetching sobriquet of Linda Fist – was almost enough to put you off sex altogether, an attribute it shared with a great deal of specialised porn. (Porn's niche markets are limited only by human imagination. You want shitting midgets? OAP orgies? No problem.) I sat in slack-jawed horror, willing myself to hit the stop button, but quite unable to do so. At one point I found myself pondering the fact that male users of straight porn will happily spend any amount of time gazing at stiff cocks and hairy arses, so long as there's a woman involved somewhere. Even if it's just the one female servicing a charabanc-load of chaps and you can barely see more than her busy little hands.

There was worse to come. Arriving on a Friday evening to collect one shipment of cassettes, Barney dropped off another assortment intended for Errol. The weekend loomed, as did the pile of tapes. Left to my own devices, which numbered among them the VCR, I inevitably succumbed.

Top of the heap was a videotape labelled *The Birthday Party*. It was not, sadly, a rump-action version of the play by Harold Pinter – although some its dialogue was sufficiently opaque to have dribbled from that eminent pen – but a homemade production packed with repugnant teenagers.

At this time, amateur porn constituted yet another British idiosyncrasy, pioneered by the magazine *Readers' Wives*, which brought forth a particularly choice item of slang, describing a type of woman hard to define but instantly identifiable when you saw her.

> ME: 'Have you met Chris's new girl-
> friend yet?'
> FRIEND: 'Yeah. Bit of a reader's wife,
> if you ask me.'

Since then, amateur porn has become big business wherever video cameras are sold, with many a hard-faced professional striving to masquerade as a genuine DIY enthusiast. *The Birthday Party* made the unfortunate mistake of attempting the opposite trick, endeavouring to pass off the risibly amateurish as professional. It even had a plot. A lump-shaped girl, upon whom congenital destiny had seared the mark of Dinner Lady with a branding iron, hosted a birthday bash. This degenerated into an orgy so unbeguiling it would have been shunned by Caligula.

Only the unfussiest of libertines could have relished this debauch. The dramatic high point saw our heroine bustle into the room to find her boyfriend, a scrofulous, weasely Welsh lad, receiving mouth-to-crotch relief from her best pal. 'What,' she demanded, in the face of unmistakable evidence, 'do you think you're doing?' It was a question I had been asking myself long before that moment arrived.

This was not nearly so outlandish as the next movie, which originated in Italy. It featured a human trio going at it like pygmy chimp gymnasts in the foreground, while in the background a woman and a pig got down to making bacon. It made me wonder exactly how jaded the viewer needed to be before he required the pig's presence to excite him. More jaded, I'm glad to say, than I was. I switched it off – although not before noting how, from one scene to the next, the same porn starlet moved from man to pig, and pig to man. I couldn't help but wonder what George Orwell might have made of that.

As a youngster I had enjoyed scarcely any access at all to pornography. Thus I had not taken on board the preconceptions about women common among British men who, from what I could gather, spent their childhoods glued (with what, I hate to think) to dirty magazines, These they found discarded in hedgerows – much as, in more innocent times, youths might have harvested blackberries.

Instead I brought with me to the UK a set of preconceptions about women peculiarly my own. If I say that my notions about women haunted the realm of fantasy, I'm not referring to the type of fantasies depicted in that grotesque video footage described above. Rather, I had an idea of women as a species of creature created by J.R.R. Tolkein – an unknowable race that belonged in the Middle Earth company of Elvish folk, but had inexplicably strayed into everyday life.

From the notion that women were creatures of other-worldly wonder, I then veered wildly towards the opinion that women were all too manifestly of this world, and that most of them were quite mad to boot. I have since levelled out, and steered a more sensible course. It's now apparent to me that it was not necessarily the women I met who were mad: it was my surroundings that were screwy. Combined with my own odd mindset, this gave me a clarity of perception to rival a funhouse mirror seen through 3-D spectacles.

When I turned up at the University of Sussex, it was not the best environment for a young chap to develop a healthy and balanced attitude towards the opposite sex. For a start, the most visible and voluble portion of the opposite sex seemed to hate my guts for no good reason. Or I thought it was for no good reason. They, conversely, would have claimed they had an excellent reason. I was a man.

On my first day at college, I was handed a leaflet, drafted by the Campus Society for Some or Other Form of Pique, instructing men how to interact with women. It could be encapsulated thus: Don't.

'If you are out in public,' it directed, 'and you see a woman that you know, do not approach her or try to attract her attention. Do not speak to her. If she wants to, she will speak to you.'

It was the era of militant stereotypes now almost extinct in Britain: boiler-suits, bovver boots and such constructive slogans as 'All men are potential rapists' – a statement which, once you reflect on it for a while, you realise is, firstly, unassailable in its logic and, secondly, altogether meaningless. It's true that all men are potential rapists, in as much as they are equipped for the offence; by the same token, all lumberjacks are potential axe murderers.

Having seen nothing else of Britain since my arrival, I had no way of knowing that these people made up a tiny and thoroughly unrepresentative fraction of the nation's females. Many adolescent males maintain, as a way of covering up for their own fear and awkwardness, that women can't abide them. In my case, that belief was down to women telling me so. Some of them had even written pamphlets, or drawn up placards, to get the message across. The fact that it was nothing personal offered little by way of comfort. If they despised all men, that meant they despised me. I didn't much mind about the other men, but felt that it would be nice if, in my case, they could make an exception.

The women in question evidently made a disproportionate impact on folk other than myself. Even today, no sooner does a variety of social malaise manifest itself in Britain than some embittered soul finds a way to link it to 'the feminists'. Nobody's too sure who 'the feminists' actually are. I picture a small group of angry-looking women in a dingy room, plotting the ruin of all that is dear and decent. This image is not plucked from the ether; rather, it's one I repeatedly encountered while at college – usually having stumbled into the aforementioned room believing I was meant to be there. This misconception never lasted more than the half-second it took for every eye to fix upon me with seething rancour. I would then back away on tiptoe – no easy manoeuvre, as you'll know if you've tried it – feeling much as Mitch Brenner must have done in Hitchcock's *The Birds*.

Despoiling the nation's social structure would have been a reach for these pockets of baleful agitators. They were more likely to be focused upon a local outrage. Something generally needed banning. A poster for a pop concert, maybe, or a magazine stocked by the campus newsagent. It was hard to view them as much of a threat to the well-being of the general populace, which is why I would later be so surprised to see them credited as such. Although not half as startled, I suppose, as they would be.

In my first term I was obliged to attend a course called 'Sexual Difference', a topic I thought I had covered comprehensively in O-Level Biology. This, however, was sexual difference as it applied to the arts. Mindful of my habit of turning up at the wrong place, I arrived early for the opening seminar and cautiously poked my head round the door. A young woman was seated alone at the large table. She looked up at me expressionlessly.

'Um, Sexual Difference?' I asked, as if I were offering her a Polo mint.

'What?' she said.

'Is this the Sexual Difference seminar?'

She stared at me like a cat watching a table lamp and said nothing. I came in and sat down. Soon the room filled up and the seminar got under way. I was one of two men there. The rest of the group glared at us with marked distaste. It bothered the other fellow more than it did me. Thanks to my repeated and inadvertent gatecrashing of such events, I was used to it.

The woman I had first spoken to did not utter another word, then or in the weeks to come. She was Swedish, and either her English vocabulary ended at 'what?' or she saw no more reason to be there than I did.

When I started working at the *Fiddler*, again I failed to realise that I hadn't come to the best place to gain an understanding of British women. Not that there was anything wrong with the few women who worked there; with one or two exceptions, they comprised the least cuckoo segment of the personnel. The trouble was the men, and the kind of women they attracted and were attracted to.

Not everyone at the paper had worked out where we stood on the Great Chain of Being (above fish, so far as I could tell, but below the larger, fur-bearing vertebrates). One colleague was a gloomy swain who put me in mind of Des Esseintes, the anti-hero of Joris-Karl Huysmans's *Against Nature*; and who rejoiced in, if nothing else, the pen name of Raynsford Fieldes. Raynsford laboured under the delusion that his role as a scribe endowed him with sexual allure. He would sometimes approach women at gigs, and initiate a conversation on the subject.

'Do you read the music press?'

'Sometimes, yeah.'

'What about the *Harmony Fiddler*?'

'I know it.'

'Are you familiar with the work of Raynsford Fieldes?'

'I think I've heard of him.'

'Well, I am he.'

It took Raynsford a while to realise that he would be

better served by introducing himself as a syphilitic boot-black. The few females who responded positively to such an approach usually turned out to be groupies too damaged and desperate to attach themselves to a band – and bands possess fairly relaxed standards about that kind of thing. Having any truck with such girls was tantamount to equipping a heatstruck gibbon with a machine pistol and giving it the run of your quarters.

There was talk at the *Fiddler* of giving Raynsford his own Agony column, wherein he would provide the agony. The mooted title was 'So You Think You've Got Problems?' The proposition, as you might surmise, was that correspondents would describe their tribulations, and in response Raynsford would tell them how lucky they were not to be him, after what had happened to him only that morning. It's a shame the idea was never put into practice, although if it had been, it's questionable whether Raynsford could have coped with the shock of something working out in his favour for once.

If Raynsford had little to commend him to the pitiless gaze of society, I was no lemon meringue pie myself. I had no illusions about the caste I had joined, nor about the quality of liaison to which it entitled me. I knew very well that only a fissure in the cosmos, a suspension of every natural law, could have allowed The Girlfriend into my life. The consorts of my fellows at the *Fiddler* amply demonstrated it. There, but for fortune – extraordinarily kind fortune – went I.

Most of my friends had desperate luck when it came to women. Admittedly, most of my friends, being of *Fiddler* stock, were not the most sane or stable individuals in the world. Or the country. Or any given room. But even so, they had an unerring knack for selecting mates of a far purer Bedlam bloodline than themselves. Often as not, these women were visibly deranged. They could not have betrayed their insanity any more plainly had they run whooping down the street waving their knickers on a stick.

My friend Terry possessed an uncommon talent for hooking up with such girls. His roster of mercurial inamoratas featured some prize specimens. There was the bulimic daughter of a suspected Nazi war criminal. After Terry sensibly severed their bond, she made a painstakingly non-fatal job of severing the veins in her wrists, and reappeared upon his doorstep, screaming and bleeding in roughly equal profusion. Terry responded in the most reasonable way he could think of: he resumed the relationship for a further, hellish year.

There was a self-professed anarchist and worshipper of all things transgressive, in appearance a living cartoon from the fetishistic Japanese school of Manga art, who simultaneously enhanced this likeness and her breasts at Terry's expense. He was still paying for her enlargement on the never-never long after she abandoned him for the dwarflike frontman of a goth band.

There was a girl who bore a strong facial resemblance to a malevolent field-vole, although in other respects she called to mind a different creature. The last time I had seen anything that matched her for both personal hygiene and gracious conduct was on the Serengeti plains, where it was squatting in a shallow mud puddle alongside the other hyenas. Among her many quirks, each more lovable than the last, she had a delightful habit of savagely kicking Terry in the shins whenever she felt he was paying her insufficient attention, which was always. At dinner in a Chinese restaurant one night, she staged a full-blown tantrum on the basis that he was 'sitting at the wrong angle'.

When the field-vole eventually fell by the wayside, in the same breath shrieking for retribution and pleading for reconciliation, she was succeeded by an affable, down-to-earth Scotswoman with whom the smitten Terry set up home. Within three weeks he had been forced to flee, her acrimonious parting shot ringing in his ears: 'Why are you always so fucking *reasonable*?'

If these were the female leads in Terry's life, their bravura turns were interspersed with characters who, on the basis of more fleeting stage time, contrived all the same to render themselves memorable: the bookseller who posted Terry's own volumes back to him, nicely charred, as though plucked from the embers of a *Sturmabteilung* book-burning; the date who illuminated a Bonfire Night party with a conniption fit that blotted out the fireworks; the girl who summoned him to Liverpool on a promise, fulfilled it and then – by way of pillow talk – cooed in his ear, 'You know, I have a knife under this bed.'

These women had one thing in common (two, if you count Terry). With the exception of the anarchist, who couldn't blink without setting off alarms and a red flag, they were closet lunatics, canny enough to keep the bats cooped up in their belfries until Terry was duly captivated. Terry could have walked into a Wembley Stadium brimful of women and picked out the functional psychopath in seconds, without ever understanding how.

Barney Flint was more typical of my peers, in that he opted for the flagrant variety of bampot every time. When I met Barney, in the early 1990s, he had recently concluded a dalliance with a girl called Maria. Suddenly, it was fair to say, that name would never be the same to him. Maria was in the habit of calling up Barney's house and issuing terrible threats down the phone. By terrible threats, I don't mean threats that were violent or spiteful, although they certainly were that, too. I mean threats that were of a very poor standard.

Maria usually managed to time these calls for when Barney was indoors. When he was out one night, his brother Dan answered the phone instead.

'Is that Barney?' said Maria.

'No, it's Dan,' said Dan.

'Right, Dan, you can tell Barney he'd better look out. I mean it this time. I've paid some skinheads to beat the shit out of him and when they're finished he'll be sorry he ever –'

'What skinheads?' said Dan.

'Nasty skinheads, horrible ones. They're going to –'

'There aren't any skinheads round here any more,' said Dan. 'Not proper ones. Where have you been? The only skinheads left are gay, and they've all got poodles. You might as well say you've hired the Knights of fucking Malta to kick his head in. Can't you do any better than that?'

Barney's gift for finding doolally women never deserted him. If they weren't teetering on second-floor window sills or gouging abstract patterns into their limbs with kitchen knives, they were running off on a whim to join the army, or auditioning for strip joints on a dare. And most of my other male friends were embroiled in similar relationships. They so often wound up with wackjobs that I came to question whether the deck was stacked. Did Terry and Barney always choose the Queen of Nuts because all the cards were the Queen of Nuts?

It took a while for me to realise that the reverse was true. The problem was not British womenfolk as a whole, but my pals. They all griped about the behaviour of their girlfriends and wives, but they took no interest in prospects who weren't completely loopy.

Like women who wonder why they 'keep going out with bastards', these men had to shoulder their share of the blame. Sane women just weren't exciting enough for them. My friends wanted girls who would have sex with them in train toilets; or spend five hours before a party transforming themselves into a sluttier facsimile of Lana Turner. Then they complained when what had been as clear as daylight to everyone else finally revealed itself to them: these girls were cracked, from shell to yolk, from tip to toe, from stern to prow.

The Girlfriend, when I asked for her opinion on this hypothesis, submitted a corollary of her own: that all the men and women we knew had been exposed, at an impressionable age, to the French movie *Betty Blue*, with disastrous repercussions.

This made a degree of sense: *Betty Blue* was the definitive arthouse flick of the late 1980s, when my contemporaries and I were – in the eyes of the law, if not by any other definition – entering adulthood. I had watched it myself, only to be so thrown by the lengthy opening sex scene that everything thereafter was lost on me. Others hadn't escaped so lightly. If *Betty Blue* had a message to impart (and let's allow right here the possibility that it didn't), that message was: there is nothing more enthralling to men than a good-looking madwoman.

It was a message which appeared to have sunk in among the film's male and female audience alike. If the character of Betty Blue was what men wanted, that's what they were going to get. I know men who've been getting it for the best part of two decades and, aside from the occasional suicide attempt, they don't seem to have tired of it yet.

Maybe it's stretching the point to attribute the Falling for Crazies phenomenon to a single work of cinema. After all, for those who didn't frequent arthouses, the key film of the era was *Top Gun*, and if that generated a lasting upsurge in homoerotic militarism, then it escaped my notice.

Perhaps a richer source of clues is to be found in advertising. Adverts are telling of their times. Not because they are honest – quite the opposite – but because they present to their audience the image of itself that the advertisers assume it wants to see. On my brief visits to the UK in the 1970s, I saw TV adverts aimed at men, featuring women as commodities, or jokes, or both. In the 1990s, the tables began to turn, until finally there was no mistaking that men were now the butts. If advertisers believe they can sell things to women by showing men as idiots, then they must also believe that those women think men truly are idiots.

One television advert of recent times sticks in my mind – a much-screened pitch on behalf of a well-known motoring organisation. It depicts a youngish couple, as they ready themselves for a social occasion, discussing car insurance. Although I should qualify that summary. Car insurance is the subject, all right, but discussion there is none. There is simply a plaintive fool of a man being read the riot act by his paramour, who weighs in on the side of the sponsor.

'But my dad –' begins the poor sap, and gets no further. His attempt to foist generations of male witlessness upon Mrs Sap is given short shrift. Not so much riding roughshod over his objections as blitzkrieging them, his lady love consigns him to perdition with a brief, brutal account of just how wrong he is and why; concluding with a snarl of, 'So everybody's happy. Except you, apparently. And your bloody dad.' Clearly, all is now set fair for a cracking night out.

You'd assume this advert was directed at women, in the hope that they would identify with the female character. And maybe they did. I couldn't say. What I can vouch for is that many of those male friends I asked about it replied that they squirmed with recognition every time the clip came on. They found themselves flinching involuntarily, in concert with the hapless Simon, as I think his name was.

It seemed to be a given among my friends' partners that my friends were imbeciles sent to try them. These men would not merit the women's patience even if the women had any. It was as if the men were wrong in thought, wrong in word, wrong in deed, wrong wrongity wrong.

And should they object to being snapped at, slapped down, interrupted, insulted, humiliated or simply trampled underfoot, then it was their own fault for being so damn wrong.

Perhaps I mistakenly ascribed to changing times something brought about by a change in my own scenery. Maybe it was always like this in Britain. But not, I suspect, to this degree. Every generation has its battleaxes, but only lately has the choice of female personae been pared down to dragon or doormat. The advert is a giveaway on that. Ads aimed at women have spent years portraying men as daft, bumbling, well-intentioned, got-to-love-'em-really, overgrown kids. Now there is a trend to represent us as insufferable pillocks who richly deserve every iota of ire visited upon us. And again, even if we warrant some of it, surely we don't warrant all of it. Yet pick any man of my acquaintance and it's even money that he's accustomed to being treated by his wife or girlfriend with instant and thoroughgoing contempt whenever she begs to differ with him, or vice versa.

I would, again, be happy to accept that this says more about my friends than it does about British women. In fact, I wouldn't doubt it, if it weren't for the advert itself, which suggests a broader tendency than my immediate circle.

The last thing I wish to do here is provide any kind of ammunition for the whinging poltroons who make up the loosely affiliated 'men's movement'. If you're going to form a movement, Lord knows there are more pressing problems in the world than a tendency among thirty-something middle-class British women to be overly brusque. My point, such as it is, goes beyond the domestic bickering undeservingly glorified by the epithet 'The Battle of the Sexes'. My point is simply that courtesy is a thing of value. Its decline across the country is lamentable, but for it to disappear from our most intimate relationships would be particularly hard to bear.

Given that I arrived in Britain in the mid-1980s and have lived here ever since, it often seems to me that I could not have timed it better had I wanted to witness the slow death in this country, not only of good manners, but also of common sense. Of course, I didn't want to witness that, not at all. But as my encounters with Barney's dodgy videotapes so instructively affirmed, once you've seen something, you can't un-see it. In both cases, I wish I could.

CHAPTER ELEVEN

THE SLEEP OF REASON

ONE WINDSWEPT AFTERNOON IN the spring of 1994, at a café in Brighton's North Laines, I sat at an outdoor table, essaying a poor impression of an urbane boulevardier, justly disregarded by all except the local panhandlers.

I had just dipped my snout into what the management called a cappuccino – although the Trades Descriptions Act might have begged to differ – when a conversation from the next table, defying the adverse gusts by dint of sheer foghorn volume, pierced the empty thought-bubble over my head and choked it with static.

'So,' blared one young woman, in a voice that smelled of tweed and wet Labradors, 'have you been to see your medium yet?'

'Oh, yah,' replied her companion, her tone more

redolent of the Harvey Nichols perfume counter. 'She says I'm basically a really good person.'

With a heroic effort, I stifled a guffaw that would have sprayed lukewarm brown water as far as the opposite pavement, where a morose hippy shared a blanket with a small selection of disheartening jewellery.

If the British are unduly suspicious of intellectualism, then at least they are also suspicious of mysticism. These traits have common roots in a mistrust of mumbo-jumbo. Or so I once thought. Sadly, I was deluded; and it was at around this time that I began to see it. While the first misgiving remains intractable as ever, the second has been visibly dwindling for more than decade. A country which, on my arrival, I admiringly associated with a blunt species of rationalism, has gone skipping down the petal-strewn path to la-la-land in double-quick-step.

Because I live in Brighton, a town largely inhabited by New Agers, I didn't at first notice how swiftly the rest of the UK was catching up. It still astounds me that by leaving a Third-World nation, and relocating to the country which engendered the industrial revolution, I could have fetched up in a more superstitious society.

Where I came from, people were scared of chameleons and witches, but they seldom let that interrupt their day. In Britain, people actively boasted about practising witchcraft (although in fairness, I have yet to meet anyone claiming to be a chameleon). And ordinary folk – not just wild-eyed adherents of Wicca cults – pursued the most extraordinary creeds. They trusted not only in newspaper horoscopes (which for the most part are guarded, vague advice columns), but in dowsing, homeopathy, aromatherapy, auras, chakras, re-birthing and – of course – mediums. How much my neighbour at the coffee shop paid her medium per hour, I can only guess. But I am willing to bet that for half of it, I too would happily have assured her that she was, basically, a really good person.

I'd once enjoyed – or at least, undergone – a shortish liaison with a girl who took a serious interest in astrology, and treated it as a science. She had textbooks, star charts, geometric diagrams, the whole *tzimmis* – and it did look impressively scientific. So, in its time, did the flight deck of the *Starship Enterprise*. You can safely label anything a science when the results are too nebulous to be proven right or wrong.

I couldn't dissuade Tessa from compiling my astrological chart. I don't think a troop of Cossack horsemen could have dissuaded her.

'With Virgo rising,' she predicted, 'as you get older, you will not look your age. As you get past your forties it's as if time freezes you.' Having had the appearance of being in my forties since infancy, I was pleased to hear this. 'But when Jupiter rises it means you'll put on weight from the age of forty-five.' That was less welcome news. I envisioned my embarking upon middle age a dead ringer for the fat kid from *Grange Hill*.

Comparing my chart to her own, Tessa deduced that she and I were highly compatible, and might well have been paired in a past life. Looking at my chart afterwards, I noticed that she'd based it on an incorrect birthdate. Perhaps we weren't so compatible after all.

On the shelves in Tessa's flat, self-help books jostled for space. She was the first person I knew who paid serious attention to such guides. I thought she must be the anomaly. It turned out that, in Brighton, she was far from exceptional; and once again, the rest of the country wasn't far behind.

I had assumed the very notion of self-help – involving, as it inevitably did, gazing like Narcissus into the shallow but captivating pool of one's own disposition – would run contrary to what I fondly imagined to be the British character. A truly British self-help book, so I'd have hoped, would be called something like *Sweep It Under Your Inner Carpet*. It would feature, among its many useful chapters: Pull Your Socks Up; Can't Complain – Won't Complain; For Christ's Sake, Get a Grip on Yourself, Man; and (for parents in need of child-rearing advice) One More Peep Out of You and I'll Give You Something to Really Cry About. As usual, I was wrong.

The key to selling self-help is the same factor that keeps mediums, astrologers and the like in work. People love talking about themselves, but even more than that, they love hearing about themselves. They will believe anything so long as it sounds like praise. Say to them, for instance, 'You are admirably simple and direct in your thinking', and they will agree. A minute later, you can add, 'There's a fascinating complexity to the way your mind works', and they will nod assent to that, too.

To do this for a wider audience all at once, you need to come up with bromides sufficiently vague to make any number of people feel you are talking directly to them and about them. There's a craft to this; any newsprint stargazer worth his or her zodiac will have worked out how to dispense bland, all-purpose homilies – usually unarguable admonitions urging either caution or zeal – while still maintaining the fiction that several hundred million people might be conjoined in both their character and their destiny by the accident of their birthdate.

The New Age tide has heaped up self-help like seaweed on a gale-struck shore. Self-help is everywhere, and the more there is of it, the more people seem to need it. In Brighton, garrison of the touchy-feely vanguard, I was well placed to witness the final, unmistakable quivering of the formerly stiff British upper lip, before open weeping and wailing broke out. Another laudable – to my mind – characteristic of the nation was about to perish, washed away in a tearful tide of self-pity.

It was the loss of Diana Spencer that finally did the trick. But it could have been anything, just so long as it was widely publicised. It felt less like the death of the People's Princess and more like the death of the People's Puppy. To my genuine bemusement, half the country appeared to be bawling like four-year-olds (the other half, although you'd never have known it from the media reports, were not much concerned).

Such a response from those closest to a young mother tragically killed would be more than understandable; of course, in this instance, they were the ones least likely to put on such a public display. It was those who knew the woman only as a fashion plate or screen image who reacted as if all the clocks must be stopped. Diana was an empty vessel into which they poured their own peculiar fixations and fantasies. I believed they cried for themselves, without knowing it, and without knowing why, that being among the chief consequences of too much fretful navel-gazing.

I'm not alone in this view. In February 2004, a think tank called Civitas issued a report in which they identified a new malady: mourning sickness, 'a religion for the lonely crowd that no longer subscribes to orthodox churches. Its flowers and teddies are its rites, its collective minutes' silences its liturgy and mass . . . but these new bonds are phoney, ephemeral and cynical.'

In my time here, I have seen much of Britain gradually succumb to the unthinking assumption that there is no distinction between a feeling and fact – surely the only explanation for the widespread perception of the flighty, manipulative and over-indulged Diana as a saint. I once watched a television documentary on genetically modified crops, in which an anti-GM activist was interviewed. A middle-aged woman, possessed of the haughty and unshakeable assurance in her own rightness that comes with a lifetime at the top of the social tree, she had this to say: 'I don't understand the science, I only understand my basic emotions and instincts. And through not understanding the science I have come to very instinctive conclusions about what I believe in . . . you rely on your intuitions, your emotions and your instincts and you basically say, "I don't trust it, stop."'

The premise behind this statement – that the impulses of a pashmina-clad society dowager should outweigh and potentially invalidate the conclusions of scientific enquiry – was so extraordinary that for a minute or more I could only gawp at the screen, wave my hands about and issue stifled squawking noises that barely made it past my tonsils. I had to seek out a transcript of the programme to make sure I had not misheard. I hadn't.

It was not the fact that this woman should think as she did that astonished me. It was the fact that she did not hesitate to voice this claim on national television, confident that she could expect not ridicule but sympathy. She did not go so far as to call for anyone to be burned as a witch, but her method of judging the issue had little to distinguish it, in terms of its efficacy, from the ducking stool.

The week Diana Spencer died, I changed the outgoing greeting on my answering machine. 'Hello,' it now ran, 'I can't get to the phone right now. I'm out on the roof putting the flag at half-mast.' I came home to find a series of indignant messages, one of which accused me of mocking the dead. I certainly wasn't doing that. I was mocking the living. The death of a human being may qualify as a tragedy; a shift in the way a public persona is perceived does not. As Elvis Presley's manager, Colonel Tom Parker, noted upon the King's demise, 'Elvis didn't die. The body did. It doesn't mean a damned thing . . . this changes nothing.'

It was Diana who defined the modern British celebrity not as somebody who Does but as somebody who simply Is. Her long shadow still shelters a host of nonentities, all of them driven not by a desire to achieve, but by a will to fame. Working at *Blasted*, you often met these wannabes, usually as they were disrobing for a photo shoot.

One young woman – let's call her Valerie – stopped by the office to discuss her appearance in a forthcoming feature. The editor presented her with a jacket created to promote the magazine. She pulled it on.

'It's nice,' she said. 'But why doesn't it say *"Blasted"* on it?'

Seb, the handsome, anxious designer, sucked in his breath through his teeth and said, 'Er, it does, Val – there on the back.'

Valerie tried to look over her shoulder. When that didn't work, she turned round. Still unable to see the lettering, she kept turning, rotating like a dreidel until Seb, with an expression of anguish carved into his symmetrical features, reached out a hand, gently grasped her shoulder and brought her to a halt.

'It's no good,' said Valerie. 'I still can't see it. And now I'm all dizzy.'

'Now?' muttered Seb.

Unhindered by talent or aptitude, Valerie went on to enjoy a career as a television presenter. You couldn't go so far as to call her a television personality, as she had no personality to speak of. And compared to what would follow her into British homes, Valerie might have been Joan Bakewell. The country was embarking upon an era where the only prerequisite for renown was the eagerness to push yourself forward. Perhaps, in an expansion of the tacit, fetishistic compact between voyeurs and exhibitionists, the curtain-twitching nosiness of an earlier age had transferred its attention to mass media. What could be more titillating to a multitude of busybodies than an unending supply of complaisant show-offs? It would explain the contemporary, misnamed phenomenon of Reality TV. The self-regarding, witless bores who populate those programmes patently hold their every utterance and action to be a source of fascination. And millions tune in, fascinated. Proving to the bores that they were right all along.

The contestants on *Big Brother* and its like are the kind of people I have spent my time in Britain trying very hard to avoid. It's difficult. There are more of them every year. If, as I do, you spend a fair bit of time on public transport, you'll know that they make it their second home. And, feeling at home as they do, they happily and loudly chat away about any topic, no matter how tedious or how intimate, on the telephone.

When I started working at the *Fiddler*'s office, I was obliged to become a rail commuter, one of a small army of lost souls who make the daily voyage from A to B and B back to A, wishing all the while that they could stay put in A and let B go rot.

The Hatfield train disaster revealed the scandalous state of Britain's rail network to the country as a whole, but it was no revelation to those of us who until then used it week in and week out. Britain's trains remain a joke throughout the mechanised world. Visitors look on them as a quaint anachronism, on a par with mule-powered funiculars in Paraguay. Instead of goats and chickens, they transport wet dogs, spoilt children, teenage gangs, fetid drunks and harassed workers. On a typical peak-hour journey all of the above clamber aboard a tiny number of carriages laughably ill-equipped for the task of dragging this babbling, screeching cargo across the landscape at speeds too low to stun a gnat. Frequent and lengthy stops are made for signal failures, broken rolling stock, sightings of the Virgin Mary and the loading of further luckless passengers into the luggage racks. Second class is worse still.

Among the most keenly cherished beliefs I had held about Britain as a nipper was its role as the epicentre of good manners. When I came here to live, in 1986, I found that reputation generally held true.

My first memories of British rail travel conjure up a golden age when everyone hid behind rustling news-papers, refusing to so much as catch one another's eye, let alone engage in conversation. Only if the train suddenly lurched off the rails, tipped onto the embankment and sat there at an angle for three-quarters of an hour without a word of explanation over the Tannoy, would one of the bolder and more extrovert passengers lower their broad-sheet, grin nervously, clear their throat and say,

'Bloody typical, eh?'

That was before the two-pronged assault on civility initiated by the privatisation of the railways and the pop-ularising of mobile telephones. On its own, each of these occurrences had the potential to turn a courteous wayfar-er into the most vulgar of churls; combined, the effect was irresistible.

Out of all the inconveniences and frustrations intrinsic to rail journeys, nothing else preys on the goodwill of ticket-holders to the same degree as the mobile phone. Screaming babies long overdue for nappy changes are tolerated as a relatively minor irritation. But the high, wild ring of that sharp little bell incenses fellow travellers beyond measure.

You can almost see the steam rising from their ears and clouding what's left of the windows.

To paraphrase the American gun lobby, mobiles don't annoy people, people do. Responsible cellphone use is both easy, and all but nonexistent. For a start, you could remember that you actually have a phone at your disposal. The person you're talking to may be in the next county, but your voice doesn't have to carry that far unaided. Potentially, you can conduct a quieter conversation with the little silver device pressed against your ear than with the occupant of the seat opposite. In fact, you should never speak to the occupant of the seat opposite, unless you know their mobile number. Nobody else in the carriage wants to hear your fortissimo discussion of office politics.

Another rule for the considerate phone owner, if such a chimera were to ever manifest itself: don't call your mother. Or your lawyer. Or anyone with whom you have just started a sexual relationship. Or anyone with whom you are about to finish one. This is as much for your own sake as your fellow passengers'. You may suddenly find yourself in a deathly silent carriage with every eye fixed upon you, and every mouth set in a cruel smirk or hanging open in astonishment. There are few humiliations to compare with realising that you have unwittingly performed a solo recreation of *The Jerry Springer Show* in front of a sizeable audience. An audience, don't forget, that you are likely to encounter twice daily for the remainder of your career.

The single most conspicuous change I have seen in British life since I moved to the UK is the crumbling of the once sturdy barrier between the public and private worlds. It may seem incongruous for a memoirist, who willingly introduces his private world into the public one, to say so, but I was very much in favour of that barrier. It was a facet of Britishness that I treasured (following years in Africa, where the division hardly exists), and I arrived just in time to see it vanish. I have no doubt at all that mobile handsets brought about its passing.

The mobile phone appeared in the wake of its only known prophylactic: the personal stereo. A pair of headphones is the traveller's one shield against the bores who never think anything that they don't say, loudly. At the time I came to live in Britain, a host of social commentators was united in the opinion that the personal stereo was a terrible thing, a contraption to detach and isolate its user from society. Those social commentators failed to grasp that this was the whole point of it. For a people as averse to uninvited social contact as the British were not so long ago (and I still possess that old-fashioned attribute myself), the personal stereo came as less of a luxury than a relief. A copy of *The Times* was a good start, but it was bound to be superseded by something with batteries.

A walkmen or iPod carries inside it your own little world. As with the mobile phone, in the hands of an inconsiderate owner that world tends to spill over into everyone else's. But without it, you would have no defence against the small child who plays pocket video games at full volume, breaking off periodically to stare at you as if you have, unbeknownst to you, a family of starlings nesting on your head; and then to shout,

'Dad! Dad! Dad! DAD! DAD!'
'Not now, Toby. I'm on the phone.'

Supping my mediocre coffee on that Brighton pavement, I could have no inkling that the conversation I'd just overheard might one day hold such resonance for me. It was Elijah's cloud, no larger than a man's hand, presaging a deluge of abject nonsense. If I had to fix upon one moment when the Britain I had hoped for became the Britain I now live in, that would be it.

'And what about your love life?' trumpeted the first young woman.

'She said nobody could really love me until I learn to love myself,' said her friend, a little peevishly, as if she held the medium and not the message culpable in her heartache. She caught me looking over in her direction and glowered at me. I quickly turned my head the other way, musing to myself that, like the medium, I would like to be an able enough bluffer to parlay a few yards of flannel into a career. Then it struck me that I wrote journalism for a living.

I stood up, blew the querulous young madam a kiss and sauntered off with a swagger only slightly impaired by a pebble, lodged in the tread of my shoe, tapping out a rhythm on the flagstones.

CHAPTER TWELVE

FORM IS TEMPORARY, CLASS IS PERMANENT

IT WOULD HAVE BEEN, I suppose, the autumn of 1995; night had fallen by five o'clock. By six, I was on a platform at Blackfriars station. A brisk wind blew down the Thames and spattered my face with drizzle. I waited in the faint hope that my train would not pull up with fewer than the required number of carriages, owing to 'a shortage of rolling stock', 'vandalism' or 'solar flare activity'.

The southbound Thameslink arrived and I boarded it. After putting in my hours at the *Fiddler*, I liked to distract myself on the journey back to Brighton by playing – quietly – a mindlessly addictive game called Minesweeper on a laptop computer. As usual, the carriage interior called to mind Dixons on a busy Saturday: the shrilling of cellphones; the clatter of computer keys; the hissing of headphones. I swung my screen open, to the umbrage of a rather rough-looking passenger a few rows along from me. He reacted like a tree-dweller whose medicine man had warned him about glowing boxes full of bad juju. No doubt he was already irked by the company he was forced to keep, but my advent provided the decisive spur. He stood up, grabbed his luggage and tramped towards the exit, pausing by the seat I was lucky enough to have snaffled.

'I didn't come all the way from Yorkshire to sit with a bunch of bloody yuppies!' he growled.

'In that case,' I said, 'you've been going in the wrong direction.'

It surprised me that I should qualify in anyone's eyes as a yuppie – a young upwardly mobile professional. I was young, granted. But any upward mobility I might have enjoyed, I did so purely by default: there was no other way to go. As a contributor to a weekly music paper, I could have diminished my social standing only by developing a partiality to meths, or by stealing from charity collection tins. As for the notion that I could be described as 'professional', it would have caused enough amusement at the *Fiddler* to leave several of the veterans in need of medical attention.

Whereas anyone else might reasonably have taken me for a vagrant who had stolen a computer, the chap on the train had called me a yuppie simply because I owned a laptop, this was the south and that was the most damning verdict he could muster.

All countries are divided by regionalism, but few are riven by it in the way of Britain. To begin with, no other country comprises four separate nations, with each of the three smaller ones bearing a longstanding grudge against the biggest. The biggest, meanwhile, may occasionally affect to despise the smaller three in passing, but in truth it has other enmities to pursue. An Englishman has only to open his mouth for another Englishman to cite George Bernard Shaw's dictum that an Englishman has only to open his mouth for another Englishman to despise him.

When I was attempting to blend in, Zelig-like, to the British backdrop, and my accent embarked on a national tour before settling on a generically southern inflection, it caused me all sorts of bother. I frequently gave the impression I hailed from somewhere that whoever I was talking to did not; somewhere, what's more, they didn't much like. This isn't hard, as nowhere in Britain do you find people who like anywhere else in Britain. Liverpudlians took me for a Mancunian, Mancunians assumed me to be from Leeds, Leeds folk had me down as some variety of cockney (not that they cared which; to their minds, the cockneys started at Sheffield).

In light of this I had developed a worse habit yet – that of unconsciously adopting the inflections of those around me. This only made things worse, as those people thereafter inferred I was mocking them.

It takes years to fathom how deeply regional grudges and resentments are bred in the British bone. As a rule, everybody dislikes everybody else; and the closer to home that everybody else is, the more everybody dislikes them. There are folk in Yorkshire, for example, who disdain southerners, detest Lancastrians, and utterly abhor the people across town. The contempt in which they hold those neighbours at the far end of the street is probably beyond the capacity of the English language to express.

The cartographer has yet to be born who could map the ley lines of territorial rancour across the UK. Football rivalries provide a chart of sorts, but one that is misshapen and unreliable – a three-dimensional cat's-cradle of tangled strands and counter-tensions. In Britain, hostilities never end; they simply transfer themselves to stadia. Any conflict in the country's history that you care to name – the Wars of the Roses, say, or the Battle of the Boyne – is still being fought out via the agency of football. This is preferable to other parts of Europe, where such disputes continue to be pursued on the battlefield, but it does make supporting a football team a tricky business. Particularly if the football team you support is Manchester United. When you're trying to blend in, and not attract opprobrium, innocently announcing your allegiance to United is very much a step in the wrong direction. A supporter of any other club will despise you reflexively.

'Another plastic, eh? Why don't you support your hometown team?'

'My hometown team is AFC Leopards. It's a bit tricky finding their games on the TV.'

Faced with the obvious fact that you aren't from Manchester, some United supporters will scorn you as a Johnny-come-lately, fair-weather fan ('fan' can be a putdown on its own, insinuating flimsy and fickle support). I have what might be considered a reasonable if unusual defence to this charge. My support for United dates back to 1974. I was six years old, and had not long since moved to Nairobi. Up the street lived my best friend, Alan Forrest. Alan was an English expatriate, a Manc – although at that stage, I wouldn't have had the first clue what a Manc was.

Alan had a table football game, with red men and blue men. When we played, the red side always had to be his. I asked him why.

'Because,' he told me, 'they're Manchester United, the greatest football team in the world.'

As they were also the only football team I'd ever heard of, I believed him. Of course, the little sod didn't mention they'd just been relegated. Maybe he didn't know himself. It was almost impossible to track English football results in Nairobi at that time, particularly if you were six. Still, 'Georgie Best, Superstar' made for an excellent playground chant – the jury was out on whether he wore frilly knickers and a see-through bra; or whether he was riding round the corner in a Jaguar, nonchalantly eluding the police by virtue of his supersonic underwear. And Georgie Best played for United. Or so I believed. In fact, George Best had left United shortly before they were relegated, but Alan didn't tell me that either. I wonder if he later went into public relations.

During my teens, my interest in football was eclipsed by my obsession with pop music (here, a devotee was unarguably a fan rather than a supporter), and dwindled almost out of existence. But just as there is no such thing as an ex-Catholic, so a football supporter can only describe himself as lapsed. Slowly, in the darkness of my subconscious, the roots regained their hold; shoots began to sprout into my waking mind. By the opening of the 1994–5 football season, I was ready to take sides again – just in time to watch the title United had won two years running slip agonisingly from the club's clutches. Even as a glory hunter, I was a dismal failure.

My passion for football had been rekindled by the 1994 FA Cup final, in which United played Chelsea. Barney Flint invited me to his flat to watch it on television, along with a crowd of his pals from south London, where he had grown up. Predictably, they were all behind Chelsea.

'Come round and cheer them on with us,' he said.

'I can't,' I said. 'I have to back United.'

He looked at me the way people usually do when I tell them which club I support.

'I thought you weren't that bothered about football.'

'I'd still have to back United, from when I was a kid.'

'Well, come round anyway – you can sit with Frederick.'

Frederick Flint, it transpired, was another Southern Red. He and I were allocated footstools at the far end of the living room; while the Chelsea mob piled around the TV, regaled each other with happy tales of fleeing from other Londoners at Stamford Bridge and The Den ('So he cornered me and said, "I'm gonna kick your fucking eyes out!"'), and bellowed the songs of their youth:

> Carefree
> Wherever you may be
> 'Cos we are the famous CFC
> And we don't give a fuck, whoever you
>   may be
> 'Cos we are the famous CFC

On the television, Status Quo began to perform United's FA Cup anthem, 'Come On, You Reds', then on its way to the number one spot.

'Why don't Chelsea have one of those?' groused Barney. 'I don't see why we can't have a cup final song in the charts.'

'You do,' said Frederick. 'You must have heard it, it's been all over the radio.'

'No, we don't.'

'Yes, you do. It's in the top ten right now. It's called "Loser".'

At the mention of Beck's hit single, a fusillade of lager cans, cigarette ends and crisp packets descended upon us. The same thing happened when Eric Cantona's first penalty went in on sixty-one minutes; and again when, on sixty-seven minutes, he converted his second. It was remarkable how much lager, tobacco and snack-food they'd managed to get through in six minutes.

Re-immersing myself in all things Red, I found out who my enemies ought to be. I was supposed to despise Leeds United. It was obligatory to hold Liverpudlians in contempt. And oddly, but in keeping with the British bent for loathing your neighbour, Mancunians were the most odious of all – if they were Blue. Matchdays aside (when red and blue shirts might be worn), Blue was mostly a state of mind, as was Red. Football is all about states of mind. As life bore down upon me more heavily, the way it does for all of us as we sink feet first into the mire of adulthood, I came to realise the true worth of football: it was the one thing you could think about that would stop you thinking about anything else at all. A true and beneficent opium of the masses, and of the individual.

Football was something you could care about deeply, even absolutely, safe in the knowledge that it was ultimately unimportant – which is not, it must be emphasised, the same thing as insignificant. There a few things, if any, more significant to a British football supporter than his (or less commonly, her) club.

There was no need for me to develop an aversion to Leeds United – everything I knew about them had cultivated in me such a distaste that it was a relief to determine it wouldn't go to waste. The Leeds sides of the late 1960s and early 1970s stood out for their savagery, dishonesty and ruthlessness – as exemplified in the nickname of defender Norman 'Bites Yer Legs' Hunter – and their supporters were cast from the same mould. The old Man United song put it neatly:

> Now, Leeds as a city's a mighty fine place
> But the fans and the team are a fucking
>   disgrace.

Liverpool was more of a stretch. I had a grudging respect for the footballing achievements of LFC – a club that in the 1970s and 1980s had won everything there was to win, and beaten every team put before it – and my friendships with Matt and Catherine had prevented me from viewing Liverpudlians through the jaundice-tinted spectacles worn by so many other Britons. It's a chicken-and-egg conundrum, whether the general British attitude towards Liverpool is a result of that city's peculiar self-regard, or the cause of it.

'You Scousers think you're a nation unto yourselves,' I once overheard Barney Flint admonish a mutual acquaintance. 'More than that, you think you're a race apart. No other city does that. I'm from south London – nobody round there thinks of themselves that way.'

'True,' acknowledged our Scouse pal. 'You south Londoners aren't a race.' He thought about it for a moment. 'But you are a *breed*.'

So Liverpudlians didn't bother me. Indeed, it wouldn't have occurred to me that I had a right to be bothered by Liverpudlians as a whole; or by anyone else who made a better fist of being British than I did, or simply made a better fist. Liverpool itself, however, did bother me. The first time I visited, a gang of scallies stole my hat from my head – the pettiest of incidents. It was a stupid hat, and I was probably better off without it, but it was mine, all the same, and I would rather it had stayed that way. Liverpool invoked in me that angry, helpless childhood sensation of falling among bullies, and the experience soured me on the place.

The city's reputation as a crime-ridden hellhole may be exaggerated, especially in recent times, but it has proved almost impossible to shake. I read a story not long ago in Brighton's local newspaper, reporting a CID raid on a drug den populated by heroin addicts. The policeman in charge of the operation described what he found there, concluding with a splendid throwaway line, unencumbered by any comment from the writer. It was, said the detective, one of the most sordid, repulsive, depraved and degenerate scenes he had witnessed in his entire career – 'and I used to work on Merseyside.'

The relationship between the four nations that constitute the United Kingdom may not be simple, but it is at least easier to unsnarl than the Gordian knot which binds together the English in a resentful muddle of claustrophobia. About Northern Ireland, there isn't much that can be usefully, or safely, added to the heavy-hearted awareness that almost all Britons already possess. The Scots scorn the English; or at least, enough of them do to make it seem that way. The English are amused by Scots, and fail to notice how often England ends up being governed by them. The Welsh, meanwhile, are convinced that everybody hates them.

For a while, I believed this myself. Everywhere I went, people sneered at the Welsh and cracked jokes at their expense. Even Blakey, who was Welsh himself, was inclined to have a go at his countrymen. He once asked me if I'd heard of Dai Guevara.

'No,' I said. The only Dai I knew of featured in a geography textbook I had studied at school, although not very assiduously. 'This is Dai Evans,' read the chapter on agriculture in the Rhondda valley. 'Dai Evans is a farmer. Every morning Dai Evans takes his sheep . . .' If I'd paid attention, I might have absorbed the makings of a few lazy, routine gags about Dai Evans taking his sheep, and that would have come in handy a couple of years down the line. But this was the point at which my attention drifted to the next desk, occupied by a heartstopping Italian girl with sienna suede for skin and lips like a cleft plum.

'No?' said Blakey. 'You never heard about Dai Guevara, the Welsh revolutionary?' He shook his head, and our colleagues around the pub table *tsk*-ed and rolled their eyes at my ignorance. 'He was a well-known figure in the seventies. He kept blowing himself up, trying to build bombs to attack power stations. They used to have him on *Nationwide*, ranting about Welsh independence, covered in bandages. Usually his arms, but one time his whole head was just bandages, like the invisible man, with a beret on top . . .'

Blakey was well aware that *Nationwide*, the show which took local news to a national audience for no discernible reason, was one more British touchstone I knew of only by reputation. It only dawned upon me long afterwards that he had made the whole thing up. I have been unable to turn up one shred of evidence for Dai Guevara's ever having existed. A pity. I would have preferred to go on believing it.

Still, I would never have dared to joke about the Welsh to Blakey. I wasn't in the practice of joking about the Welsh to anybody. I was alone in that. The Welsh, I soon learned, were stooges and straight men for the whole of Britain, whether in the pub or in the media. I didn't get what it was about the Welsh that precipitated so much mockery. None of the Welsh people I'd met seemed out of the ordinary. Or at least, bearing in mind Paul Worth was also a Welshman, none of them seemed out of the ordinary owing to their Welshness. If there was such a quality as Welshness, I couldn't see what defined it.

At last I worked it out. There is one reason and one reason only that everyone pokes fun at the Welsh: they react. The Welsh are the national equivalent of the boy at school who invariably erupted in impotent fury when provoked – so nobody could resist giving him a prod and watching him go off. The Scots know better, collectively speaking. A

cheap stereotypical joke aimed at the Scots in a newspaper or on television will not, as a rule, result in a post-
bag bursting with indignant rage. The same stunt aimed
at the Welsh almost invariably will, which is why it happens so often.

This disposition frequently betrays itself in conversation, too. Incensed at yet another slur upon his country-
folk in the pages of the *Fiddler*, Paul Worth launched
himself into an agitated polemic, worthy of Dai Guevara.
The fact that he happened, at that moment, to be wearing
a beret and a small beard only heightened the likeness in
my mind's eye.

'It isn't funny. You wouldn't think it was funny if it was
about anyone else . . .'

I didn't think it was funny even when it was about the
Welsh, but I thought his reaction hilarious.

'. . . having a go at the Welsh is just the last acceptable
form of racism.'

'No, it isn't,' I said.

'It is. Tell me – why isn't it racism?'

'Because nobody ever got beaten up for walking down
the street looking Welsh. Except, perhaps, in Wales.'

At this, Paul began to imitate a large and unsecured
Catherine Wheel, and I judged I had taken the subject far
enough.

My comprehension may have broadened enough to encompass regional rivalries, but there was still the matter of
class to contend with. Compared to class, territorialism
was a game of tic tac toe (or noughts and crosses, as I now

knew to call it). The intricacies of class in the UK are such that I've yet to meet a born-and-bred Briton who can explain them. An outsider has no more chance of making sense of them than a fruit fly has of mastering astrophysics. Perhaps even less; the laws which govern astrophysics are, if not immutable, at least consistent. The laws which govern class, depending as they do entirely upon perception, are infinitely and arbitrarily changeable.

The phrase generally used in Britain is 'the class system'. This – much like that other favourite, 'unwritten constitution' – is misleading to the point of self-contradiction. There is no system. The exercising of class prejudice, in either direction, is random and capricious; and the biggest mistake any newcomer can make is to believe that his alien status renders him exempt from it. Naturally, that is exactly the mistake I made; when it came to cocking up, I didn't deal in trifles.

The friends I made when I arrived at college ranged from working-class Liverpudlians to upper-class Londoners. I was too callow to understand that this difference was in any way significant. I noted class the way I might have noted a conversational quirk or an unusual haircut. It might be the seventh attribute of a new acquaintance, or the nineteenth, to gain my attention; it didn't register on me that for Britons, it was invariably the first.

Where I came from, race mattered, and money mattered more. Class, in the sense of breeding and manners, did not. There wasn't time for that. For the haves, protection of privilege was at stake; for the have-nots, survival. The slogan 'It's not where you're from, it's where you're at' applied in the most ruthless fashion. Compared to my new social circle, I was in most ways staggeringly naive. But my upbringing had taught me one thing theirs had not: that people, any people, are only as civilised as they can afford to be. I don't use 'afford' in the financial sense, but in the sense that consideration for others tends to be conditional upon one's own sense of security.

Only Matt and Catherine, I think, intuitively appreciated this principle, having found themselves at the sharp end of it often enough. I had never before known people like Catherine and Matt. Their instinctively adversarial, unapologetic stance towards just about everything was entirely new to me. The Britain to which I was trying to adjust myself was a different Britain to the one they came from.

Several years after leaving college, I interviewed the American film director and *Monty Python* alumnus Terry Gilliam. I was struck by how much I recognised in his own account of the notions that lured him to the UK in the 1960s.

'I arrive,' said Gilliam, 'and all I know is what a Jolly Good Place it is, with very polite people who can queue and all that. And then little by little you begin to realise that, no, they're all at each other's throats. But they've developed this ability to behave civilised . . . [Britain] knew where to pull the punch – just before it hit your nose. America had to go right through your nose and out the back of your head. And that's civilisation; to stop the punch just there.'

Gilliam's expectations of Britain closely reflected my own. And it was through Catherine and Matt that I learned of the alternative Britain, one from which they had briefly broken free. It was Disraeli's other nation, where the punches were seldom pulled, etiquette was a low-priority luxury and the veneer of civility, stretched thin, could rip at any moment.

In a rare lapse into self-righteousness (he habitually displayed remarkable forbearance towards me), Matt on one occasion sneered at what he called my 'bourgeois preconceptions'. He was right about the preconceptions, but mistaken as to their provenance. They weren't bourgeois, they were outlandish. In Africa, I had seen the extremes of what the world had to offer by way of beauty and horror, luxury and desperation. In Britain, life occurred between narrower margins, but managed to be far more complex than my imagination yet knew how to take in.

Eventually I came to understand that the problem in Britain is not class-consciousness. It is class-subconsciousness. Active snobbery and its counterpart, resentment, are plentifully evident. But it's far more typical for Britons to make class judgements without being aware of it. This renders class doubly difficult for the neophyte. When you at last attempt to reckon with it – which happens, usually, when it starts to work to your disadvantage – you find yourself dealing with strictures that are not even explicable to the people who implement them. Generally speaking, asking a Briton to account for class is like inviting a bat to explain sonar.

In the late 1990s, my byline made a brief appearance in an upmarket fashion magazine. I was invited to contribute on the subject of styling products – face creams, powders, potions and the like. Stanley Elton, the editor who commissioned me, was a fellow of the old school, considered an authority on manners. His own were exquisite. I thought this a good thing. I had finally begun to catch on to the way class permeated and influenced Britain, outweighing merit by a factor so high it defied any bid to gauge it. That said, good manners were always a pleasure to encounter. And if the upper classes weren't wonderfully polite, then what, I had to ask myself, was the point of them?

Stanley's assistant, Fenella, obtained her vowels exclusively from the Webb Corbett crystal company. Stanley was as debonair a creature as ever set its hand-tooled shoes down upon a discreetly luxuriant carpet; but seated in his office across from Fenella, he might have been a costermonger bundled into a waistcoat for a wager.

I stopped by, one breathlessly hot summer's day, to collect a small skipload of men's moisturisers. Inside my suit, my shirt and underclothes were clinging to me with sodden tenacity, as if fearful I might dispense with them altogether. And admittedly, it was a temptation.

Stanley and Fenella were experts on toiletries, so I thought I would seek their advice.

'You folks would know,' I said. 'On a day like this, what's the best anti-perspirant to try?'

H.M. Bateman is a cartoonist best remembered for his series 'The man who', which comically detailed parvenu errors that, however paltry, triggered such revulsion they paralysed all around them in a tableau of outrage and disgust. I'd assumed these class-inflected caricatures pertained to a long-gone era. I was wrong. Had I lit my cigar before the royal toast, or bid half-a-guinea at Tattersall's, I could not have made a more ghastly faux pas.

It was as if the heat had been sucked out of the room by an air conditioner of instant and absolute efficacy. The temperature plummeted. Everything froze – and nothing more markedly than the expressions upon Stanley and Fenella's faces. It was one thing to dispense guidance on such matters in print, to the readers – but to bring it up in conversation? Stanley was a gentleman, in every sense, but this was patently beyond the pale. Into the bottom drawer marked 'Oiks' I went, never again to defile Stanley's pages.

Class in Britain forms a mesh so fine that, in certain lights, its presence may be impossible to discern. But it certainly is there, acting as the most scrupulous of screens. I lost count of the occasions it filtered me out, often so gently that only with hindsight did I twig to what had happened.

For a while, the *Fiddler* provided a unique environment. Everybody there was an outcast, an exile or an interloper. That pervasive, subliminal question, of whether or not a person is 'one of us', was relevant here, too, but with the criteria reversed. What mattered was not your background, nor your instinct for what was and wasn't done (a rule that applies across the social strata). If you could tell a good story, crack a few gags, or cut feeble artistic efforts off at the knees, you were in. We had all left somewhere to end up there and, more importantly, each of us had abandoned an idea of how his life ought to be. I once heard it described as 'Oxbridge for pariahs'.

One of the least prepossessing side-effects of the British immersion in class is that, once you become cognisant of it, you may start to blame it for everything, if you're not careful. It took me the first half of my time here to appreciate how class exerted a pull upon British life equivalent to that of the moon upon the tides. And it took me the second half to realise that, for all its power, you can't blame class for everything. If people don't like you, it's not necessarily because they've adjudged you The Wrong Sort of Person. Sometimes, they simply think you're a git.

CHAPTER THIRTEEN

W.C. FIELDS WAS RIGHT

FOR AN OUTSIDER attempting to make sense of Britain, there are two issues above all that cannot be ignored, and I speak as someone who's tried. One is animals, and the other is children.

I've tried to ignore these issues because, when I don't, I all too frequently find myself running away from angry people – something in the style of a silent film comic who has inadvertently incurred the wrath of a portly, dyspeptic, walrus-moustached elder. Folk are very touchy hereabouts when it comes to children and animals. You never know what will set them off. Or rather, *I* never do.

On the matter of animals, the country maintains something close to unanimity. It is, to varying degrees, *for* them. On the matter of children, things are not so simple. The British seem polarised between those who would indulge children in every way, and those who yearn for the days when a clip round the earhole was yet to become a breach of human rights legislation. I have to admit that the closer I have come to assimilation (or more accurately, some mildly effective form of camouflage) within the UK, the more I've veered towards the latter sentiment.

I think it began in the mid-1990s, when for the first time I briefly felt flush enough to pay my way in a decent restaurant, in the company of The Girlfriend and a quartet of bumptious kiddiewinks. The kiddiewinks weren't included in our own party; but that didn't stop them running up to the table, knocking over water glasses and offering candidly lavatorial critiques of our chosen dishes, while their adoring progenitors looked on from across the room.

This was also the first time I heard that now familiar lamentation, so often recited by a certain type of parent. 'Restaurants just aren't family-friendly here,' griped the mother of the poppet who was at that moment wrestling my napkin from my grasp. 'It's so different on the Continent. They welcome kids there.'

They certainly do. And speaking as someone who considers restaurants one of life's great pleasures, the moment British kids show one fraction of the decorum that those French, Spanish and Italian kids display from an early age while eating out, I'll be happy to share my mealtimes with them. Perhaps parents who want their offspring to be accepted in public dining rooms should avoid raising them to be fractious, whining brats.

As The Girlfriend and I hastened from the restaurant, our enjoyment of the evening both overshadowed and curtailed by the voluble tykes, we were followed all the way by the resentful glares of the parents. They evidently held it against us that we should not find their brood as winsome as they did.

'I really do despair sometimes,' brayed the mother loudly, for our benefit, as we passed. 'It's almost as if some people hate children.'

This was too much. I stopped by her table. 'I can assure you,' I said, boldly, 'that we don't hate children. Not a bit of it.' Judging by her expression, she wasn't convinced. 'We hate *your* children.' At which point, before the affronted paterfamilias could rise from his chair and administer a thorough drubbing to me, I boldly dragged The Girlfriend through the exit at speed and boldly bundled the pair of us into a cab, not glancing back once.

Where children are involved, class once more comes into play. *My* children are boisterous; *your* children are a menace. *My* children have experimented with drugs; *your* children are criminals. *My* children will be shielded by their innate respectability; *your* children are beyond redemption.

When a teenage joyrider contrives to despatch into oblivion either a hapless pedestrian, a law-abiding driver, or himself, we are treated to the inevitable interview with his haggard Fag Ash Lil of a mother. She declares that her boy may be 'no angel', but remains 'a good kid, really', and indignantly pins blame for the whole mess upon the police for being so insolent and reckless as to chase him.

If this view differs, in essence, from that of the middle-class mum who interprets her children's rotten public behaviour as a form of self-expression that bystanders should consider themselves privileged to endure, then the distinction is too fine for me to grasp. The effects may be very different, but the causes are identical.

In the two decades I've been acquainted with it at first hand, I've seen British culture develop into something of a youth cult. Back in 1986, the opinions of the young were more or less confined to patronising specialist outlets on TV and in the press. When I reflect on what I, at the age of eighteen, had to say for myself, I have to allow that's exactly where they belonged. Almost twenty years on, the idea that kids are inherently fascinating (to anyone besides other kids, that is) has been all but enshrined in everyday life. Gone is the premise that, in order to attract interest, you should be interesting. Attention – serious attention – is now your birthright. The young are Britain's household gods.

'The voices of young people,' said an interviewee on a TV news programme I was half-watching the other day, 'too often go unheard.' In the unlikely event that the lady in question is reading this, I can assure her that they don't – not on my street, anyway.

My front window faces onto the main drag leading to and from the city centre. Up this road, every day, walk Billy and Angie, a teenage couple. I've never met Billy and Angie. Yet I know their names. I know their favoured tipple – Diamond White cider. And I know a fair bit about their relationship, which is on the tempestuous side. I can tell, because Billy and Angie never walk together.

Some days, Billy will be in the lead, striding ahead in his hooded top, broad trousers and lurid trainers. It's odd how little the underclass male uniform has mutated since the 1980s. The haircuts are different, as are the labels and logos, but the basics remain much as they were when first adapted from American ghetto style: a crumpled morass of baggy vestments, the chief purpose of which, in its country of origin, is to confuse potential assailants as to which bit to shoot.

Shuffling behind, her jeans low enough on her capacious hips to reveal the narrow gusset of her underwear, and her crop top riding high above a spare tyre of a size more commonly found bolted to the underside of a tractor, comes Angie, clamouring stridently after her beau like a champion hog-caller in full cry.

'Billy!'

'Fack off!' Billy replies, gutturally, without turning his head.

'Billeeeee!'

'Fack off!'

'BILLLLLLEEEEEEEE!'

'FACK OFF!'

I hear this little procession as it arrives and passes, the twin components of the dialogue rising then fading, in a slow-motion demonstration of the Doppler effect. The next day, it repeats itself; only this time it is Angie who is the aggrieved party, waddling furiously up the hill with her can of cider twitching in her hand like a metronome and her cigarette bobbing upon her underlip, trailed at thirty paces by the beseeching Billy.

'Angie!'

'Fack off!'

'Angieeeee!'

'Fack off!'

'ANGIEEEEEEEE!'

'FACK OFF!'

If more than two days go by without Billy and Angie sluggishly pursuing one another up the hill, I start to worry. But they always come back. Perhaps, eventually, one of them will catch up with the other and the argument will be resolved. But like Achilles and the tortoise, they seem destined never to meet. To make the paradox even more confounding, Achilles (if you can picture Achilles as a slouching ne'er-do-well or a sundae-shaped xanthippe) is the one in front, while the tortoise brings up the rear, yet the distance between the two never seems to alter.

It's understandable that any society should be jealous of youth (Billy and Angie excepted). Youth has looks. It has confidence. It has fun. It has the darling belief that life may yet work out for the best. Enviable qualities, all.

But for a society to be solicitous of youth's opinions is another tureen of bisque entirely. The fact that the young are, on the whole, just as boring as everyone else is somehow disregarded. Bluntly, who cares what teenagers think about non-teenage matters? It's not as if the young need any further motivation to place themselves at the centre of the universe. The reason we shouldn't solemnise the views of children is the same reason that we don't let them smoke, drink, drive, vote or choose adult sexual partners: they're children.

Parents often tell me that I'll feel very differently if and when I have children of my own, and I'm sure those parents are right. If and when I have children of my own, I won't let them dress like prepubescent vamps either. Not even the girls.

I recall with a shudder an evening in 1999 when I was persuaded to attend a show at the Brighton Centre, featuring some of the most popular bubblegum bands of the moment – freakishly sunny Irish poppets N*Chanted; curiously trousered line-dancing karaoke act Strides; stupefyingly bland boy band 192; and, for all I know, Simon Smith and His Amazing Dancing Bear. I say 'for all I know', because I didn't make it inside the venue for the show.

I had arranged to meet Terry at the front entrance; he had bagged some complimentary tickets and was taking along his young son, Olly, and a few of Olly's schoolchums. It was Terry, no doubt desperate for grown-up company, who had talked me into showing up. Which was more than he did.

'Go on,' he'd pleaded. 'It'll be a laugh.'

'It won't, you know.'

'Oh, go on. We can nip out to the pub once the kids are in their seats.'

So against my better judgement, I agreed. My better judgement was, inevitably, spot-on. At seven o'clock I found myself leaning on a lamp post at the corner of the street while certain little ladies came by. Dozens of them; not a one over twelve years of age, and all of them dolled-up like Louisiana jailbait. They were, naturally, accompanied by their parents, who scowled at me with ever more profound suspicion as I lurked alone in wait for Terry, looking for all the world like somebody's funny uncle.

I grew more nervous by the moment. Where the hell was

Terry? I shrank into my jacket, expecting at any instant to be collared by stern policemen and hauled off to the cells, my protestations in vain and my name permanently tarred with the ugliest of slurs. I pulled out my mobile phone and called Terry. He did not answer, and the expressions on the passing parents' faces suggested that they now believed I was furtively contacting an equally reprehensible accomplice. Couples began conferring among themselves, while casting hostile glances in my direction. After fifteen minutes of this, I could take no more. I legged it while still at liberty to do so, and spent the rest of the evening at home, waiting for my heart to stop hammering, and summoning curses upon – in ascending order – high street fashion retailers, the demise of childhood innocence, and Terry.

'Oh, right,' said Terry, the next time we met. 'I went around the back, in the end, where the guest list was kept.'

'And you failed to tell me this, why?'

'Ah, you know, I was distracted keeping track of the kids. Slipped my mind. Sorry about that. Hope you didn't wait too long.'

Every second was a second too long. I don't blame the parents for their misapprehensions. If I'd been in their place, I too would have thought the worst. But if they want to discourage the type of person they mistook me for, it might help if they also discouraged their daughters from dressing up like a drunken hen party on a nightclub manhunt.

If this seems to veer uncomfortably close to the notions of modesty espoused by certain societies less tolerant than Britain's, allow me to correct that impression. The wardrobe space between the burka and the peekaboo thong is a broad one – a walk-in, really.

As for the British view of animals, it is, for outsiders, one of the country's oddest attributes. It's a stereotype of Britons that they prefer animals to people, but it seems to have some foundation in truth.

Animals, wild and domestic, were everywhere during my childhood in Kenya. Our home was inhabited by a succession of pets, and we were surrounded at various times by cows, goats, sheep and chickens; and invaded by monkeys, mongooses, bats, birds and a honey badger, which pensively chewed its way through a set of burglar bars one night to get at a tray of raw meat which had been set out for drying into biltong.

I was aware of a parallel organisation to the RSPCA – called, unsurprisingly, the KSPCA. It was a fringe group, largely a colonial holdover, which drew little support from indigenous Kenyans – or, for that matter, from non-British expatriates. It followed the model of its British parent, in that it was essentially concerned with being nice to dogs and donkeys. Not, I'd add, that there is anything inherently wrong with being nice to dogs and donkeys. But in a country where more than half the population is scratching a living at subsistence level, being nice to dogs and donkeys is accorded a lower priority than it might be otherwise.

I was devoted to my family's own dogs, and wished no harm to anyone else's (which was more than could be said for my family's own dogs – particularly Achilles, a Jack Russell terrier of peculiar and single-minded belligerence). But it never entered my head that people outside my family would care about our animals. They had other things with which to concern themselves.

On coming to the UK, I encountered an attitude towards animals very unlike the one I was used to. Initially I took this to reflect the contrast between a poor country and a rich one. That wasn't so, as I later found out. British views on animals are substantially different, for instance, to those in continental Europe. In Spain, cruelty to animals is the basis of sport. The French would probably find that approach as odd as they do the British one. In France, they have no particular interest in causing animals to suffer, nor in preventing it. The dining table is their principal concern. As you might have guessed, I'm with the French on this one.

The exceptions in France are Parisian dog-owners, who coddle their canine treasures to a degree that the most canophile Briton would approve of, and blithely permit them to crap where they please. Walking through Paris one day, I heard the deep thrumming of a powerful engine as it approached swiftly from behind me. I jumped hastily aside and narrowly avoided being struck by a futuristic white-and-green vehicle resembling a cross between an outsized motorcycle and a hovercraft. It nicely complemented the Pompidou Centre, a hundred yards ahead of it. This craft pulled to halt, and a fellow accoutered in the style of Robocop jumped off, then detached from the bulky abdomen of his vehicle one end of a giant segmented hose, which hissed with subdued menace. This item he applied to a large pile of dogshit. The dogshit vanished with a satisfying whoosh and a conclusive thunk, leaving the pavement as clean as if the mess had never been there.

I was delighted at this. 'He's the James Bond of street cleaners,' I enthused to The Girlfriend. 'He's got the gear. He's got the moves. He's got it all. If you were told you had to clean up dogshit for a living, you'd be miserable. But then they give you that, and suddenly it's the best job in the world.'

I was disappointed to learn, a few months later, that this gizmo had been taken out of service; although not a fraction so disappointed, I'm sure, as the chap who had been using it and now had to revert to more traditional methods. It's a pity no enterprising British local authority, if such a thing exists, thought to buy up the disused machines on the cheap. When it comes to giving their dogs excretory leeway, the British are second only to the Parisians. Sadly, they have yet to devise so stylish a solution to the problem. Or, if the pavements near my home are a guide, any solution at all.

Not long since, in the car park of Brighton railway station, I stopped in at what its organisers would call an open market and anybody else would call a car boot sale. In the midst of the milling throng, a collie – coupled via an expensive leather leash to a woman whose outfit must have cost more than the entire stock of goods on offer – squatted down and deposited a mound of stinking ordure onto the tarmac. The woman waited until the dog had voided itself, then without a word turned and walked off, the dog following behind.

'Hey!' shouted a stallholder, justifiably miffed. 'Aren't you going to clean up after your dog?'

'Why should I?' retorted the disdainful owner. 'He's never cleaned up after me.' She stalked haughtily away. The part I found hardest to figure out was that she did so to a round of applause, from folk who would now have to pick their way around a foul heap of collie crud. In any other country, the crowd would have lynched her with her own dog lead.

As the couple in the restaurant did with their children, so this woman evidently regarded her dog as an extension of her own person – and thus as far beyond reproach as she no doubt deemed herself. If anything, the British are even more protective of their pets than of their kids. The parallels don't stop there. 'In the eyes of its mother,' runs a salient Arabic proverb, 'every dung beetle is a gazelle.' This truth has been a comfort to metaphorical dung beetles everywhere, myself not excluded. But there are also Britons who cherish actual dung beetles – or whatever exotic pets they can get their hands on – as if they were children.

There is something deeply tedious about both exotic pets and their owners. I think it may come down to the uniformity of their pretension, the typical stance of the unimaginative would-be rebel, who mutinies against conformity by doing exactly what every other self-proclaimed individualist does.

Inevitably, it was my friend Terry who one day opened the door to find Petunia, the girl he then lived with, standing on the step, clutching a hefty and testy-looking lizard under her right arm, and flourishing a soporific tarantula in her left palm. She had rung the doorbell with her nose.

People like cats and dogs because they're furry, they do a good impression of liking people back and they offer a blank screen on which to project notions about their apparent personalities. Lizards and spiders – along with snakes, scorpions and all other creatures favoured by those with a taste for piercings and transgressive tattoos – lose what little appeal they have very swiftly. There's only so many times you can watch an iguana impassively swallow a cricket before the entertainment value starts to pall.

Within a week, all chores relating to the new pets had been delegated to Terry, because Petunia 'hadn't realised how boring they would be'.

'I don't find them any more interesting than you do,' protested Terry. 'And you're the one who bought them.'

'God, you just won't support me in anything I do, will you?' seethed Petunia, and stamped out to practise taking pictures of dead flowers with the expensive camera equipment he had purchased for her the month before.

It wouldn't be fair on The Girlfriend's bosom pal, Jamila, to class either her, or her mouse, in this category. The mouse was, if not an exotic pet, then certainly an unconventional one; and in this much it was well suited to Jamila, who was a genuinely unconventional woman. It was 1994, and I was still living at Green Street, when Jamila obtained the mouse from the RSPCA. Jamila was a lovely person, a kind, gentle, considerate and sweet-natured fruitcake. She had originally wanted a cat, but George, the landlord, adopted a no-pets edict; and so,

come to that, did The Girlfriend and I. We had been resident the longest in the house on Green Street, so we held
some sway in these matters.

'But I just want something to look after,' said Jamila.
'Something to take care of. Something to nurture.'

'How about a fish?' said The Girlfriend.

'Fish would be nice,' I said, thinking of the Cheeky
Chip, five minutes' walk away, which did a very pre-
sentable battered cod.

'Can you nurture a fish?' said Jamila, doubtfully.

'Of course you can,' said The Girlfriend, firmly.

So Jamila went off to the RSPCA shelter, to see if they
had any fish.

'Can't she just buy one?' I said to The Girlfriend.

'She can't afford it.'

'They can't cost that much. And why would the shelter
have fish? You don't find stray fish in the street. People
don't abandon them in lay-bys.'

'She wants to check. Then if they don't have any she'll
go and buy one.'

The shelter didn't have fish, of course. And Jamila did-
n't go and buy one. Instead she came home with a bulky
object concealed beneath a sheet and a nervous, concilia-
tory grin hovering over her face.

'Now don't be cross with me . . .' she began. My heart
sank. When Jamila asked you not to be cross with her, she
generally followed up that request with a statement such
as, 'I forgot I was running a bath again' or 'I invited the
congregation from the Spiritualist Church over tonight'
or, in this instance, 'I got a mouse.'

'Why did you get a mouse?' said The Girlfriend.

'I felt so sorry for it,' Jamila said. 'People always want dogs or cats, but nobody wants a mouse. That's why it was there, because somebody didn't want it in the first place. Look at it. Don't you feel sorry for it?' She drew back the sheet and revealed a wire mesh cage containing a bed of straw, a plastic water bottle and no mouse. The cage could not have been more mouseless had a large and satisfied tabby been couched atop the straw licking its lips.

After I'd looked for a while, I realised the mouse was there after all. It was just very hard to see. Jamila's mouse was tiny – small enough to hide head-on behind an old sixpence. And it was grey, the kind of grey that absorbs and nullifies light, so the eye must strain to find it. This was not a drawback when the mouse was in its cage, as it did nothing in there but chew its own tail, and that wasn't fun to watch anyway.

Mice are normally bright, bristle-whiskered and button-eyed, fearfully alert and alive, but this one was as listless a mouse as ever twitched its nostrils, and it could barely summon up the interest to do that.

'It's depressed,' said Jamila.

'It's a mouse,' I said.

When, inevitably, Jamila's mouse escaped from its cage, its near-invisibility became a problem. Being by then the only man in the house, it fell to me to recapture the animal.

There was no one I could call on for advice in what was, to me, an entirely novel situation. The only person I knew who had any experience in hunting mice was Pugsley, Barney Flint's Yorkshire chum. And Pugsley's experience wasn't much to go on. When he was much younger, Pugsley played in a band with a pair of fellow Leeds men, and an eccentric singer from the Home Counties with an Oxford degree in botany. The singer, owing to his short stature and black clothing, was nicknamed the Gnome of Darkness. His bandmates routinely beat him up, sometimes for being an intellectual, sometimes for being Southern, but usually for being annoying.

Pugsley came home one night, several pints to the good, to the house he shared with the band. It was blanketed in darkness. He stumbled into the living room, felt for the light switch, and was greeted by an odd sight. Sitting cross-legged with his back to the wall was the Gnome. An air rifle lay cocked in his lap. Propped against the opposite wall, directly across from the Gnome, was the living-room door – which, Pugsley recalled, had still been hanging on its hinges when he left for the pub.

'What the fuck are you doing?' said Pugsley.

'Shhh!' hissed the Gnome. 'Turn the light off!'

'What the fuck are you doing?' repeated Pugsley, not a man to let a question go unanswered.

'Behind that door,' said the Gnome, 'there is a mouse.'

'How did a mouse get behind the door?' said Pugsley. 'And how did the door get against the wall?'

'The mouse,' said the Gnome, 'did not get behind the door. The door was placed in front of the mouse. By me. Now, there are only two ways out. There' – he indicated to the left of the door with the gun barrel – 'or there,' he indicated to the right. 'And when he does – boom.'

'You're fucking cracked,' said Pugsley

'Tell that to the mouse,' said the Gnome.

At that moment, a scuffling noise sounded behind the door. Instantly, the Gnome swivelled the rifle and fired, punching a small hole in the woodwork, alongside several others that ranged across the door's lower portion.

Pugsley took the gun from the Gnome's hands and – with minimal zest for the task, because it was late and Pugsley was tired – gave the Gnome a brief slapping rather than a proper beating up.

'What's' – slap – 'wrong' – slap – 'with' – slap – 'a' – slap – 'bloody' – slap – 'mousetrap?'

Then he went over to the opposite wall and picked up the door. There was no longer a mouse behind it. It had fled while he was slapping the Gnome. He put the door back on its hinges and went to bed.

The Gnome had an advantage in his mouse hunt that I did not; he wanted the mouse to die, which you would have thought multiplied his options beyond removing the door and shooting at the mouse in the dark. I, conversely, wanted Jamila's mouse to live. Or rather, Jamila wanted her mouse to live; The Girlfriend didn't want to upset Jamila; and I certainly didn't want to upset The Girlfriend. The effective chain of command ran from Jamila's mouse at the top to me at the bottom. There was only one thing to do: draft in a subordinate.

That was how my friend Rob and I found ourselves in the narrow kitchen at Green Street, armed respectively with a tea strainer and a colander, looking for all the world like a brace of disreputable ghillies after a shoplifting spree in Woolworths. We could hear Jamila's mouse scrabbling around behind the panels beneath the floor cupboards, where before there had been nothing but woodlice. Armies of woodlice. So many woodlice that one day I had teamed up with another, now departed male tenant, removed the panels, plugged in the vacuum cleaner, and hoovered up several pounds of them, in half a dozen shifts. Each time the vacuum cleaner bag filled up, we emptied its squirming contents into a heavy black bin liner, sprayed in a hefty dose of insecticide, and waited for it to stop writhing.

Now I was left with no option but to take the panels off again. If I didn't, it was only a matter of time before George turned up at four in the morning and took them off himself in one of his nocturnal home derangement frenzies. The thought of George coming face to face with Jamila's mouse as it gnawed through the gas pipe in the small hours was not a happy one. George was a tolerant chap, but he was understandably of the view that nobody except himself should wreak any kind of damage upon his property.

With the aid of a long-handled serving spoon, which I scraped back and forth underneath the cabinets, I succeeded in driving Jamila's mouse out into the open. As I hurriedly propped the panel back into position, Jamila's mouse scuttled towards Rob. Alert and agile as a ninja warrior, Rob dropped into a crouching position. A crack sounded in his knee.

'Yow!' squawked Rob, synchronously grabbing his patella and dropping the tea strainer, which came within a whisker of providentially trapping Jamila's mouse. Jamila's mouse turned on a pinhead and skittered straight towards me. I held the colander ready. I had the wee beastie now. It had nowhere else to go. I drew my breath in and waited for the precise moment. Not now, not now, *now* –

The door opened behind me and I reflexively half-turned my head over my shoulder as I heard Jamila say:

'You're not going to hurt it, are you?'

Jamila's mouse scampered between my feet, past Jamila and out into the hallway.

I gripped the colander hard in both hands and exhaled slowly. Then I summoned a limping Rob into the hallway and we struck up our fandango, once more, from the top.

The most galling aspect of the whole episode was that, once we'd recaptured Jamila's mouse, and Jamila had obtained a cage with a smaller mesh, she then released the rodent into the window box over the patio, 'To cheer it up a bit.'

'Christ on crutches,' I groaned, as The Girlfriend summoned me to take up my colander once more, 'why couldn't she just have had a baby?'

Jamila's mouse was a nuisance, but a minor one. One couple of my acquaintance, Ian and Olivia, proponents both of 'animal rights', matched deeds to convictions by giving a home to several rabbits either liberated or purloined (depending on your viewpoint) from a laboratory by bala-clava-clad trespassers. Most people would have built a hutch in the back garden of their newly acquired and expensively refurbished house. Olivia and Ian gave the rabbits the run of the place. Obliged to leave the rabbits unattended for a fortnight, the pair rigged up an automatic system designed to replenish the fluffy house-guests' feeding bowls as these were emptied.

Within half a day, at the best estimate, the rabbits had eaten the lot. They spent the next thirteen days methodically chewing their way through the plaster, which – in addition to its innate lagomorphic irresistibility – offered the appetising quality of freshness. Olivia and Ian returned to discover a ragged trench skirting the base of every wall in the house. Had their home been disfigured by vandalism, they would have been furious. As it was rabbits that did it, they didn't seem to mind at all.

The idea of Britain as a nation of animal lovers had not come as a shock to me. I had known a fair few 'doggy' people in Kenya, all of them British. What I did find startling about Britain – and still do, every time I think about it – is that notion of 'animal rights'. At first this might seem a logical extension of sympathy for animals and the consequent eagerness to protect them from harm. But it isn't. There's nothing logical about it at all; and between those who abhor the idea of pointless savagery towards animals, and those who believe that animals have rights, there exists not so much a gap as a chasm.

I first encountered 'animal rights' at college, where I took it for yet another of the wacky crusades that would engage temporary firebrands for a year or two, before being shrugged off in favour of rudimentary common sense. Somewhere on campus there always seemed to be a folding table decked out in photostats of disembowelled foxes, smoking dogs and tormented apes. It was generally manned by nose-ringed hunt saboteurs, who took your refusal to sign their petition as a sign that you actively endorsed all the cruelties pictured, and probably indulged in them by way of weekend relaxation.

I supposed 'animal rights' to be a form of politics for those who had nothing better to worry about. In doing so I misunderstood at an axiomatic level the nature of the movement. To champion the concept of 'animal rights' is not a political position. It is, to all intents and purposes, a fundamentalist orthodoxy. The premise that an animal life is of a worth comparable to a human one doesn't bear debating. You either accept it or you don't.

In the late 1980s, I saw 'animal rights' agitprop everywhere I looked. On the wall of my local butcher's shop there appeared, daubed in red paint, the words 'murderer' and 'criminal' and, in capital letters, 'ALF'. I took Alf to be the butcher thus maligned. It was explained to me that 'ALF' stood for 'Animal Liberation Front'. That kept me amused for days, until it was further explained to me that the Animal Liberation Front was not a prank, but an underground organisation operating in deadly earnest. That struck me as even funnier. Subsequently, in the wake of bombings, arson, break-ins, intimidation and general low-level terrorism, I found it not quite so funny – but still no less preposterous.

Another preposterous feature of British views on animal welfare is that you're not allowed to shoot seagulls.

You really should be allowed to shoot seagulls. Or at the very least, I should be allowed to shoot seagulls. They're a nuisance, a menace, a health hazard. They have criminal tendencies, too. I remember the first time I noticed how audacious they had become. I was standing at a bus stop outside a supermarket one day in 1994, when I spotted a gull surreptitiously stalking my shopping bags.

'The bugger's after my prawns,' I thought. It caught my gaze and strutted away with feigned nonchalance, darting glances back at me to check if I was still watching it. Had it possessed pockets, it would have thrust its wingtips into them and whistled.

I have a friend who went so far as to buy an air rifle, so fed-up was he with these objectionable birds. Before he could take the law into his own hands, his wife told him that she would divorce him if he fired a single shot. It was a close-run thing, but after giving it some thought, he laid down his weapon, and both the seagulls and his marriage survived.

Once seagulls never ventured beyond the shoreline. Lately they have been spotted as far inland as Birmingham, which is all Birmingham needs. Not that Birmingham should worry, because any seagulls en route to the Midlands can be relied upon to stop off in my front garden instead, and strew garbage across it in the small hours. After which they congregate on the chimney pots and shriek their requitals. The friskier ones then couple noisily on my bedroom ceiling, dislodging the tiles, while their pals tap at the window with their beaks and peer at me with sideways mockery when I blearily pull up the blinds. They remind me very strongly of the malevolent brats in hooded tops and trainers who infest town centres around the country. All they lack to perfect the appearance of feathered scallies is a selection of gull-sized alcopops and contraband cigarettes.

The seagulls share with their human equivalents a

streak of anti-social violence. They bully, harry, intimi-
date and even assault pets and people. Several dogs and
cats have been done in by seagulls, and even one person –
the unfortunate Mr Wilfred Roby of Anglesey, who, in the
summer of 2002, perished of a heart attack after being set
upon by gulls in his back garden. Mr Roby was eighty
years old, and – one might conclude – relatively frail, but
this is still no excuse. If anything, that makes it worse.

To curb these avian delinquents, I favour the Short
Sharp Shock treatment so beloved of self-proclaimed law-
and-order champions. In this case, and in the absence of
firearms, I think it should be applied literally – at a suitably high voltage. Anywhere else in Europe, I suspect, it
already would be. Even in the modern, compulsively risk-
averse Britain, had poor Mr Roby been felled by an
agency other than animal – a low-flying balsa-wood glid-
er, say, or an unusually colourful shirt worn by a neighbour – there would have been calls for an enquiry within
minutes of his hitting the deck; followed by hasty and ill-
conceived legislation pushed through parliament.

Perhaps if the seagulls were not so evocative of
Britain's maritime heritage, you could get away with taking a pop at them. Or perhaps not. Rats played a far more
prominent role in the nation's history; yet neither the law
nor the populace in general seems at all troubled by the
thought of rats coming to grief. It's a good thing rats
aren't cute. Cute animals enjoy grace-and-favour residence in the penthouse suite of the British heart.

During the 2001 foot-and-mouth crisis, pyres of burning carcasses reproduced across the British countryside
the atmosphere of Pieter Bruegel the Elder's *The Triumph*

of Death. News reports invoked such words as 'massacre' and 'carnage'. As most of this livestock was destined for the abattoir, a more accurate front-page headline (which we never saw) would have read 'Animals Killed A Bit Early'.

Then, unscathed from the slaughter, emerged 'Phoenix the Calf' – saucer-eyed, pure white and adorable. This event was greeted as a miracle, and Phoenix became the most celebrated creature since the fondly remembered 'Blackie the Donkey'. It was in 1987, the year after I came to live in Britain, that Blackie became a tabloid hero after his rescue from cruel and ruthless Spaniards, who planned to kick, batter and eventually crush the poor beast. I got in all sorts of trouble one evening when, in response to what felt like unending outrage from my companions, I uttered the words, 'For God's sake, it's only a donkey.' Had I not jumped off my barstool and fled into the night, I might well have suffered the fate originally intended for Blackie.

By the time Phoenix arose from the ashes, I knew better. I kept my thoughts to myself – in public at least. My thoughts being that many of those celebrating the survival of Phoenix were probably not averse to a bit of veal now and then. Nor am I. I was walking through a back-street near my home around that time, when I spotted a sticker in the back window of a parked car. 'Veal,' it declaimed, 'is a bloody awful meal!' I looked up and down the pavement. There was nobody in sight. I took a pen and pad from my pocket, wrote out a note, folded it and placed it under the windscreen wiper on the driver's side.

'You should try the *saltimbocca alla Romana* at La Macelleria,' it read. 'That's really nice.'

Then, mindful of what usually happens to me at such moments, I scurried away before any angry people happened along. Cowardice may be an uncommon trait in both the United and the animal kingdoms; but I was raised in neither.

MENTIONING THE WAR

STORIES SHOULD HAVE AN ending. 'And that's how I became British' – curtain down, lights up, a brief ripple of polite handclaps from the few occupied seats. But life is never that neat, and nor am I, as the clutter strewn around my desk will testify.

Becoming British is always a work in progress. Whenever you think you've got it nailed down, up pops another conundrum. Who do you, and who mustn't you call 'mate'? Why does 'cheers' signify, variously, a thank-you, a farewell and a toast, and which use applies where? Are you the only one who thinks that a fair few people from the north-east of England should come with subtitles? This particular difficulty, I must admit, is not confined to Tyneside. I still have moments when I overhear conversations, and cannot tell in what language they are being conducted. I once shared a train compartment with three voluble Russian teenagers for half an hour, before I realised they were native Anglophones from Gypsy Hill.

One of the advantages of getting older is that eccentricities which formerly marked you out as foreign are now attributed to your being, simply, eccentric. It is a tenet of national self-image that the British love an eccentric. I can affirm from experience that this is not, generally, the case. I consider it a measure of my increasing Britishness that I too am alarmed by other eccentrics. I'm worried they may want to talk to me – and like most Britons, I just want to be left alone.

In the summer of 2004, I boarded a bus in Greenwich, bound for London Bridge. I sat on the top deck. I heard a young man across the aisle and one row behind me begin to talk, loudly and without pause. I didn't turn around. But I began to feel sorry for his companion, as the speaker reeled off a never-ending spiel of London gangsta-isms dotted with patois. Each turn along the bus route brought forth a banal, repetitive and patently fictional tale about some violent conflict that he'd been involved in on that spot.

'. . . 'Cos that's where they came runnin' out at us, blood – right there, from that house, twenny of them. Boosh! Down on the concrete, kickin' in the head. So then we fetched up your bro' and your cousins from their crib on the mobile. But the mobile wasn't workin'. We're like, shiiiiiit. It's like the time right here' – as the bus pulled up to a DIY superstore car park – 'where that business-man took it in the face from both barrels. Man in a suit, just like yours. Boo-ya! Mash up completely, man, no face left, gone. What do you drive? Audi? BMW? That was what he had. Stuck it through the window. Blam! Then they run . . .'

On and on he went. People got on the bus, and people got off. After a while, I noticed that the people getting on the bus were getting off very soon afterwards, often at the next stop. And shortly after that I realised that there was nobody left on the top deck but me and the orator, who hadn't ceased for a second. He had no companion with him. That explained why the conversation was entirely one-way. I was the man in the suit. He had been talking to me all along.

The nutter on the bus is a fine old British tradition, of course, and this chap had simply updated that tradition to fit in with the times. But when the nutter is hurling into your left ear a ceaseless torrent of bloodthirsty narration, casting you as the victim in one grisly scenario after another, it's hard to dismiss him as the harmless kook he probably was. I pressed the buzzer, headed for the stairs and, with some relief, dismounted the bus. My relief was short-lived. It was twilight, and I was standing at a bus stop in a grim and dingy part of south London unknown to me, wearing a summer suit and carrying a fold-up umbrella, which, as a defensive weapon, would not have been much use against a medium-sized moth. The fact that my pockets contained a railcard, £7.36, an obsolete model of mobile telephone and nothing else was little comfort. I began to suspect I had probably been better off on the bus with the nutter.

At moments like this, ample experience of feeling out of place can come in handy. When you've faked fitting in for eighteen years, you get an instinct for it. I'm sure I managed to make myself look as much a typical bystander at that bus stop as any man in a single-vented, three-button, green linen suit could do. My apprehension was, anyway, unjustified. Nobody approached me, or even walked past me. The street was deserted. I was just a nervous outlander scaring himself with phantoms born of jaundiced unfamiliarity. Perhaps I hadn't changed that much in those eighteen years after all.

Another problem with assimilating yourself into a country is that the country itself changes even as you learn about it. Britain has become ever more what some describe as a 'multi-cultural' nation, a phrase I dislike – partly because it implies that culture is something each of us wears like a lapel badge to define and identify himself; and also because 'multi-cultural' has become a sniggering euphemism for 'non-white', among the kind of people who then go on to use, without irony, the phrase 'political correctness gone mad'. It's been a good ten years since I heard this complaint from a person who didn't turn out to be some species of bigot.

For 'multi-cultural' read 'lots more foreigners than there used to be'. Of course, most of them aren't really foreigners. They just look 'foreign', which is a disadvantage I never had to contend with myself. I like having lots more foreigners around (it beats the 1980s, when approximately 17 per cent of Brighton's ethnic minority population was my girlfriend). It makes me feel less conspicuous. Which I admit is not a very commendable reason. But I've heard worse.

In 1996, during the build-up to the British handover of Hong Kong to China, there was a great deal of talk about issuing UK passports to the Hong Kong Chinese. The issue was much debated both in the newspapers and in the Wothorpe Arms, where the sundry soaks, layabouts and outcasts who comprised the *Harmony Fiddler*'s crack editorial team gathered in lieu of putting out the paper.

By and large, the *Fiddler* crew practised what you might call 'pub morality', as exemplified by Barney Flint, who at that time based his appraisal of individuals principally on how they behaved in the saloon bar. It's a good thing he was born too late to experience the Third Reich: 'Say what you like about Josef Goebbels, but he always got his round in.'

On the issue of Hong Kong, the views in the Wothorpe echoed the views in the press, and distributed themselves across the same spectrum of opinion.

'We should let in anyone who wants to move here. They're hard-working people' – this was rich, coming from anyone on the *Fiddler* – 'and they'd be good for society.'

'Yeah, but there could be millions of them. You can't take in that many people in one go, wherever they're from.'

'What makes you think they'd all want to come? It'll probably just be a few thousand, but we owe them the chance if they want it.'

The discussion became quite heated, with splenetic references to Enoch Powell countered by angry denials. Then it simmered into rancorous silence. It was only now that Frederick Flint spoke up.

'I say we should let them all in,' he stated, gravely.

'Why's that?' said Blakey.

'Because,' said Frederick, 'it exponentially increases my chances of sleeping with a Chinese girl.'

At the time of writing, I sense an ugly mood drifting, fog-like, across the British Isles. The famous British quality of tolerance towards newcomers is, in my experience, largely mythical. The native population of the country – and this sometimes includes those whose forebears arrived not so long ago – is not uniformly welcoming to those who appear different, and never has been.

But a significant minority has received immigrants warmly, and continues to do so. Perhaps most important-ly, as a matter of policy, successive post-war governments have, until recently, repeatedly defied the electorate's meanest instincts on the issue. Having been born a British citizen, this was never something I needed to worry about. All the same, I would not like to be arriving in Britain to take up a new life today.

I have a British passport because in the 1960s, my par-ents – finding the Apartheid regime intolerable – left South Africa and took up the option of residency and citi-zenship here. For that alone I have reason to be grateful.

It is open to question whether they would have sur-vived to do so had Germany prevailed in the Second World War. Very likely, Jews in overseas territories would have been rounded up with the same ruthless thorough-ness that the Nazis showed in Europe. My parents, then mere tots, would have shared the fate of their uncles, aunts and cousins in Lithuania.

This is why, for as long as I have known about it and understood its significance, the war has formed the back-drop to all my ideas about Britain. When I came to live here, this turned out, to my surprise, to be the most British thing about me. A fascination with the Second

World War is a trait I share with most other Britons. You need only turn on the television, read a Sunday newspaper or scan the shelves in a bookshop to see how deeply the war is rooted in the British psyche.

Churchill, like Hitler, was given to predictions measured in millennia. Hitler's Thousand-Year Reich disintegrated after a bloody dozen. Over sixty years into its own projected thousand, Churchill's prophecy is faring better. Men still say of the moment Britain stood alone against the Nazis, 'This was their finest hour.'

Except, of course, Britain did not stand alone. As Churchill's own speech acknowledged, it was 'the British Empire and its Commonwealth' of which this sentiment would be expressed. Those who fought, suffered and died came not just from the British Isles, but from Asia, Africa, the Americas and the Antipodes. The British, with their keen sense of history and their understandable fixation on the war, are liable to forget this aspect of the story. People who are now reviled as a foreign 'tide' often hail from countries without which that brave stand against the Nazis would have been doomed.

When war was declared, my maternal grandfather Herbert was among the first to enlist in what was then Rhodesia. He died in August 2004, in his late eighties, more than six decades after he was left for dead on the battlefields of North Africa. My pride in what he did is as strong and imperishable as that felt by any Briton over the war. When it mattered the most, and even if it had not done so before, Britain acted as a lightning rod, a channel for the forces of decency and freedom. No wonder Britain may at times appear, to its European neighbours, obsessed with the past; it is largely thanks to Britain's past that those European neighbours now dwell in the broad, sunlit uplands of modern democracy.

In one important way, then, I was primed to be British before I moved to Britain. I can't help snickering at jokes, no matter how crass, about loud noises inducing the French spontaneously to surrender. The sight of an SS uniform on the television draws the eye as reflexively as does nudity, a nigh-on pornographic national compulsion that explains the astonishing number of broadcast hours devoted to the Third Reich.

One of my many visits to Germany was made in the company of a Welsh rock band. The tour manager was a strapping, exuberant fellow by the name of Kelsey, with an accent so richly redolent of the valleys that when he spoke, you could all but smell the green, green grass of his home. As Kelsey spoke all the time, to be in his company was to be engulfed by a demented and hugely entertaining Welshness.

Kelsey was having a marvellous time, in part due to the free availability of the most explicit and indecent films on German hotel televisions. '*Anal Adventures* was on last night,' he would impart, with relish. 'I was wondering, what kind of adventures can you really have? I mean there's in, and there's out – but what else are you going to do? Go camping? Meet some pirates? It's pretty limited, when you think about it.'

I didn't much want to think about it. Fortunately, talk shifted to Kelsey's sister, who had once enjoyed a rendezvous with one of the musicians, a coupling that Kelsey had only just found out about. He did not seem overly concerned.

'You shagged my sister?'

'Of course I did. For three weeks. I was twenty, she was thirty and up for it.'

'My sister' – here he turned to me, politely, clueing in the stranger in the group – 'is a total slag.' He said this without any hint of judgement or malice, much as you might in passing allude to someone's interest in stamp collecting. 'Honestly. If you had only that description to go on, and you saw her in a crowded room, you would know which one was her.'

Kelsey stopped having a marvellous time when we reached Hamburg. There he became aggravated in the extreme. The band's German record company, we were given to understand, had appointed a promoter in Hamburg only a week before the show. This had given the promoter no time to do what he did best: promote. There was every chance that the show would be attended by nobody whatsoever. Not even the band's German record company, in whose absence Kelsey was having to make do with being aggravated in the extreme at Germans in general.

'Fucking hell, they're supposed to be so fucking efficient here. That's what they're meant to be good at. Efficiency. They can put five channels of hardcore anal filth into your hotel room, but can they organise a gig? Can they fuck! Adolf shoots himself,' he spat out by way of summary, 'and the whole country goes to pot.'

I can't imagine anyone who wasn't British saying that. I can't imagine anyone who wasn't British hearing it and thinking it was funny. I can't imagine anyone who wasn't British hearing it and being anything other than deeply appalled and scandalised.

It took me five minutes to stop laughing.

It's a sorry thought, but if a country is divided by its varying loves and beliefs, then maybe it's united by its common prejudices. To find out that you have shared some of these prejudices from the start, even if you're not proud of them, goes some way towards helping you blend in.

Winter is on its way, as I sit typing in a suitably writerly garret, draughty and dim – an attic dormer box nudging into the sky, vainly fending off the north winds with thin, hollow walls. I can feel the cold air swirling around my ankles. The radiator gurgles ineffectually on the opposite wall, its small warmth swallowed up long before it reaches my desk. At moments like this, I feel as British as can be. In a colder country, the house would have been built with proper insulation. In a warmer country, the house wouldn't need it. Here, in this in-between land, with its deceptively intemperate temperate climate, I might be tempted to conclude that I have settled into the worst of both worlds.

But still, here I am. There is no law to stop me leaving. No restriction other than my own caution prevents me striking out for somewhere new. Something more than docile habit must be keeping me here, and I know – or I believe that I know – what it is. I have practised so relentlessly at British as a second language that I no longer have a first one. I may not be fluently British, but nor am I anything else. For an in-between person, an in-between country may be just the ticket.

I've had it easy, in many ways. For one thing, I look the part. My once tanned skin has assumed a pallor bordering on translucence. Light doesn't pass through it, but gets trapped inside. At a London office where a few years back I routinely came to work in a black suit, I had bestowed upon me the nickname 'Death'. Arriving late one day, I explained that I'd been delayed when an unfortunate soul threw himself under my tube train as it pulled into Barons Court. 'Saw you coming, did he?' said a colleague.

Britain has treated me well, so far. No other country would have paid me a living wage to do what I do all day. Nor, for that matter, has Britain. But it has occasionally come close. I've been the victim of no crime more serious than petty theft. Most of the people I meet are nicer to me than my own behaviour probably merits. These are things that can change in a moment. But I'd be foolish not to acknowledge that I was lucky to fetch up here, after a turbulent if exhilarating upbringing, in this relatively safe and gentle in-between land – where things more often than not work as they are meant to; where events tend to happen as expected; where dotage beckons, sooner than I might have guessed.

Hm. Time, I think, for a cup of tea.